AF477673

The Natural History of
VEDOVAMAZZEI

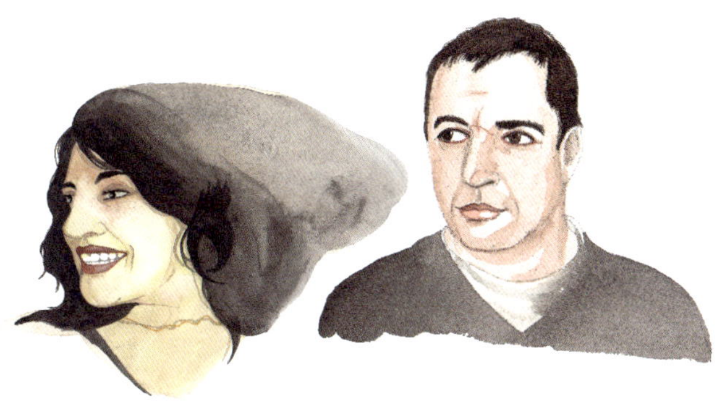

EDITED BY

MIRTA D'ARGENZIO

TROLLEY

Index

	fig.	p.

Preface

Art my life and Art my Way
See us painting in Mud and Clay
See us dancing and smiling too
Let us hope that Art is True [1]

The Natural History of vedovamazzei is a kind of taxonomy of the *vedovamazzei species.* It aims to use art to investigate this species in so far as it represents a creative being in constant evolution, to analyse its genetic make-up, determine a physiology for it, define the process of artistic production the species adopts and its field of action. This *Natural History* aims to present vedovamazzei's work as a kind of entomological series with scientific, illustrated tables, as if vedovamazzei were artist-insects being studied in their natural environment. For the artists, this publication is like a personal version of Baudelaire's *Mon coeur mis à nu* and has been compiled deliberately without passing the censor. Thus, the challenge of providing a completely open portrayal of their own lives, including their most intimate experiences, such as the trauma portrayed by Stella in *Identikit* or the first corpse discovered by Simeone as a child, becomes in itself subject to analysis. The experiences are transformed and exorcised by art, via memory.

Both artists demonstrate a peculiar strength in their capacity to exalt violence and life's torment. Such a capacity can be clearly seen throughout, even in the early pictures in Chapter 1, which focus more on the duo's individual personalities which are presented here as two distinct identities for the first time. This capacity is undoubtedly rooted in their experience of living and growing up in Naples and represents a determination to confront reality and make everyday life a constant source of inspiration, even in its wretchedness. What forms the basis for vedovamazzei's male and female nucleus and constitutes the duo's karyotype is a feature common to both artists. It is the strength to objectify reality and, with this detachment, to ironise and then transform it. Or even to attempt the same feat as Icarus and escape reality, while still maintaining the low-key tone of everyday life. *Specie vedovamazzei* is an atypical, hermaphrodite union because although its sexuality remains a strong feature, the male and female elements are equivalent.

In 1974, a charismatic man from the North arrived in Naples proclaiming: *'We Are the Revolution.'* He used to give out postcards of commonplace icons with notes in German to a small crowd who rushed to listen to him. Beneath a holy picture of Jesus Christ he had written 'the inventor of the third principle of thermodynamics.' With his distinctive boots and his hat permanently pulled down over his mesmerising blue eyes, he used to broadcast his theories, and turn them into poetic forms of social sculpture. He would reiterate that the only resource for the future available to everyone could be found right there. They were it. This art that was at everyone's disposal was the only means of obtaining freedom. Joseph Beuys was this great shaman. His performances and the art he produced in his beloved Naples from the early 1970s until his death in 1986 left a strong impression on many people's minds. vedovamazzei were still in embryonic form at the time but they were there. They were at the chrysalis stage, wrapped in the double cocoon of their individual identities. What was driving them was a specific will, from which they metamorphosed into vedovamazzei. Like real lepitdoptera, they immediately started to use their proboscis to pierce and suck the sap out of their short life cycle. And since launching themselves with their multicoloured wings, they have never stopped interpreting the harsh reality we are all trying to navigate.

Many of their projects are such flights of fantasy that they seem to defy common sense. At first they look like picaresque and ingenuous exploits that are always poised between a mock-heroic vision of science and weak or totally groundless hypotheses. Then it emerges that many of these absurd fantasies, which produce their most blissful visions, in fact originate in a direct observation of reality. They originate from a profound curiosity about life's big issues, which are examined using the Galilean method.

It has been noted that by giving up their personal identities in 1991, the duo have placed themselves within the Dadaist and Post-Conceptual movement, whose roots lie in the early twentieth century European avant-garde, and are inevitably related, therefore, to Duchamp. Ambiguity and ambivalence coexist in both. An evocation of the widow and her duality is undeniable. *Mutatis mutandis.* While Duchamp debuted as his female alter-ego, Rrose Sélavy, with the work *Fresh Widow* (1920) and thus in dissociation made his renowned digression into the subjects of life, femininity and death, vedovamazzei's birth has a different kind of mourning behind it. While Duchamp happily splits into two and makes a frivolous association of ideas on the subject of death, vedovamazzei's case consists of a mournful union and all that this involves. For the former, the first pun in Rrose's rose-coloured life lies in the assonance between the work's title and an evocation of the guillotine (*Fresh Widow* sounds more or less like *French Window)*, whereas for vedovamazzei the play on words lies in their choice of just one out of many names on the tombstones in a Neapolitan cemetery. It is a married woman's name which buries her maiden name forever. It is true that vedovamazzei expunge any reference to the woman's real name twice in their choice of pseudonym, since we can deduce her husband's surname but will never know her Christian or maiden names. They do not, however, expunge her gender. She was also a woman. For Rrose, her name was everything. vedovamazzei no longer has a name and has therefore lost everything.

So, vedovamazzei is a woman, like Rrose, perhaps as a tribute to the great Duchamp's game. But not only for this reason. What can she, with so little left, play at? Her ironic banter and provocative games are not always frivolous. Unfortunately. Like many other women whose lot at a man's death is to burn together with him on the pyre, vedovamazzei also makes a sacrifice; her own name. Indeed, the two artists have dedicated much of their work to identification and personality dissociation. The fusion of the two genders plays an important role for vedovamazzei. But as a woman, vedovamazzei is an anti-Rrose Sélavy. In fact, this anonymous creature shows little sign of self-satisfied narcissism. This unassuming side, the antithesis to Rrose's egocentricity, is the creature's most interesting characteristic and its name denotes a bitter yet general existential condition. vedovamazzei's depersonalisation truly embodies 'the isolation of the human being which is the isolation of all humanity.' And throughout their work, the desire to focus on everyday issues emerges distinctly. A clear demonstration of this is *The Portrait of Jesus Dressed As Stella,* which expresses a real desire to see femininity at the heart of the Catholic religion, as it would often merit. vedovamazzei might be more accurately considered as a tribute to the absolute yet forgotten figure of woman. Like a kind of memorial to the Unknown Soldier but instead to the distinct abilities and unacknowledged creative female intuition that has acquired the art of survival. A memorial to her isolation, to the cage of iconic clichés which has imprisoned her forever. Not everyone can escape into Rrose Sélavy's world because life is less rosy than the pun would suggest.

In 1991, when vedovamazzei was created by Stella and Simeone's artistic fusion, the first thing they did was to take off their masks and *Masks Self-Portrait* portrays their own empty effigies. The same effigies are found in the faces of two children leaning over a balcony. The image is disturbing. They have the features of two adults, of Stella and Simeone. *What are we playing at? At vedovamazzei* (1991).

Mirrored in Stella's and Simeone's art, and specifically in their study of portraits and self-portraits, the subject of personality dissociation often emerges. They analyse it by modifying the image contained in an icon, even in a Barbie doll. It is precisely as a kind of doll that Stella undergoes dissociation in the video *Pupa quae etiam carne humana veciutr* (1994), where she appears in a depersonalised state while at the same time feeds on her own flesh. This self-sacrificing aspect is particularly interesting because it goes against the general trend and because it is developed throughout the body of drawings making up this *History*. Perhaps vedovamazzei's frustrated hope in her life as a woman was for the contemplative dimension of the process which they elaborate here with a completely free hand. And it is this absolute freedom of thought and action which is the basis of Stella and Simeone's exceptional artistic journey.

MIRTA D'ARGENZIO
Salina, 29 July 2003

---

1 *A day in the life of Gilbert & George, the sculptors* (1971).

I

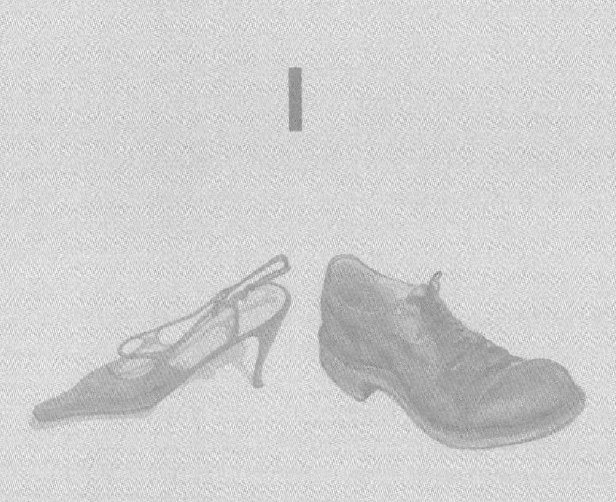

The Structure of vedovamazzei's World

The Natural History of vedovamazzei opens with an inventory of their world.
This is presented in pictures, as a symmetrical catalogue of the possessions
belonging to both artists, which were divided up at the time of the couple's
separation. Here, the two separate identities of Stella and Simeone appear, with
the whole personal store of garments, fetishes and shared memories in which
they are reflected. After vedovamazzei's birth in 1991 Simeone and Stella spent
some time as a couple in life as well. This chapter also includes a collection of
tokens from their adolescence and their private lives. These represent memories
which would often come to be used as raw material for their early collaborative
works. The classic subject of the portrait and self-portrait also constitutes such
raw material. Both artists analyse it right from the start, taking a very liberal
approach towards it, and the subject will remain a constant field of enquiry in
their work.

WARDROBE: CLOTHES

ALL ABOUT STELLA

1.01 ——

A flowery dress, made of real daisies. It is a wonderful present, received at 11 o'clock on a Sunday morning, which joins all that Stella kept in her wardrobe and loved the most. Stella wore it, photographed it and drew it.

1.02 ——

A vintage sheepskin coat from the 1970s. The choice of clothes from Stella's wardrobe and the corresponding pictures are linked to the desire she feels towards the object in itself.

1.03 ——

A vintage blue taffeta dress. The idea of the object and the dress is always tied to a personal motif. Stella and her little girl's dresses, which her mother made out of remnants. The dress as a fetish. The 1960s and Barbie dolls. These are some of the motifs of her world.

1.04 ——

Perhaps her wedding dress.

1.05 ——

A flowery dress.

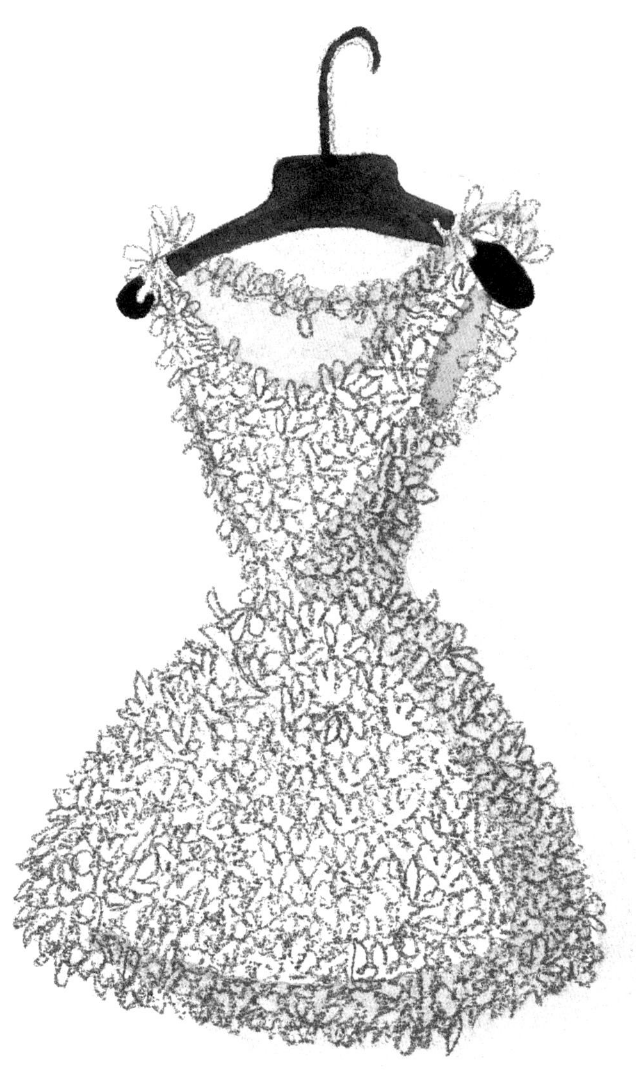

1.01 —

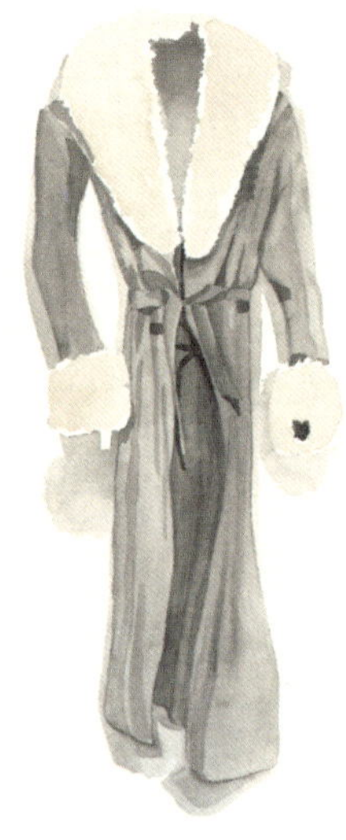

1.02 ——

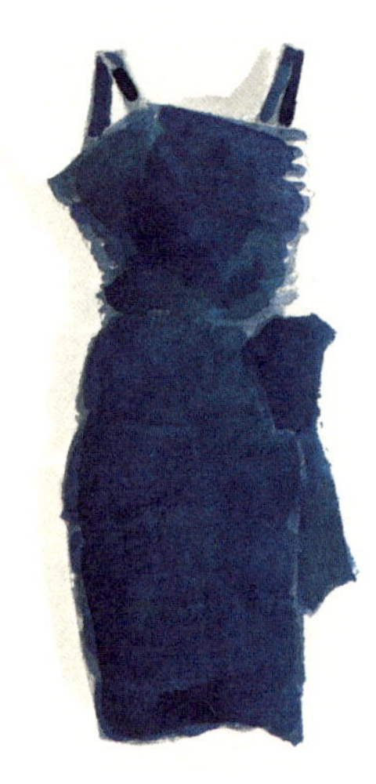

1.03 ——

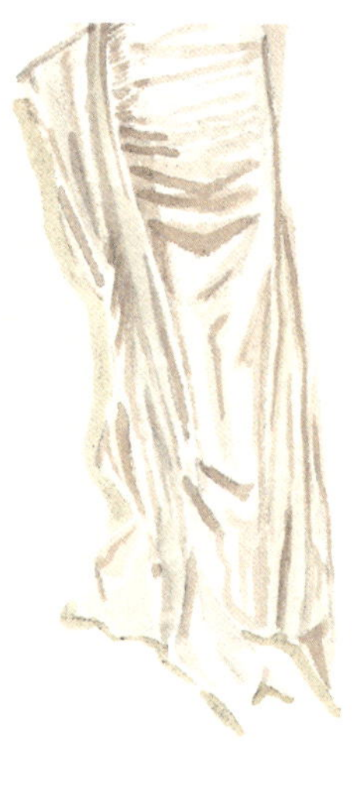

1.04 ——

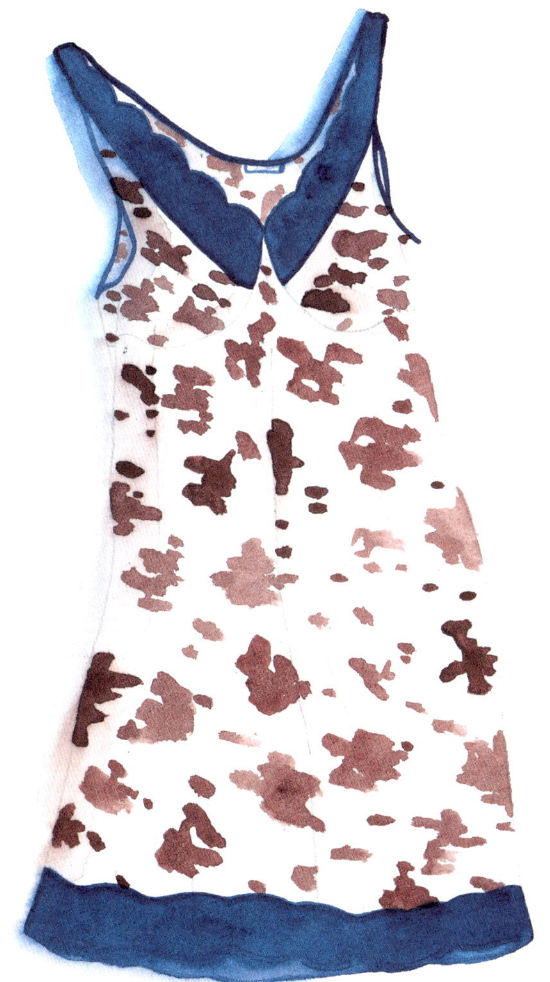

1.05 —

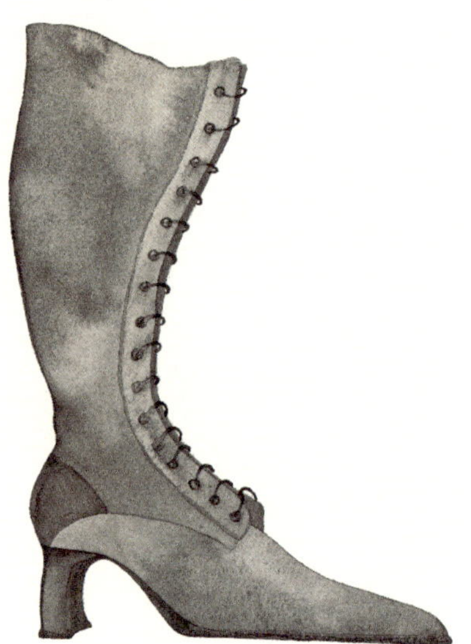

1.06 ——

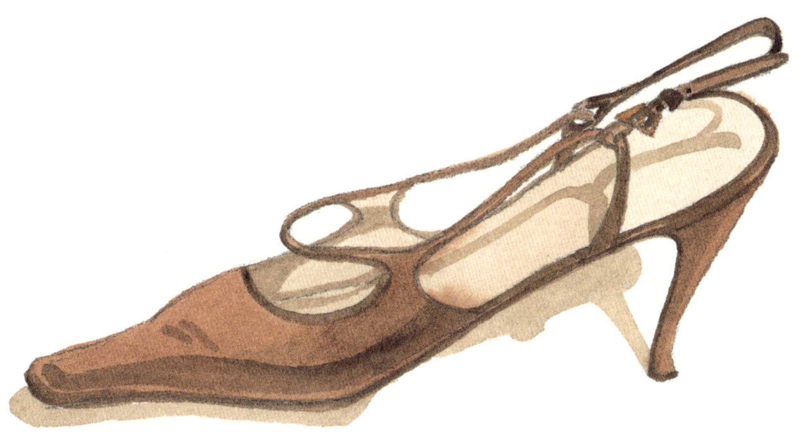

1.07 —

WARDROBE: SHOES

1.06 — 1.13 —
Stella's shoe collection combines a series of real designs
and inventions.

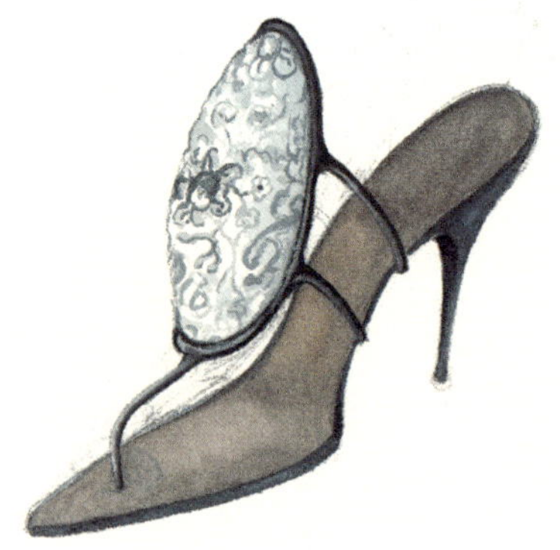

1.08 ——

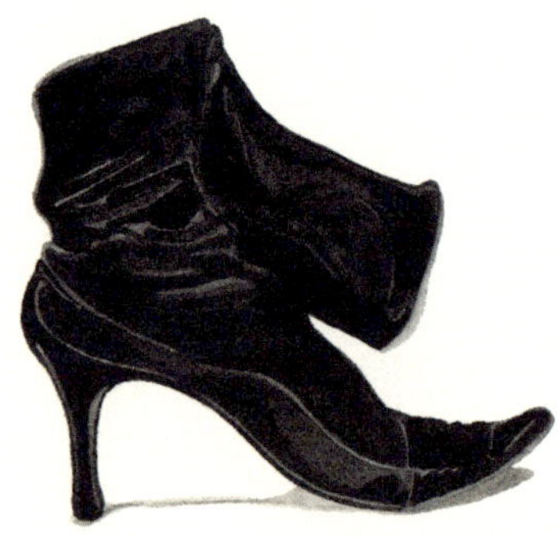

1.09 ——

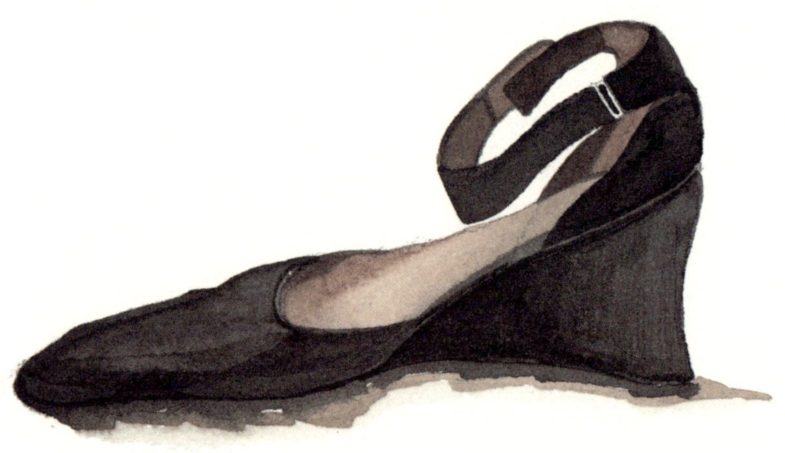

1.10 ——

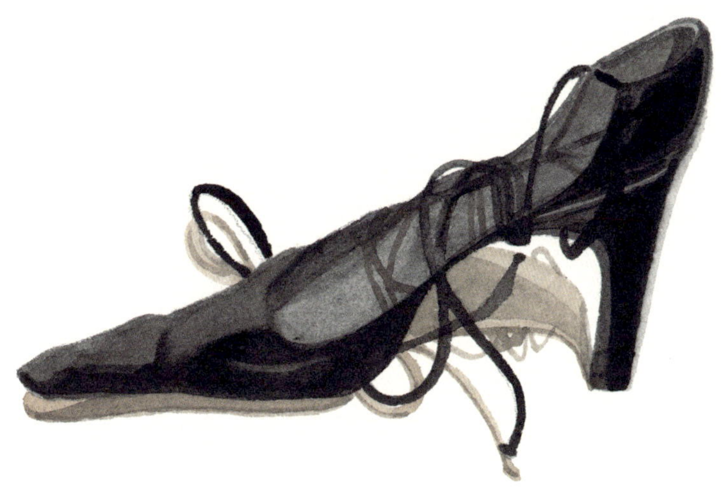

1.11 ——

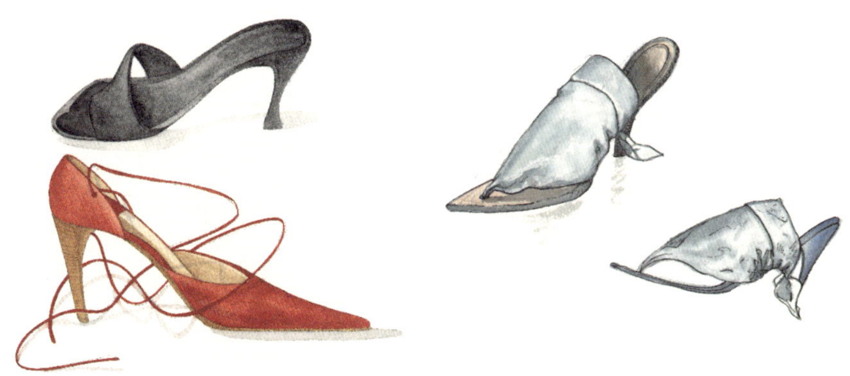

1.12 ——

1.13 ——

1.14 —

A floral plastic bag which Stella only uses on Capri.

1.15 —

Details of gloves, shoes and hands from Stella's Barbie
collection. Clockwise from the top, study of gloves and
feet from Barbie as Audrey Hepburn in *Breakfast At
Tiffany's*. Clockwise from the bottom, study of hands
and feet from Barbie as Marylin Monroe in *Cabaret*.
Stella owns thirty-five Barbie dolls.

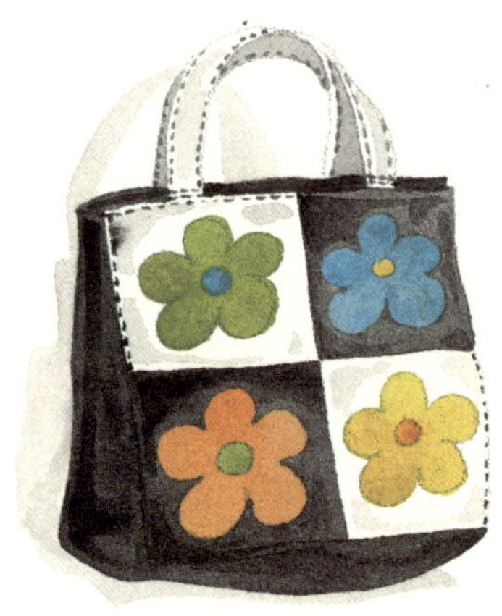

1.14 —

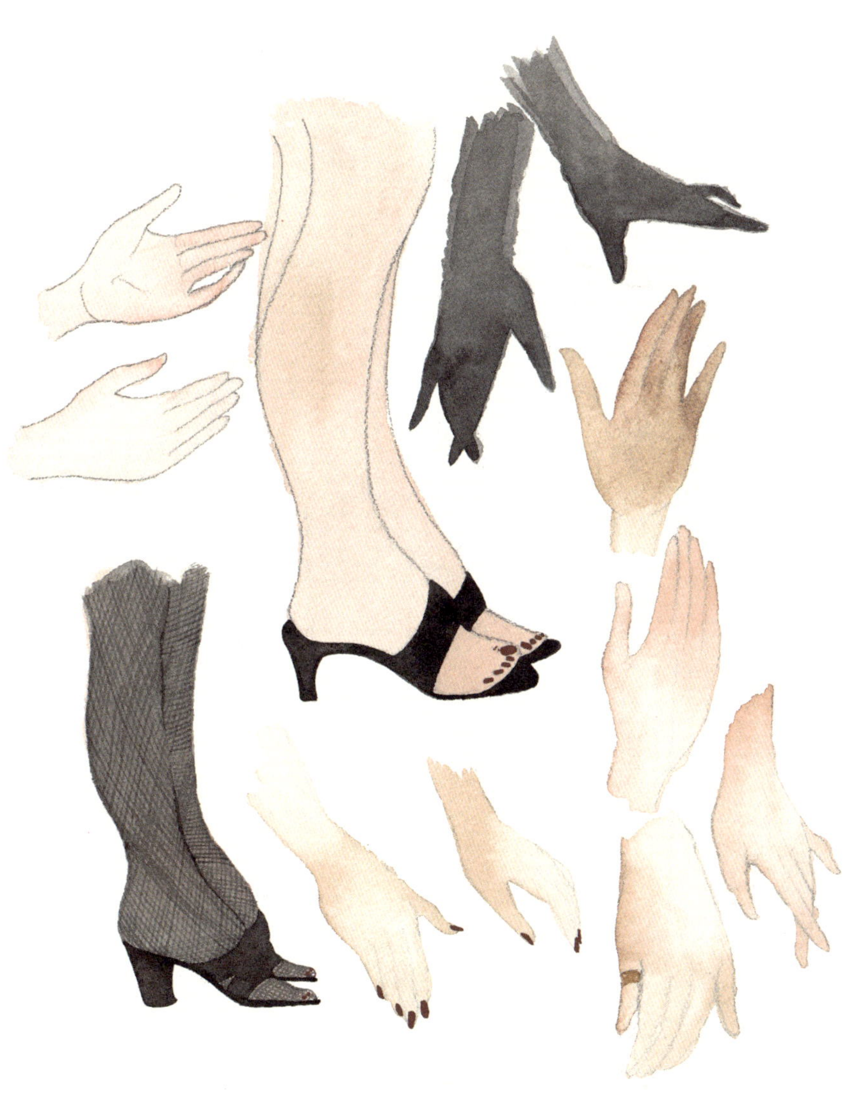

1.15 —

WARDROBE: UNDERWEAR

1.16 — 1.18 —
A series of Stella's underwear.

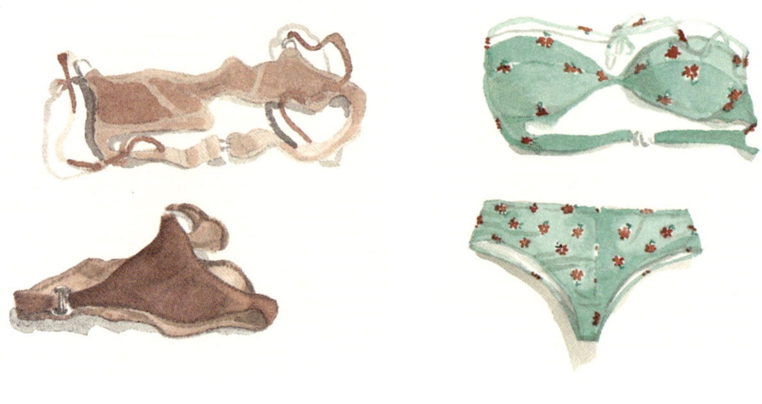

1.16 —

1.17 —

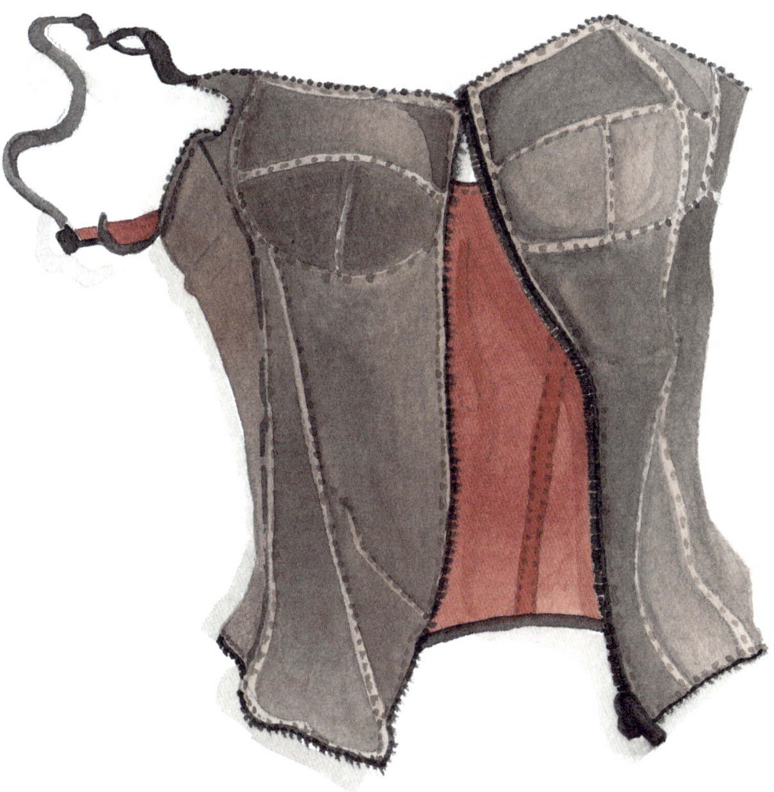

1.18 —

IMAGINARY SELF-PORTRAITS

1.19 ——

Self-Portrait of Stella as Greta Garbo. Stella, who identifies her alter-ego in the diva, has made a slight alteration to a photo taken from the film-star's website. In the picture, Stella has made Garbo's hair redder and more like her own hair. The text and image on this sheet are associated, as often occurs in Stella's notebooks, the text and image on this sheet of paper are detached from each other, as if they were jottings in a diary. The text is a quotation from the *Code of the Samurai:* 'My heart burns like fire but my eyes are as cold as dead ashes. Each day of my life, before dressing, I shall burn incense and mediate; I shall go to bed at the same time, I shall feed myself at regular intervals. I shall eat in moderation and never to my fill. I shall receive a guest with the same demeanour I have when alone. When alone, I shall have the same demeanour that I have when I receive guests. I shall be careful about what I say, and whatever I say, I shall do. When an opportunity occurs, I shall not let it escape me, but before acting I shall think twice. I shall not regret the past. I shall look to the future. I shall take the intrepid stance of a hero and the tender heart of a child. As soon as I go to bed I shall sleep as though it were my last sleep. As soon as I get up I shall leave my bed behind as if I had thrown away an old pair of shoes.'

Il mio cuore brucia come il fuoco ma i miei occhi sono freddi come ceneri morte.
Ogni giorno della mia vita prima di vestirmi brucerò dell'incenso e mediterò;
mi coricherò alla stessa ora; mi nutrirò a intervalli regolari.
Mangerò con moderazione e mai a sazietà.
Riceverò un ospite con lo stesso atteggiamento che ho quando sono solo. Ma solo, conserverò lo stesso atteggiamento che avrò quando riceverò ospiti.
Baderò a ciò che dico, e qualunque cosa dica, la metterò in pratica.
Quando si presenterà un'occasione non me la lascerò scappare, ma prima di agire ci penserò due volte.
Non rimpiangerò il passato. Guarderò al futuro. Avrò l'atteggiamento intrepido di un eroe e il cuore tenero di un bambino.
Non appena andrò a letto, dormirò come se quello fosse il mio ultimo sonno.
Non appena mi sveglierò, lascerò subito il letto dietro di me come se avessi gettato via un paio di scarpe vecchie.

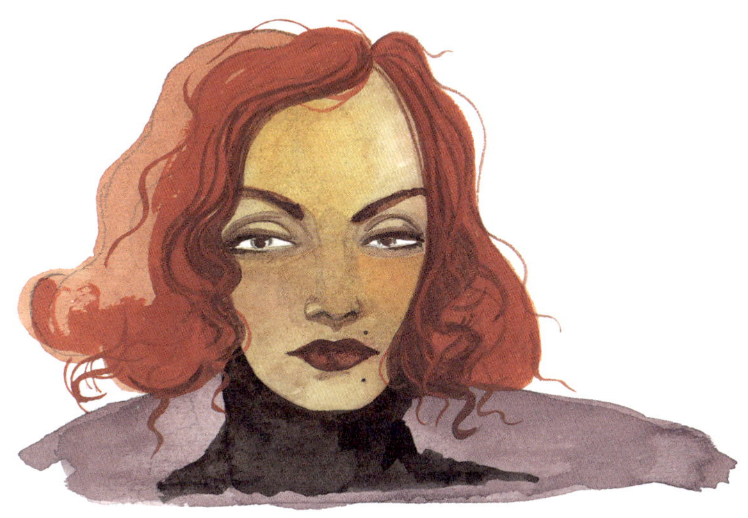

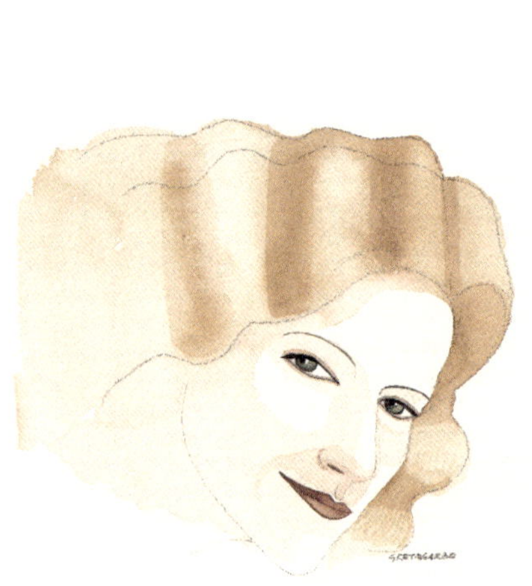

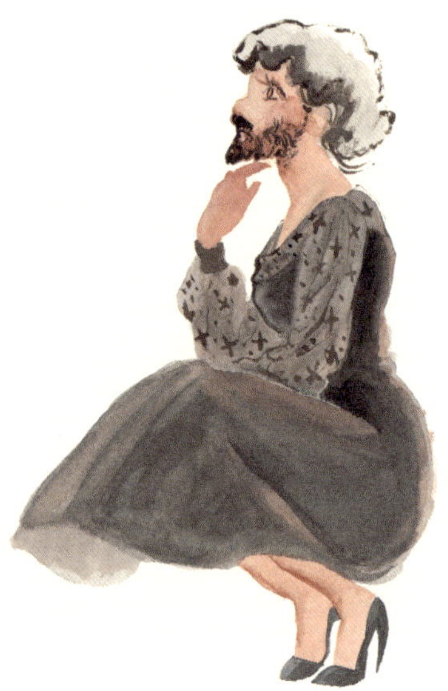

1.20 ——

Self-Portrait of Stella as Greta Garbo. Stella professes that her second name is Greta. Here she is drawn in a gentler version. Stella's identification with the personality of Greta Garbo dates back to her childhood.

1.21 ——

Self-Portrait of Jesus Dressed up as Stella. One of the imaginary self-portraits, this Jesus wears one of Stella's evening dresses. The idea was to invent a female Jesus, to imagine woman as the central figure in conventional religious iconography.

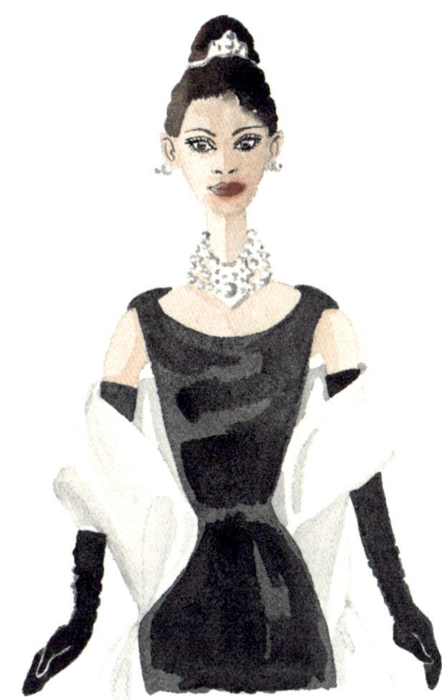

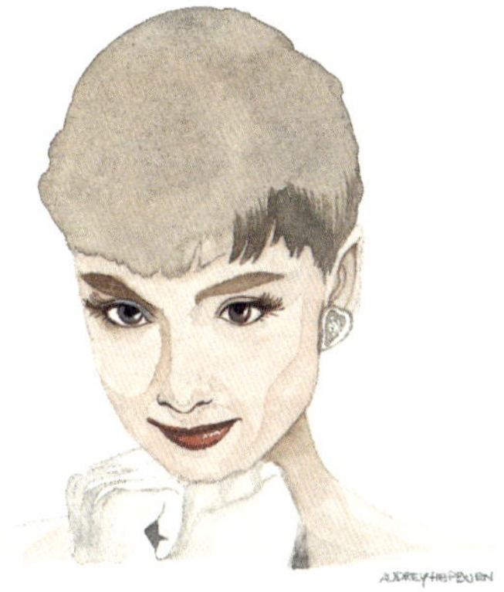

1.22 —

Self-Portrait of Stella as the Audrey Hepburn in
Breakfast at Tiffany's *Barbie Doll.*

1.23 —

Self-Portrait as Audrey Hepburn. As the incarnation
of emotiveness and fragility, Audrey Hepburn belongs
to a series of icons of female stars and celebrities from
the 1960s whom Stella identifies as being a part of
herself and who form her innermost world. Like a
contemporary Olympus, Hollywood divas have
influenced and genetically modified the childhood
imagination of generations in Europe.

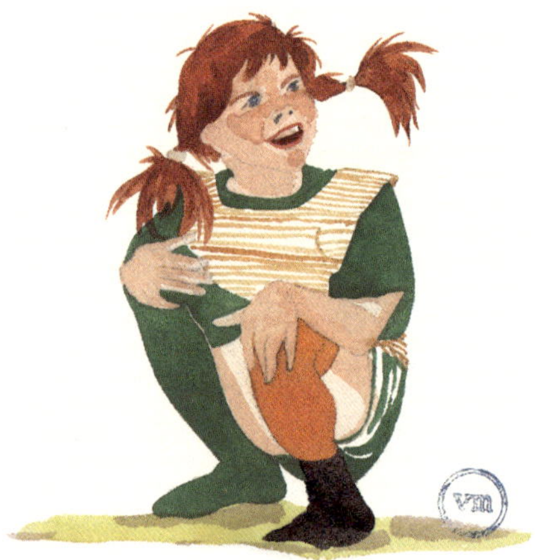

1.24 —

Watercolour Self-Portrait of Stella as Pippi. When
Stella was seven, her first reading-book was *Pippi
Longstocking.* She has still got her copy, illustrated
with her collages, and it is one of her most important
possessions. Stella often states that one part of herself
is Barbie and another part is Pippi. She has got all
the episodes of the TV series and films about Pippi,
whom she considers a heroine and Pinocchio's
female counterpart. In Italy, an icon of feminism is
established in Pippi, who anticipates the work by
many contemporary female artists when she makes
a patchwork quilt or draws a spotted horse, and not
on the blackboard, or invents the talking tree.

PHOTOGRAPH AND VIDEO SELF-PORTRAITS:
DIVIDED-UP OBJECTS

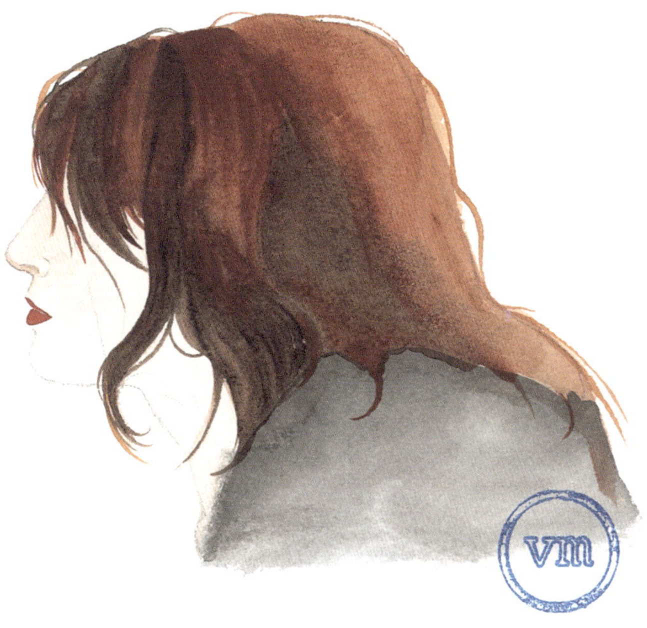

1.25 —

Stella's profile. In her self-portraits, Stella pays
special attention to her hair. This is a legacy from her
art school training and the study of hairstyles in the
Roman portraiture collection in the Naples'
Archaeological Museum.

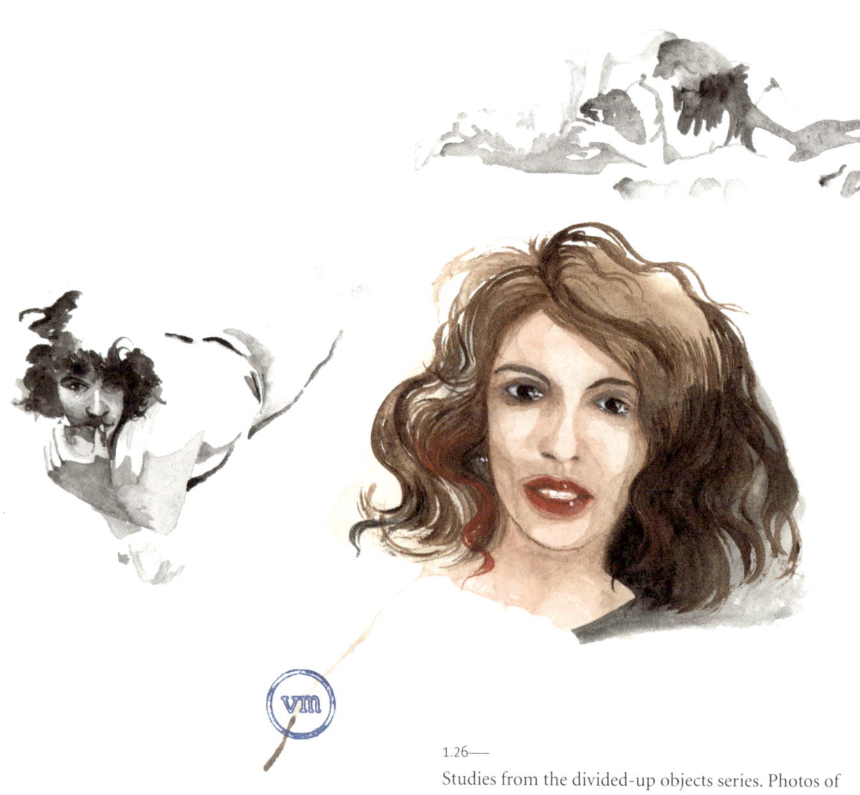

1.26—

Studies from the divided-up objects series. Photos of
Simeone and Stella, which Stella has recreated as
duplicates and separated from each other. In the top
right, self-portrait of Stella and Simeone embracing
and set on a bench in Venice. On the left, portrait of
Simeone taken by Stella at the 1987 Venice Biennale.
Portrait of present-day Stella in the centre.

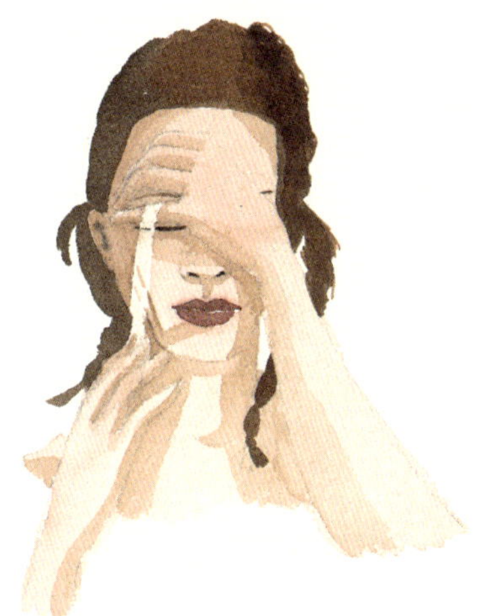

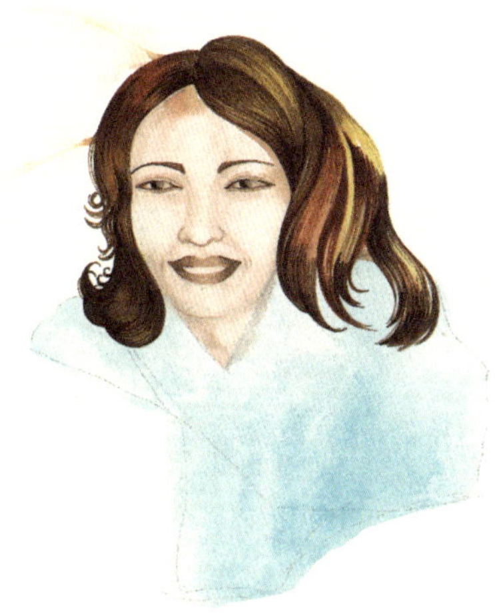

1.27 —

Stella self-portrait with sellotape on her nose. The
image appears again in the video by vedovamazzei
Pupa quae etiam carne humana vecitur (1994). This
picture precedes the super 8 video of 1994, which was
then re-recorded on VHS and presented by Guenzani
in Milan for vedovamazzei's first solo exhibition.
In the 1970s Stella asked her father to lend her his
videocamera to make this film. Her mother asked to
be allowed to name it. In the film, Stella disfigures
herself by sticking sellotape on her face. First she sticks
it over her right eye, then over her left, and finally over
her nose and mouth. When her mother saw the film
she said that it looked like a doll in a horror film that
is swallowing itself. And, since she was a Latin teacher,
named the work *Pupa quae etiam carne humana
vecitur*, or *Doll Which Also Feeds On Human Flesh*.

1.28 —

Stella self-portrait. Here, the portrait's distinctiveness
also lies in the treatment of her hair.

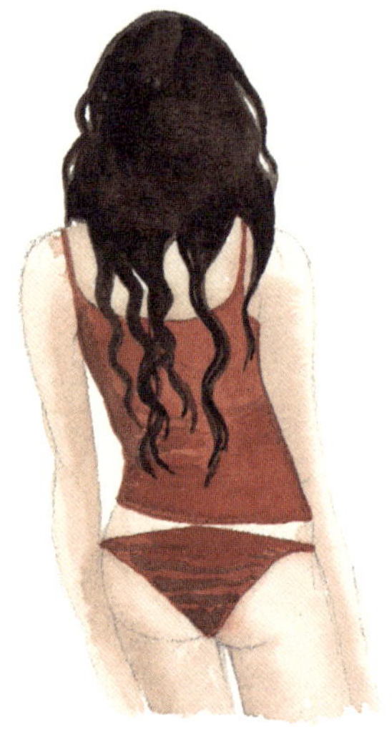

PHOTOGRAPH AND VIDEO SELF-PORTRAITS: NUDES

1.29 ——

1.29 —1.34 ——
Self-portraits and nudes by Stella. The pleasure of depicting oneself in studies and real and imaginary details. Here, the picture takes up the theme of hair as the only form of clothing, with a variation.

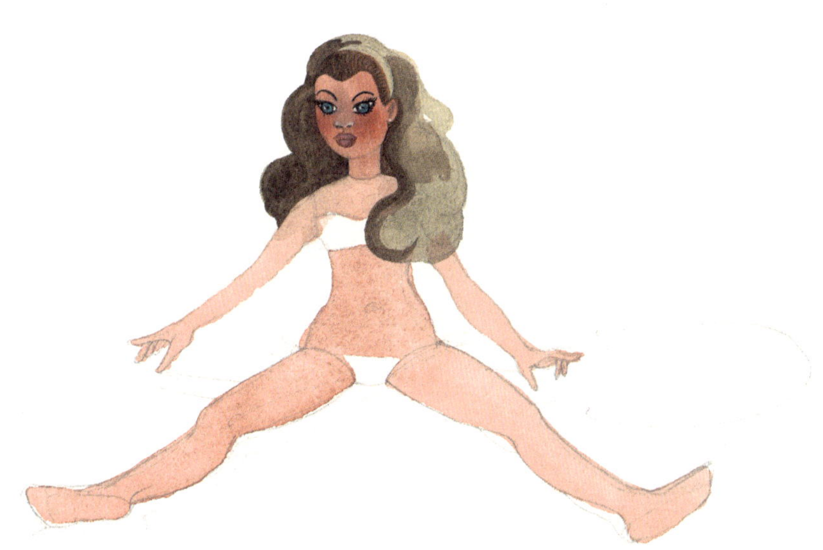

1.30 ——

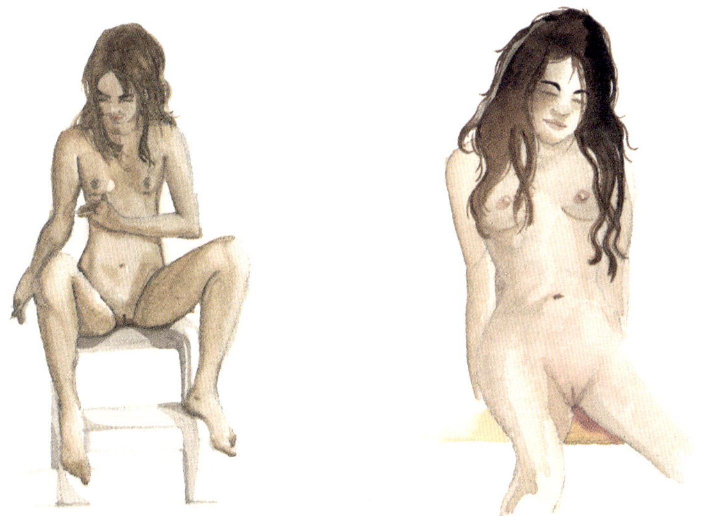

1.31 ——

1.32 ——

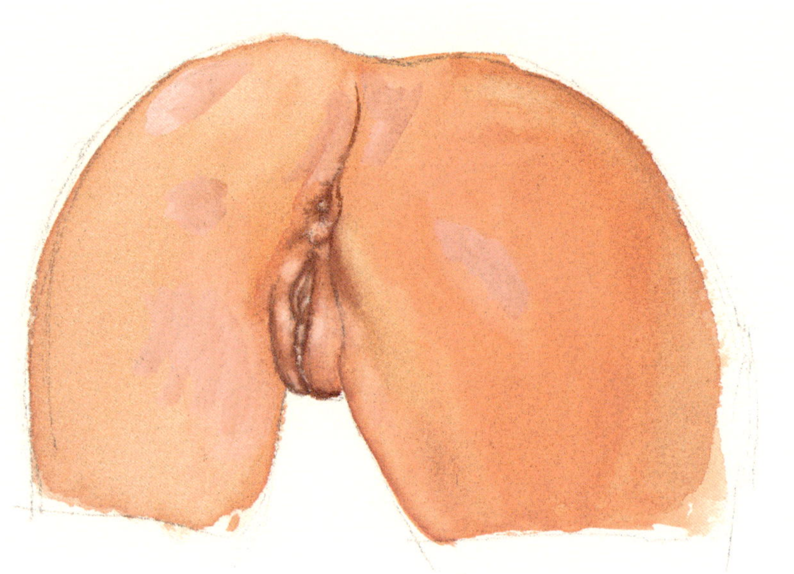

1.33 —

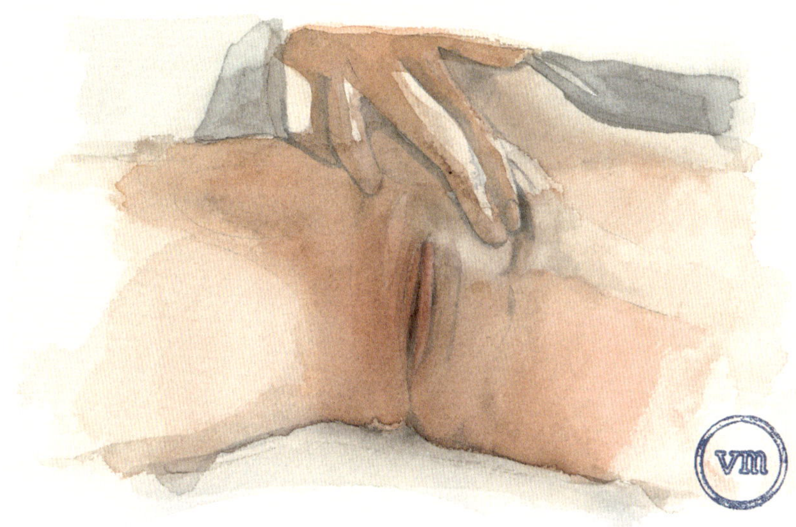

1.34 —

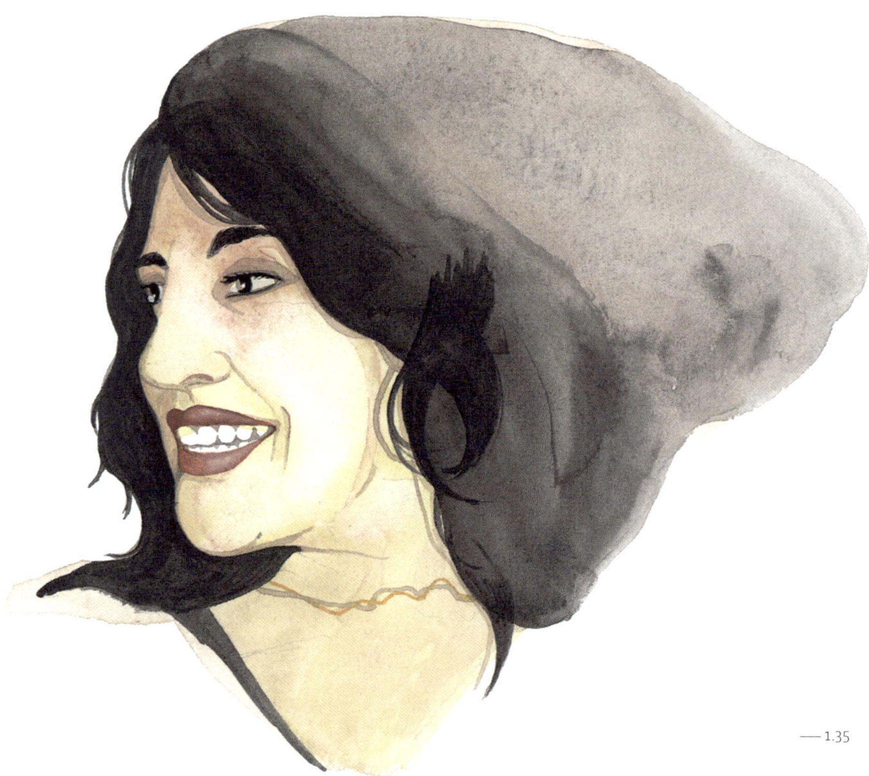

— 1.35

PHOTOGRAPH AND VIDEO SELF-PORTRAITS: STELLA

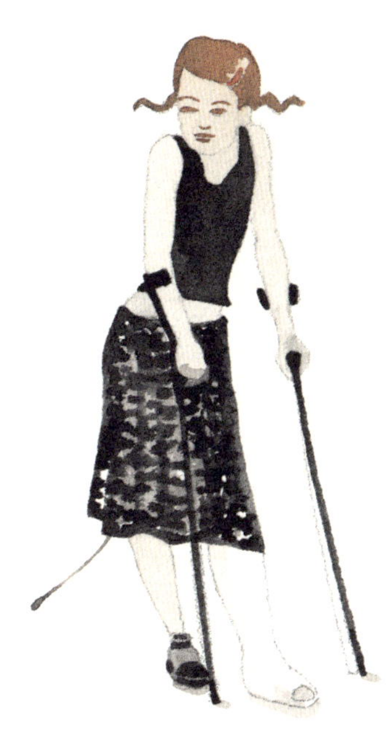

1.36 ——

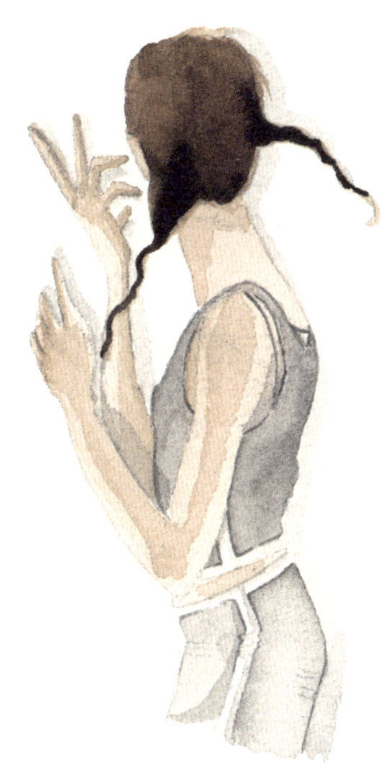

1.37 ——

1.35 — 1.40 ——
Real self-portraits by Stella at different times in her life.

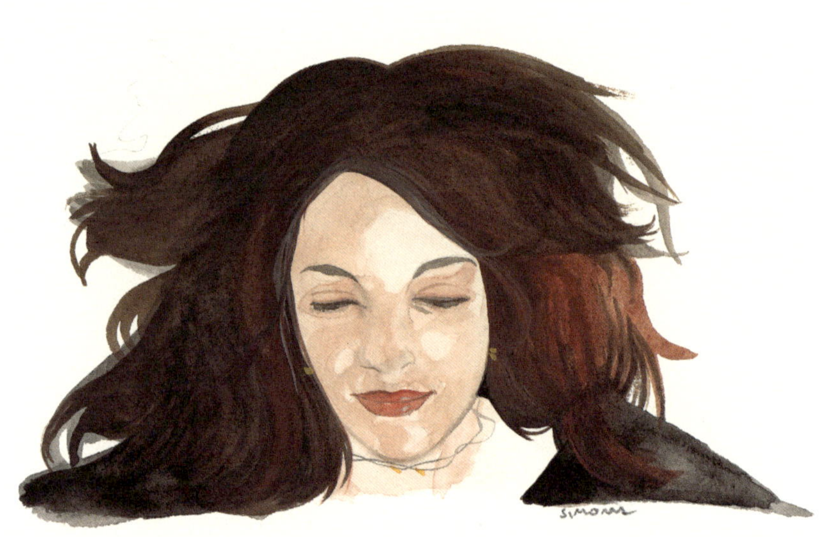

1.38 —

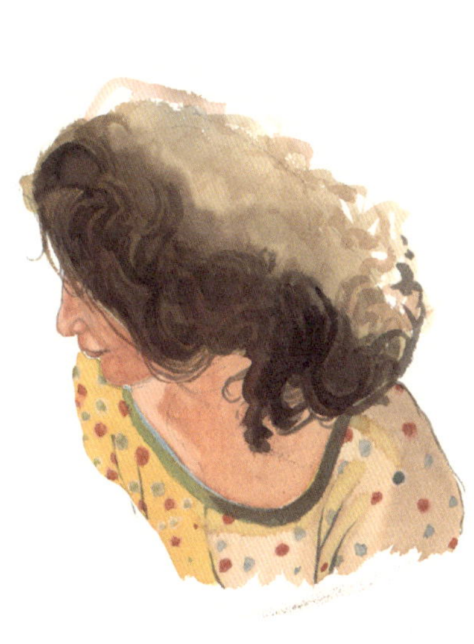

1.39 —

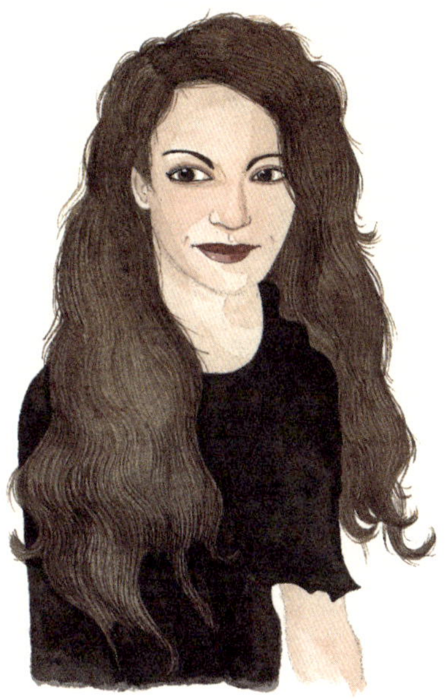

1.40 —

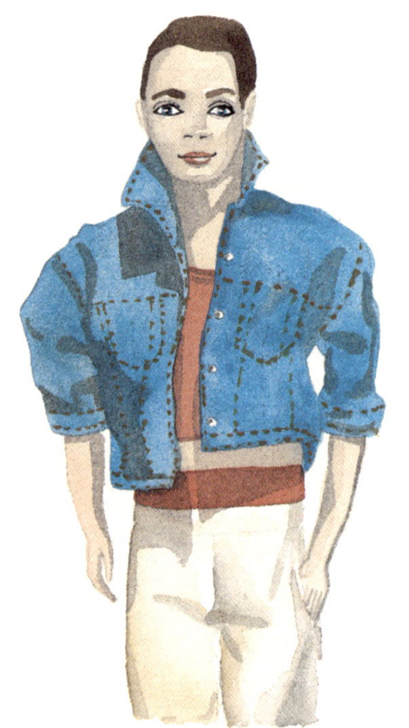

PORTRAITS: KEN AND SANTA LUCIA

1.41 ——

1.41 ——

One of the first Kens, from 1959. Simeone bought it in
New York for $120 for Stella's collection.

1.42 ——

St. Lucia. An Italian religious icon seen as an icon of
Japanese pornography and a hybrid of the two cultures.

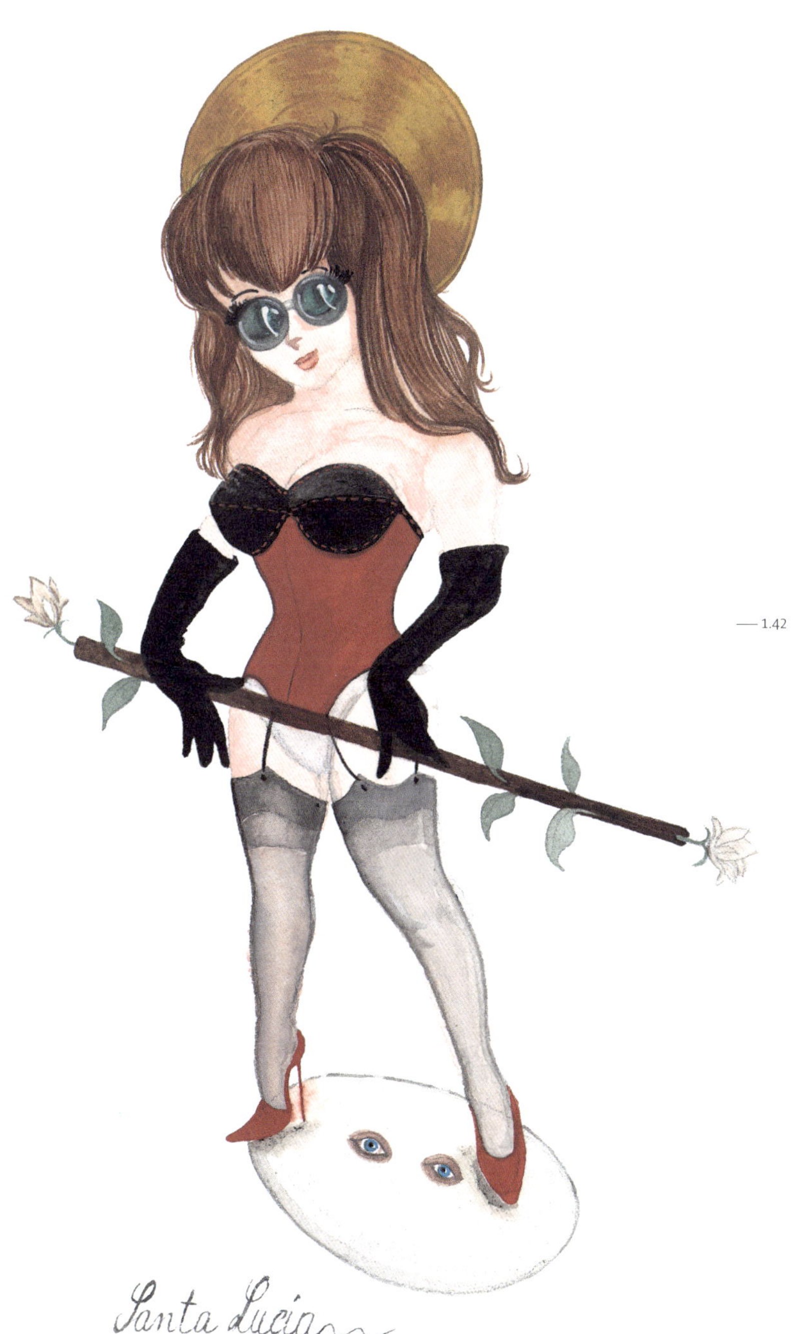

—— 1.42

IDENTIKIT

1.43 ——
Drawings of sweets used as bait by the offender.

1.44 ——
Identikit is Stella's memory of a trauma, of being raped as a child, taken from her personal journals. The text, a piece of almost mechanical writing on the memory, appears together with a portrait of the man who molested her and a self-portrait of herself as the small soft toy, used as bait.

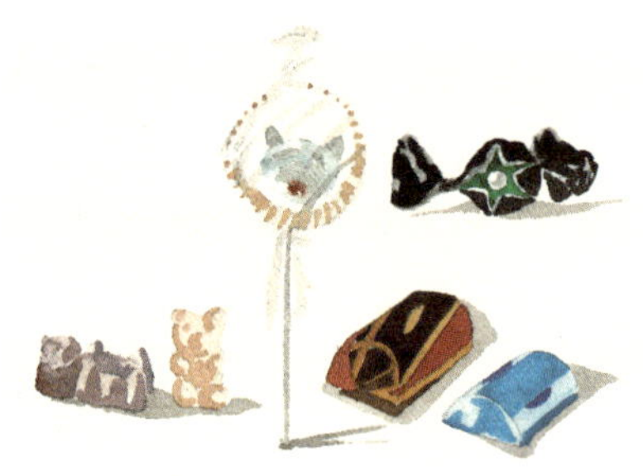

1.43 ——

Il metodo che seguito per calmarsi consiste
nell'inghiottire saliva. È bene considerare
il mondo alle stregua di un sogno. Quando
abbiamo un vicino, ci svegliamo e diciamo,
o non spesso di aver solo sognato, si dice che il
mondo nel quale viviamo non sia affatto diverso.

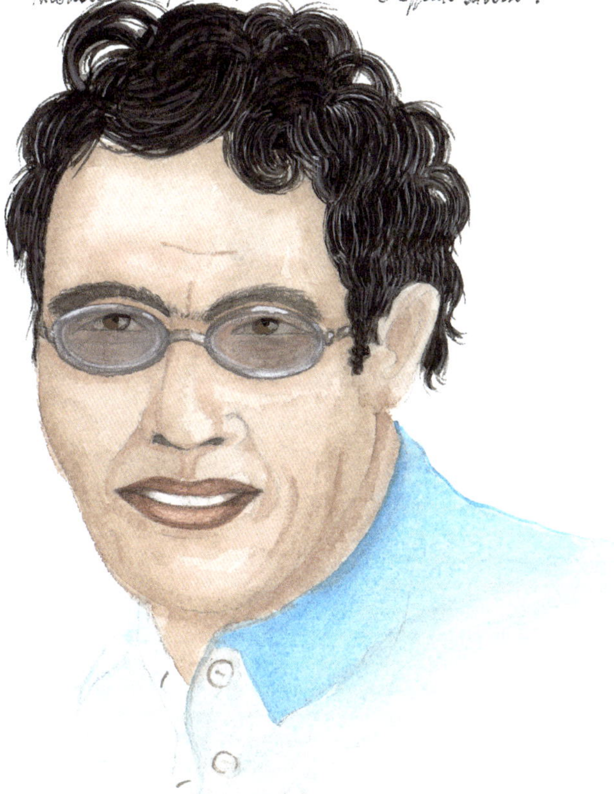

Gente Nova a facchiopena
un giorno, perdonare e
dimenticare
un uomo la cui reputazione
si basa nella sua abilità tecnica
è uno stupido. Concentrando
tutta la sua energia in un solo
campo, certamente vi eccelle, ma non è
ritornato ad altro. Un uomo simile è inutile.

1.44—

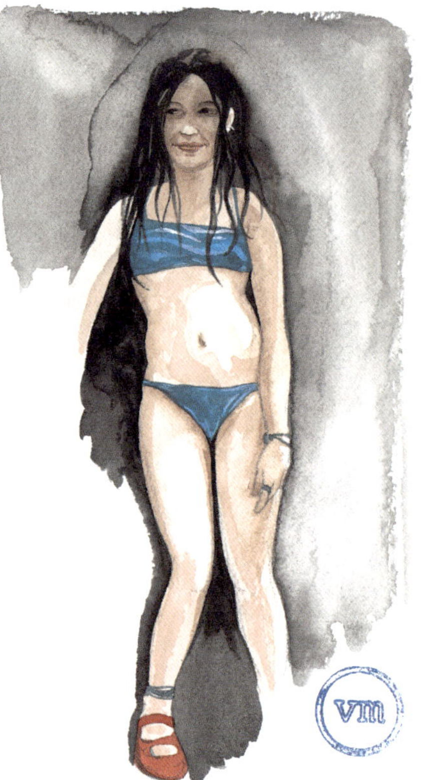

PORTRAITS: THE FAMILY

1.45 ——

Portrait of one of Stella's Nieces with a red shoe.

1.46 ——

Portrait of Stella's Mother playing dead in a swimming
pool on Capri.

1.45 ——

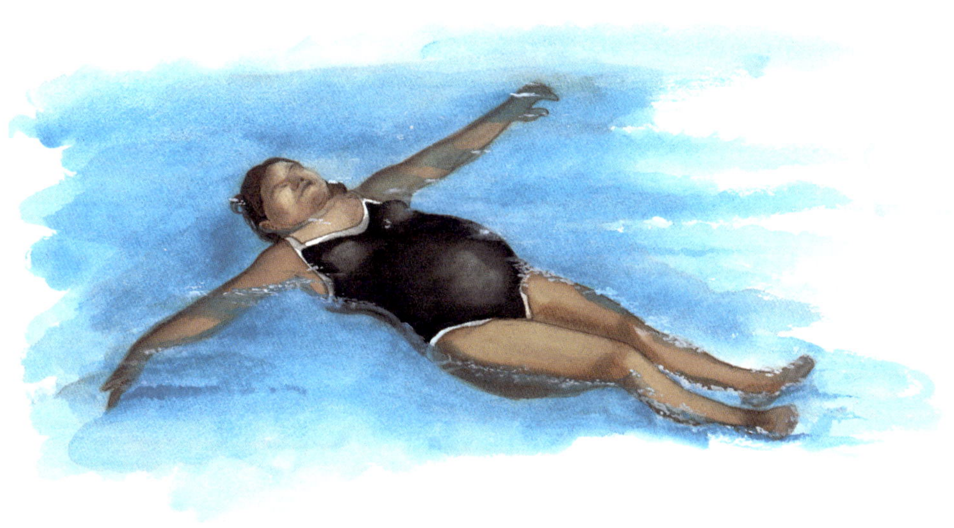

1.46 ——

WARDROBE: CLOTHES

1.47 ——
This second section of Chapter I mirrors the first
and is devoted to everything that belongs to Simeone.
Selected and portrayed in watercolour, Simeone's
possessions are organised according to the types of
garments from his wardrobe. The inventory of
belongings begins with Simeone's beautiful banana-
coloured Burberry coat.

ALL ABOUT SIMEONE

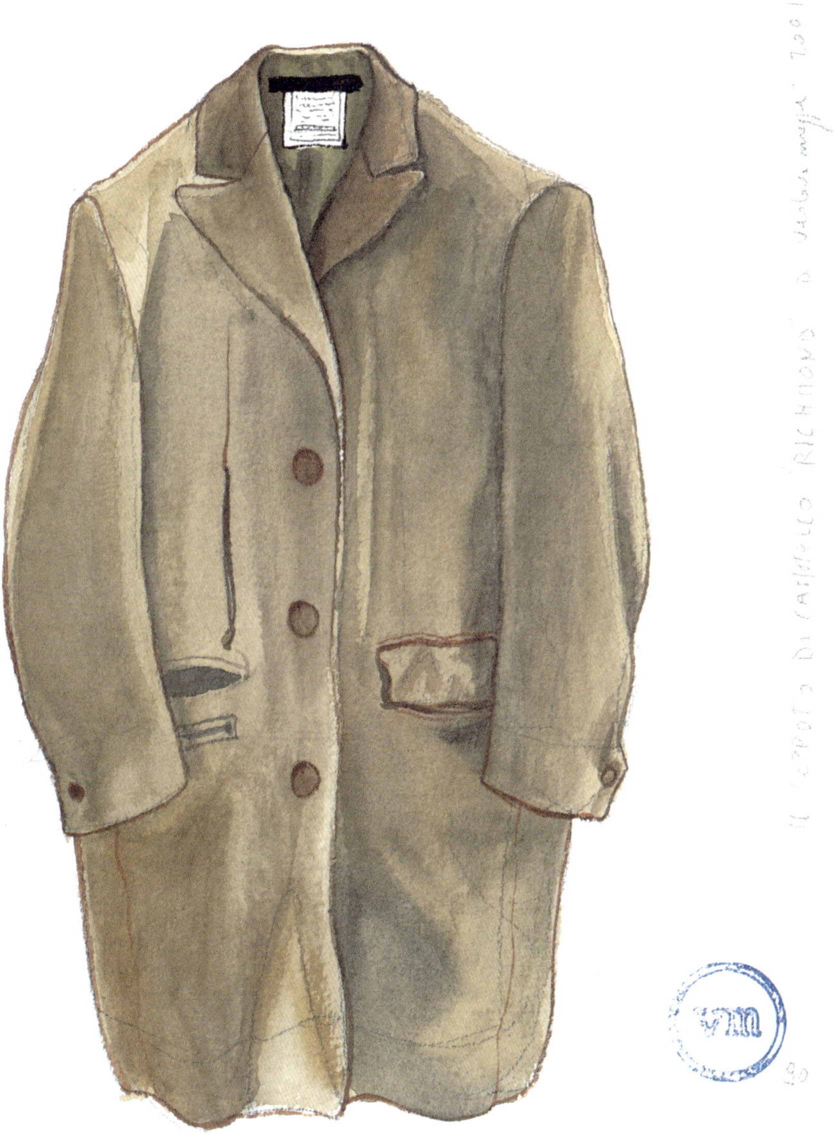

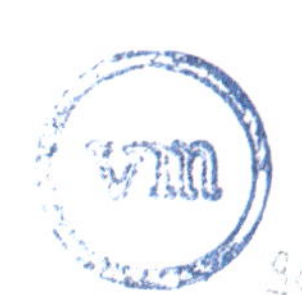

Il cappotto di cammello RICHMOND a falda morbida 1997

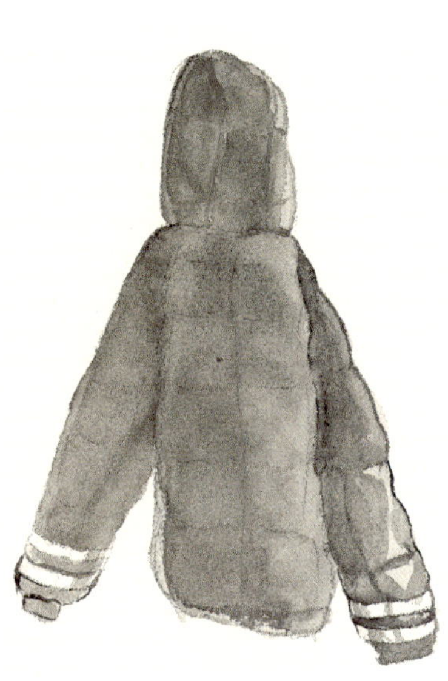

1.48 ——

1.48 ——

A DKNY windcheater from 1999.

1.49 ——

A Dries Van Noten glove from 1999.

1.49 —

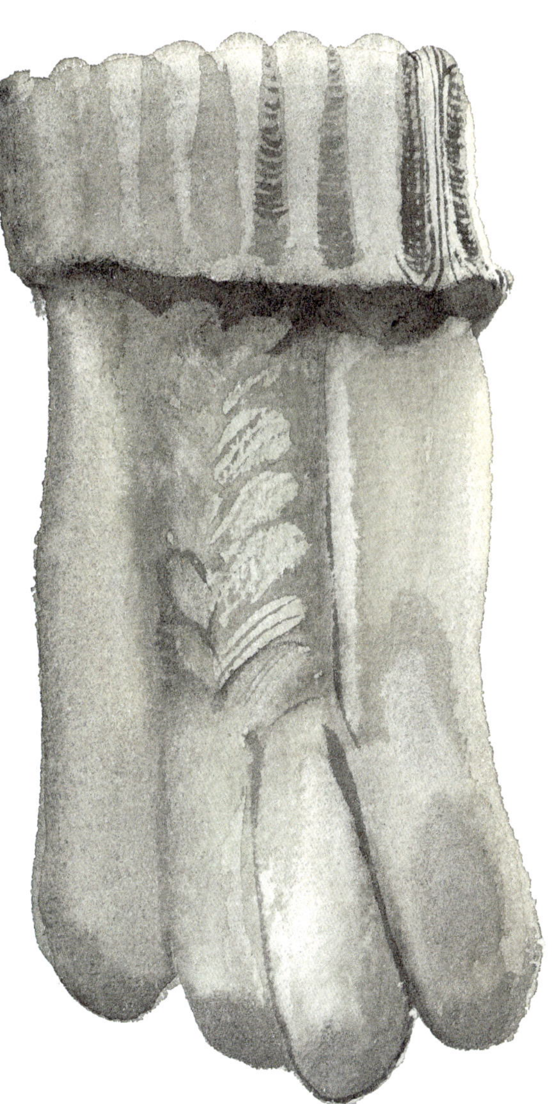

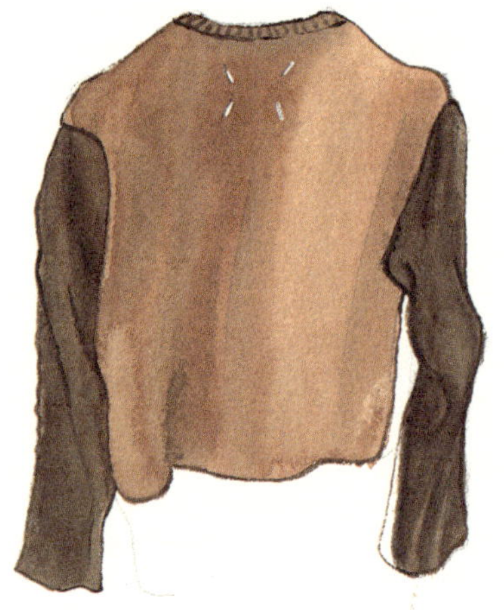

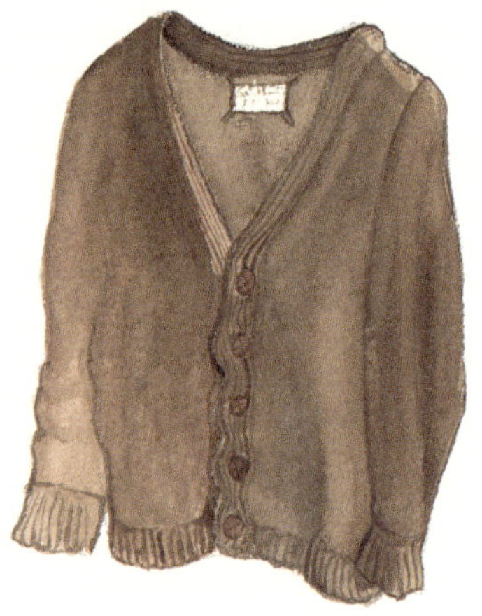

1.50 —

A Martin Margiela cotton sweater with leather sleeves from 1999.

1.51 —

A Martin Margiela cardigan.

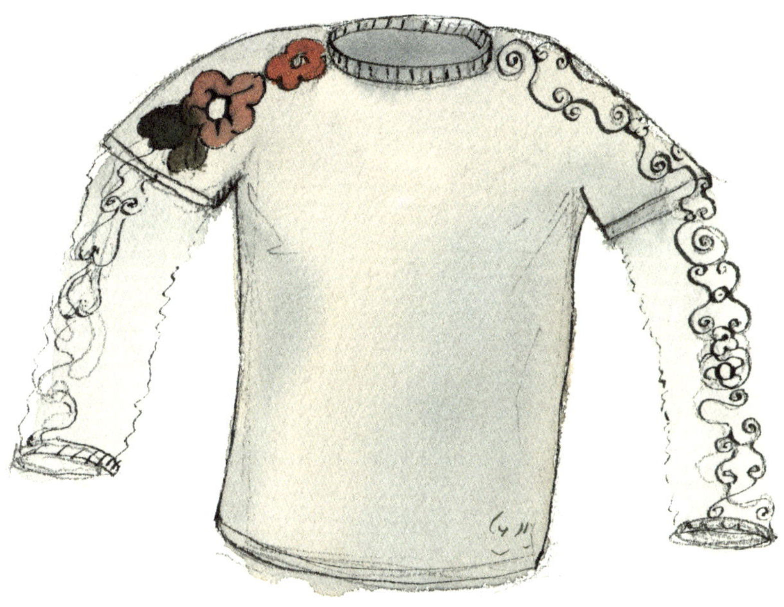

1.52 ——
A vintage flowery sweater, bought at the flea-market.

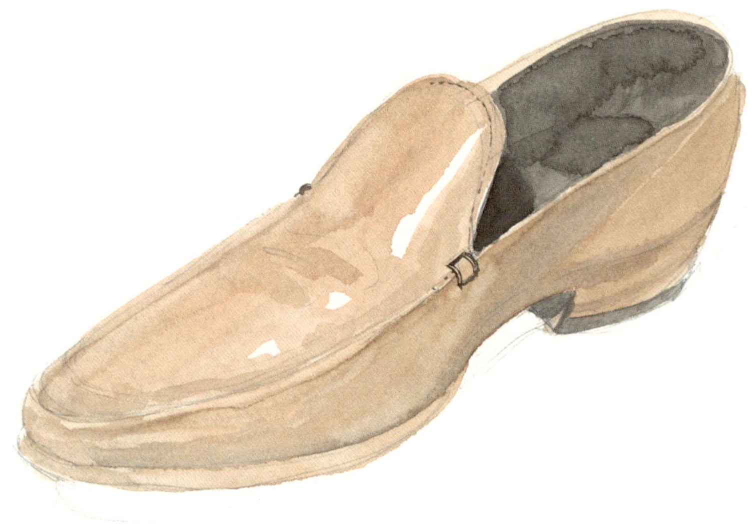

1.53 —
A Fendi slip-on shoe from 2001.

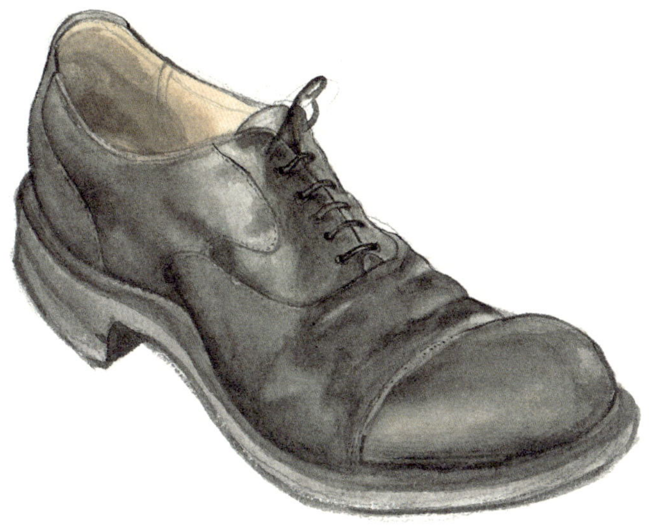

1.54 —
A black Church's shoe.

IMAGINARY SELF-PORTRAITS

1.55 —

Simeone and the Baby Jesus. Self-portrait of an adolescent Simeone at boarding school, masturbated in a dream by the infant Jesus. The composition demonstrates great familiarity with religious iconography and is the first picture on the subject by Simeone. The extremely liberal treatment of the subject makes this piece the ideal companion to the self-portrait of *Jesus Dressed As Stella.*

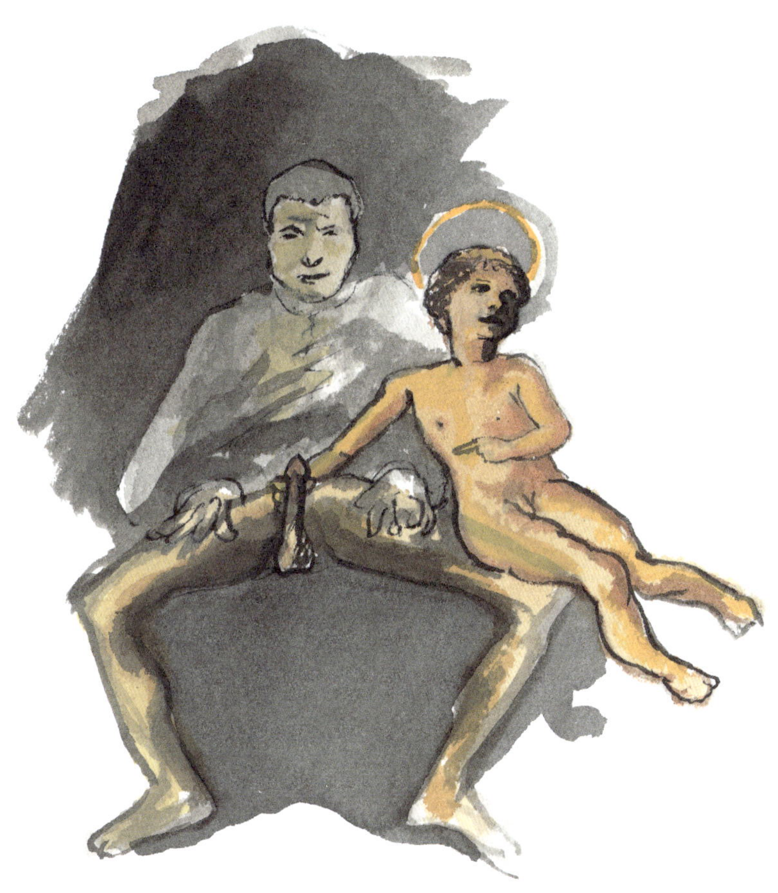

1.56 —

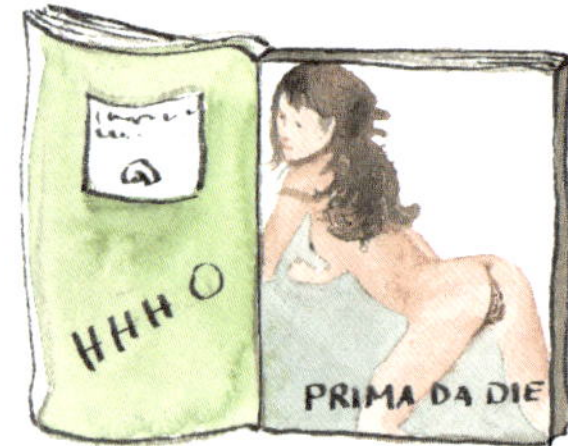

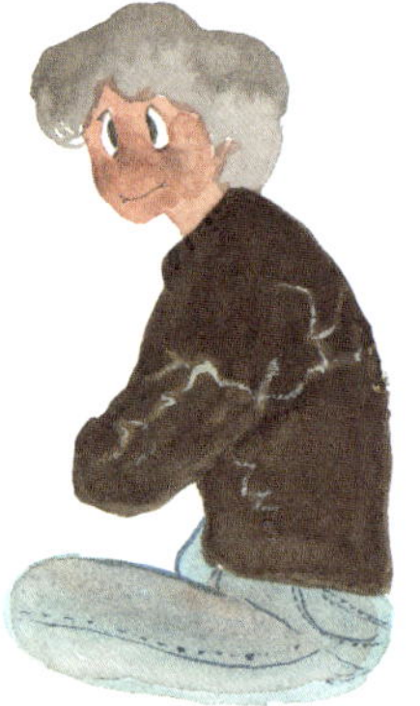

AVEVO 13 ANNI
ERO IN COLLEGIO
A S. MARINELLA.
FUI SORPRESO
CON UNA RIVISTA
PORNO. MI SONO
FATTO ROSSO IN
FACCIA. LA PRIMA
VOLTA CHE PADRE
GIUSEPPE MI
FECE IL DISCORSO.
ECCO…

le erbe sono
buone da mangiare

il primitivo ESPANSIVO e catena
'chi è'?
UNO CHE aspetta la civiltà
o che l'ha inventata e la
domina?

— 1.57

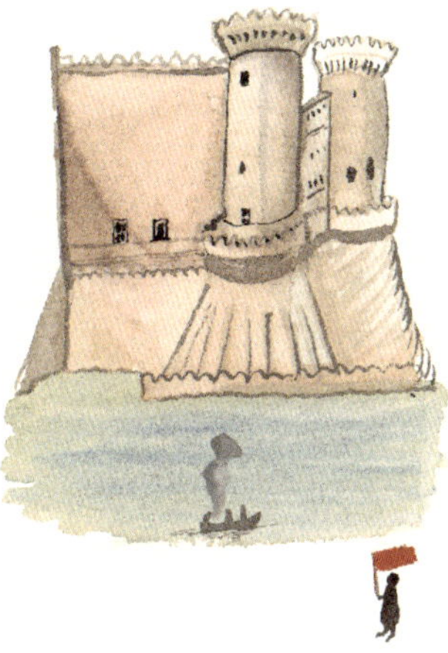

1.58 ——

1.56 ——

Self-Portrait of a Thirteen-Year-Old Simeone, caught at boarding school with a pornographic magazine. Between the ages of nine and fifteen, Simeone grew up in a religious boarding school. The Jesuit and Murialdine school was 56km north of the Via Aurelia and artists and intellectuals, including Pier Paolo Pasolini and Orson Welles, often gave lessons there. Simeone also remembers a visit by Pope Paul VI.

1.57 ——

Self-Portrait of Simeone as a Seal. In this watercolour, Simeone has depicted himself at the age of ten, just before a test at boarding school, as a seal on the verge of being attacked by a shark. As often occurs in Simeone's sketch-books, brief, apparently nonsensical remarks accompany the pictures. Here he writes: 'Who is the effusive and courteous primitive? One who awaits civilisation or one who has overtaken and dominates it?' This self-portrait is the companion to a 1994 vedovamazzei work in which Stella is depicted as a dog. A photograph portrays her just as she saw herself without her contact lenses, naked in the bath with a dog mask on her face.

1.58 ——

Self-Portrait of Simeone at the Angevin Fortress at the age of fifteen when he was first stopped by the police with a joint in his hand.

SELF-PORTRAITS

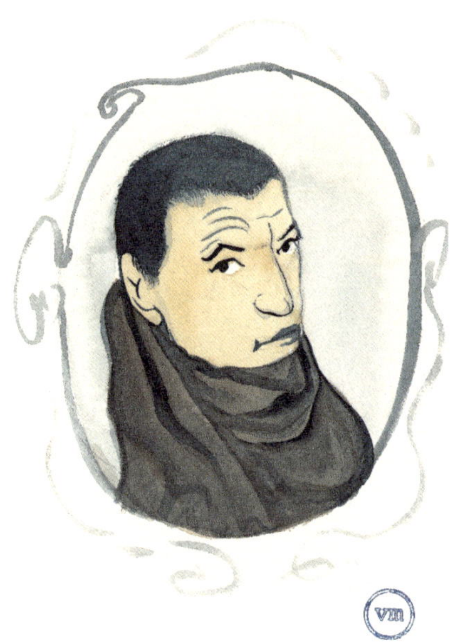

1.59 —

1.59 —
Self-Portrait in a Japanese Style (2001).

1.60 —
Self-Portrait of Simeone as the Reincarnation of Trajan,
as seen by Mario Merz (2001).

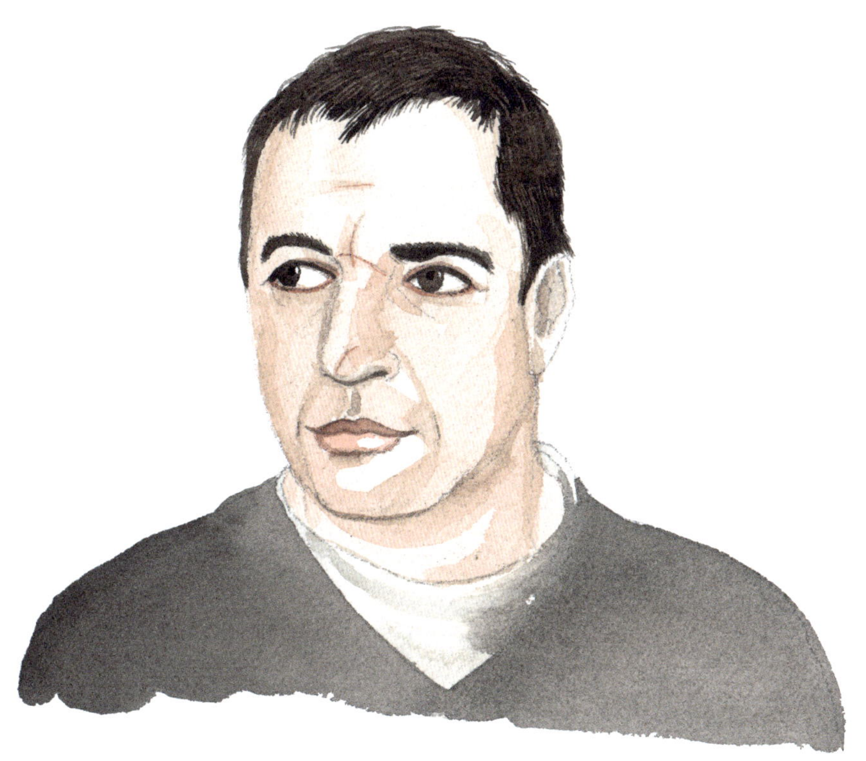

— 1.60

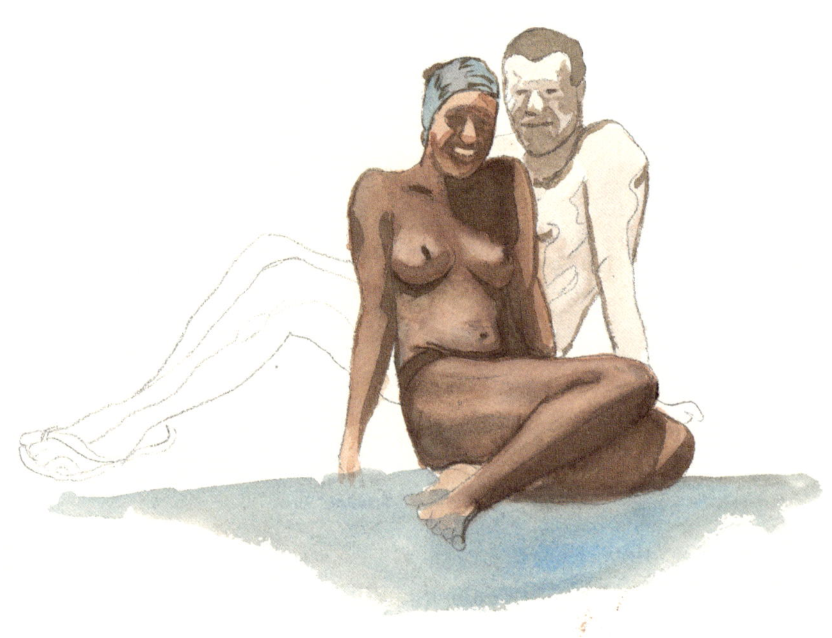

1.61 —

1.61 —
Self-Portrait with Roberta A. in Alicudi (2001).

1.62 —
Self-Portrait as Zeus, in Alicudi (2001).

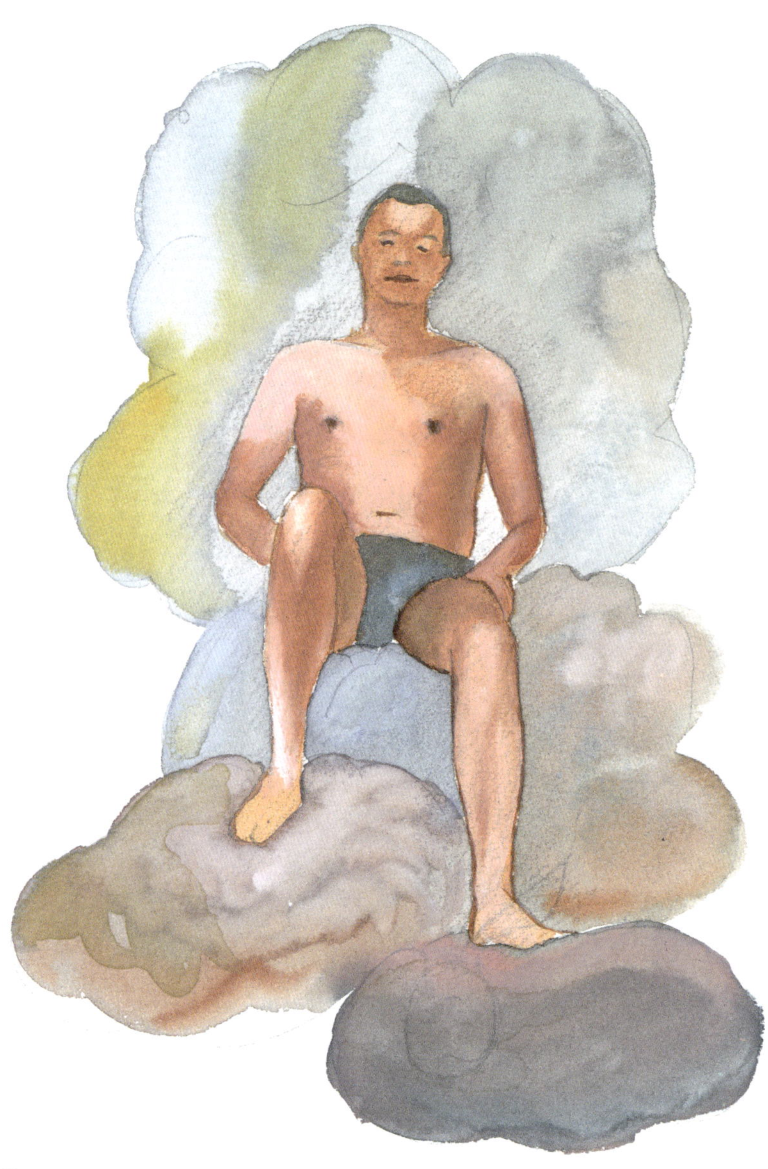

1.62 —

SELF-PORTRAITS: PUBIC MEMORIES AND FEET

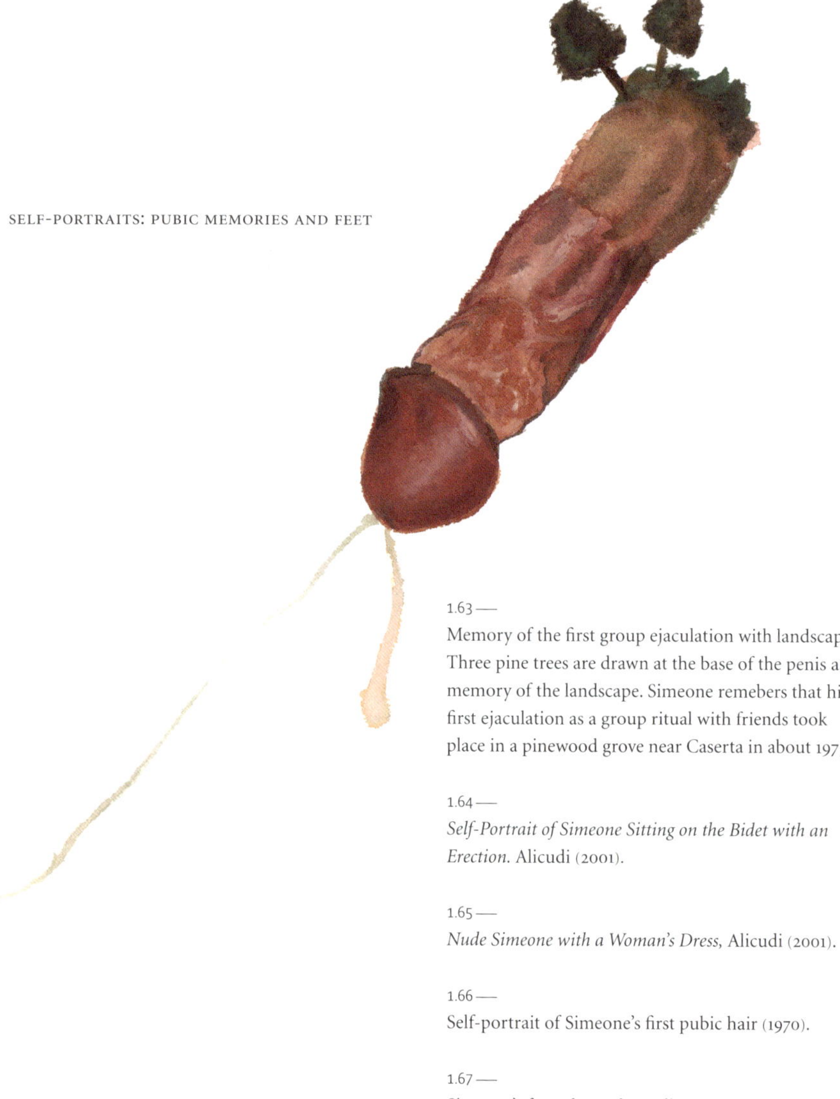

1.63 —

Memory of the first group ejaculation with landscape.
Three pine trees are drawn at the base of the penis as a
memory of the landscape. Simeone remebers that his
first ejaculation as a group ritual with friends took
place in a pinewood grove near Caserta in about 1975.

1.64 —

*Self-Portrait of Simeone Sitting on the Bidet with an
Erection.* Alicudi (2001).

1.65 —

Nude Simeone with a Woman's Dress, Alicudi (2001).

1.66 —

Self-portrait of Simeone's first pubic hair (1970).

1.67 —

Simeone's foot, drawn by Stella.

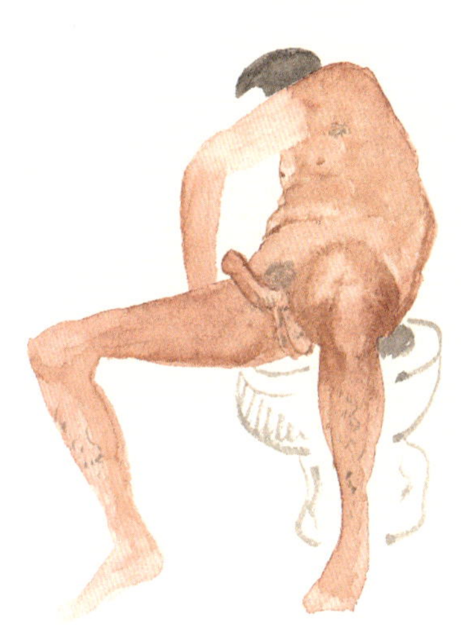

1.64 —

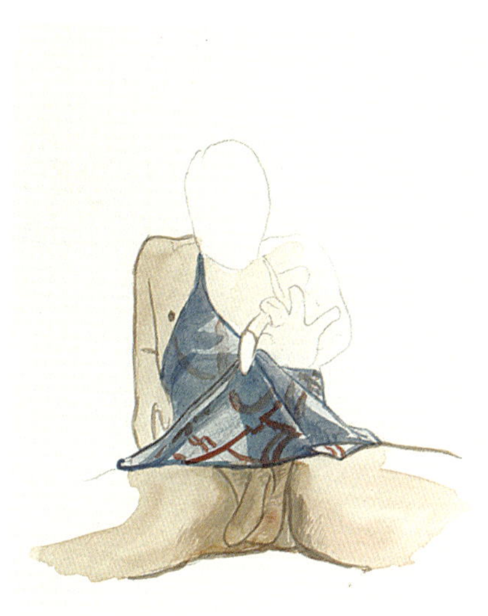

1.65 —

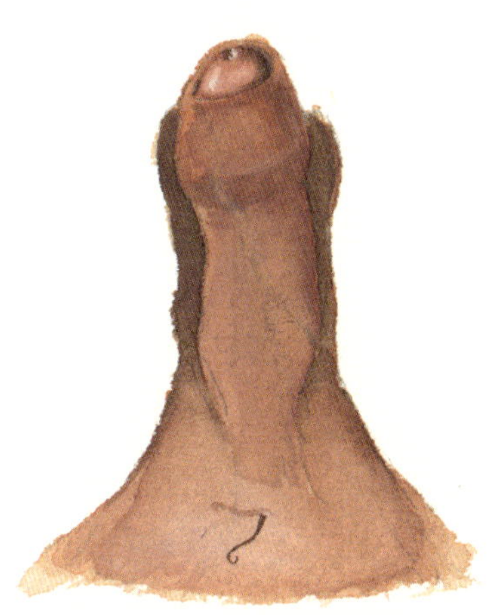

1.66 —

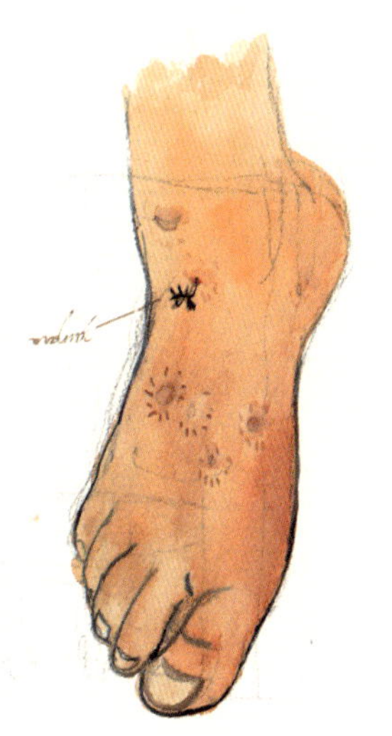

1.67 —

IDENTIKIT

1.68 ——

My First Corpse. A story about Simeone, drawn by
Stella. The first corpse found in the country at
Frattaminore by Simeonr, who was seven at the time,
and his brother Lazzaro, who was nine. The picture of
the dead man is accompanied by a list of objects
belonging to him, sharply defined in the childhood
memory.

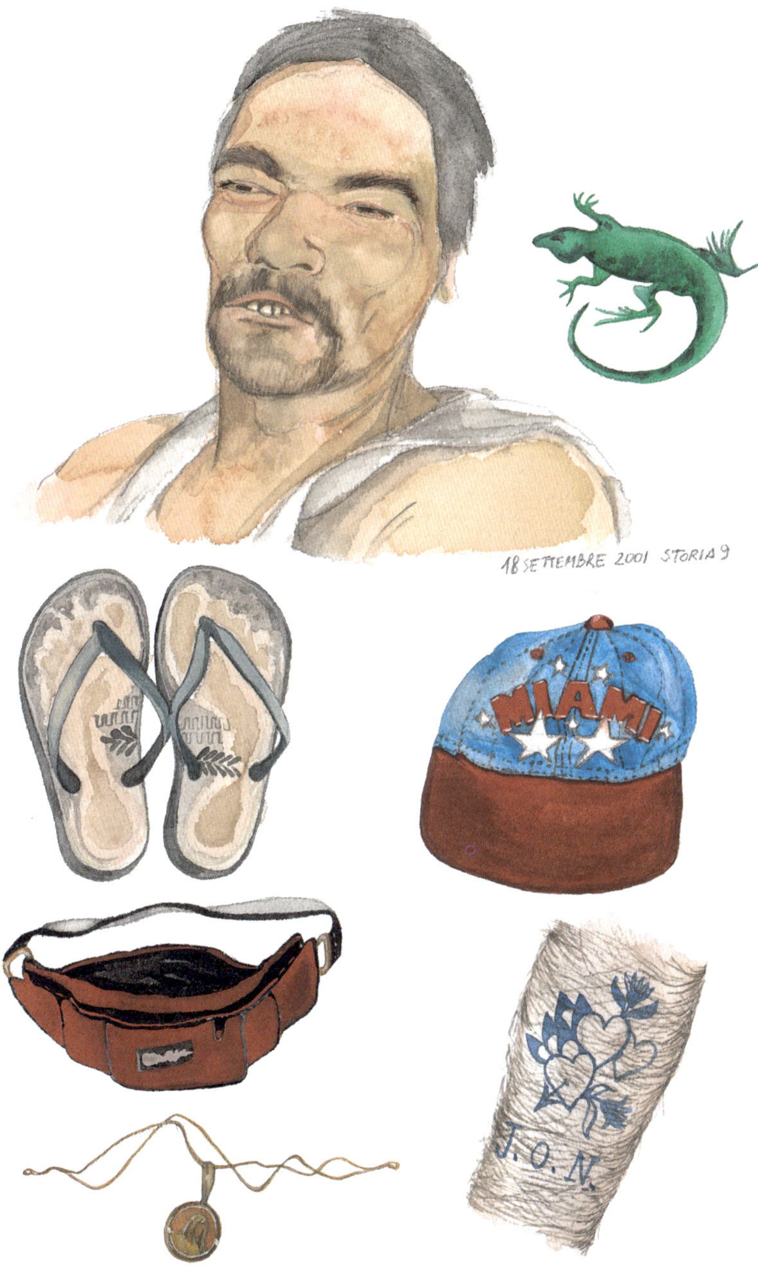
18 SETTEMBRE 2001 STORIA 9
MIAMI
J.O.N.

VEDOVAMAZZEI SEX ITEMS

BLUE TOYS

Cataloguing and studies of sex items and fetishes.
The blue toys belong to vedovamazzei's collection of
items sold in sex shops. The artists used some of these
drawings to create *T.I.M.I.T.W.* in 1995, a photographic
work featuring Simeone dressed as Mao Tse Tung.
This Is a Man In The World is a close-up of Simeone's
hands stretching a clitoral stimulator in serrated latex
rubber. By distorting it in this way, he seems to turn it
into the wide-open jaws of a crocodile. Here again is
the idea of a man with his collection of symbolic icons
telling the story of his life. According to vedovamazzei,
'These drawings are blue because blue and pale green
are vedovamazzei's colours. They started off as
drawings in a notepad, then they became a series.'

1.69 —
Sketch of an anal dildo with small pump. 'Everything
viewed from close up is pornographic,' says
vedovamazzei.

1.70 —
Sketch of a shell vibrator with electric motor.

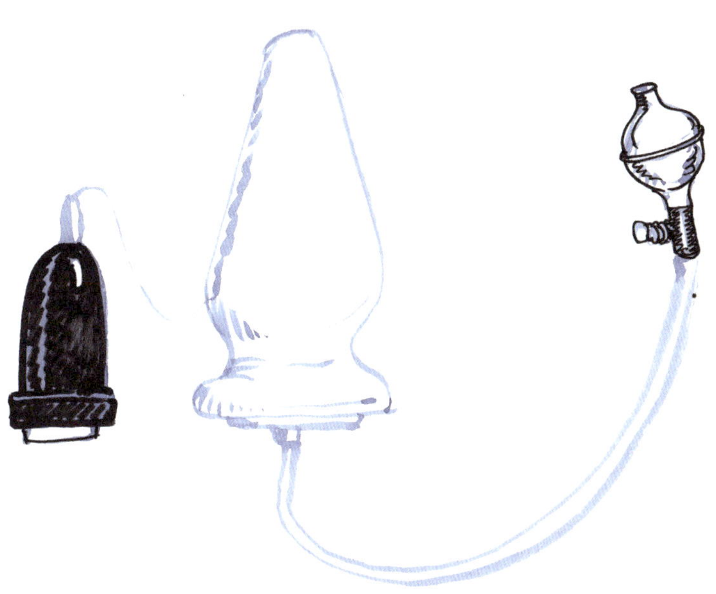

1.69 ——

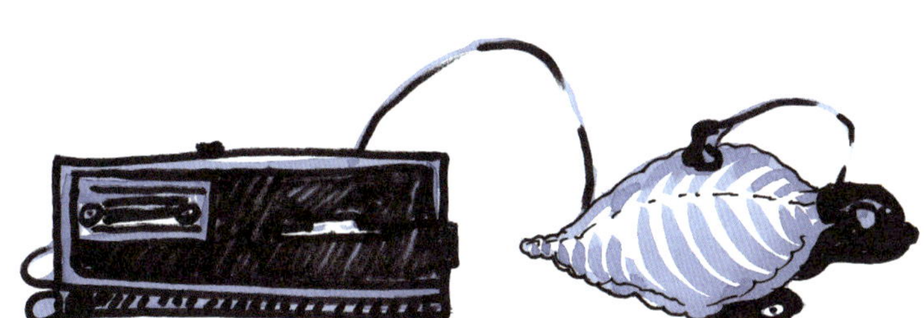

1.70 ——

1.71 —

Sketch of a multiple anal dildo with beads.

1.72 —

Sketch of inflatable leather mask.

1.73 —

Sketch of penis in latex.

1.74 —

Sketch of hand and arm in latex.

1.75 —

Sketch of black latex gloves.

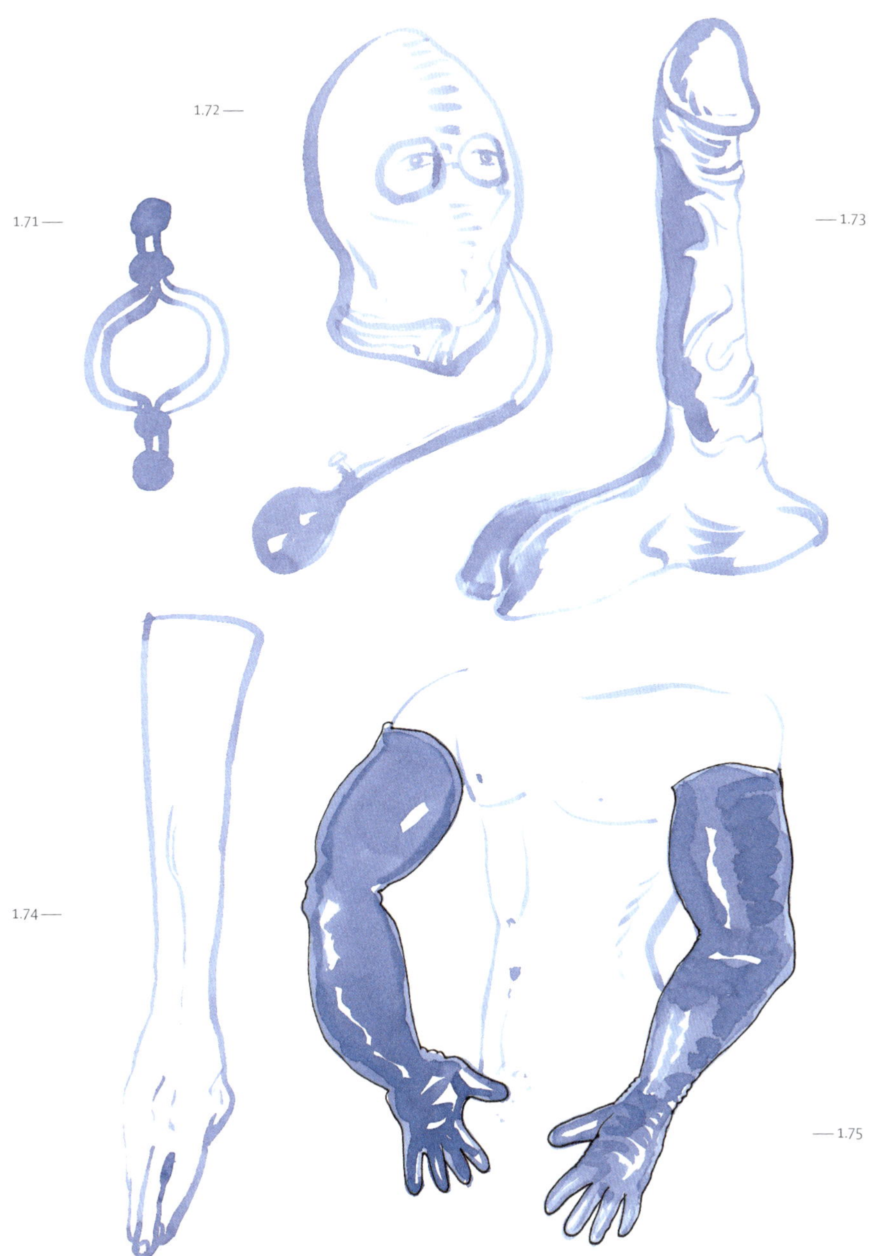

1.72 —

1.71 —

— 1.73

1.74 —

— 1.75

1.76 ——
Sketch of testicle pouch.

1.77 ——
Sketch of briefs with open penis sheath.

1.78 ——
Sketch of multiple anal dildo.

1.79 ——
Sketch of anal dildos.

1.80 ——
Sketch of two penises in latex.

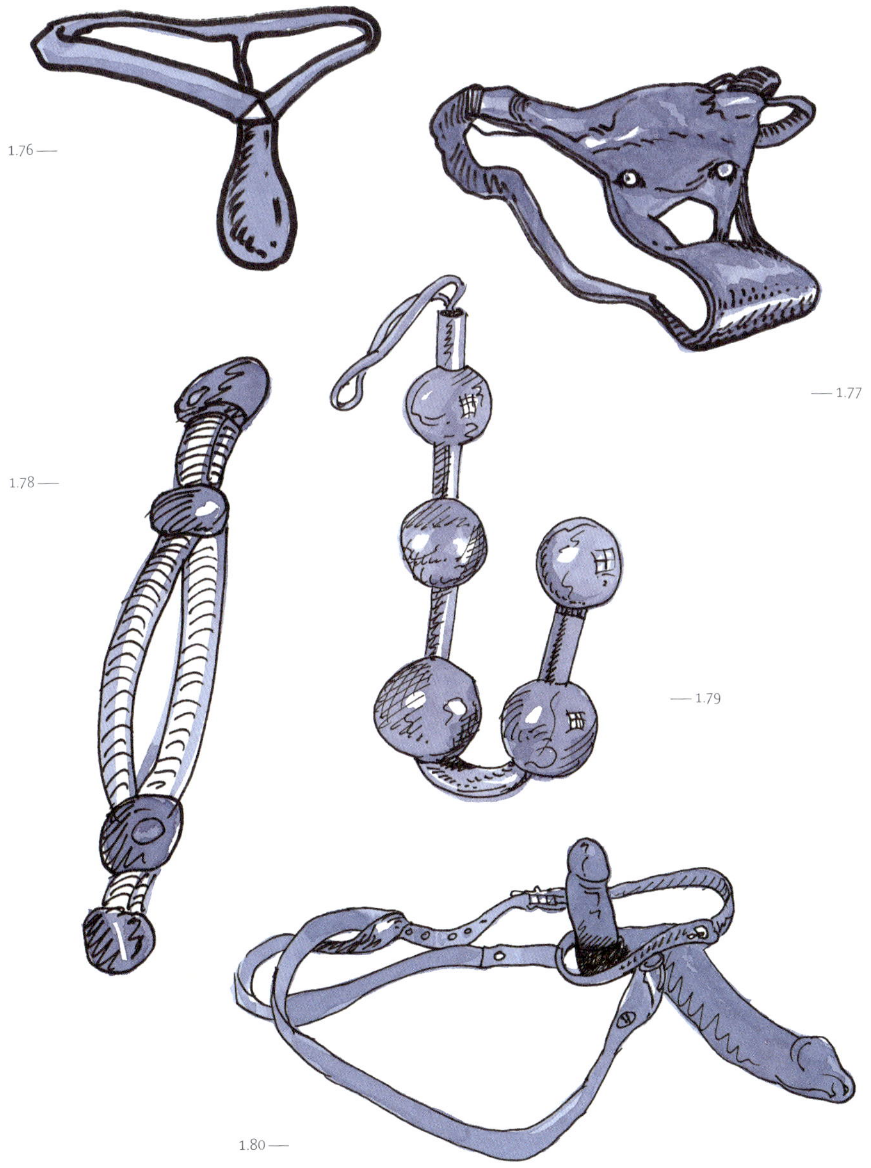

1.76 —

— 1.77

1.78 —

— 1.79

1.80 —

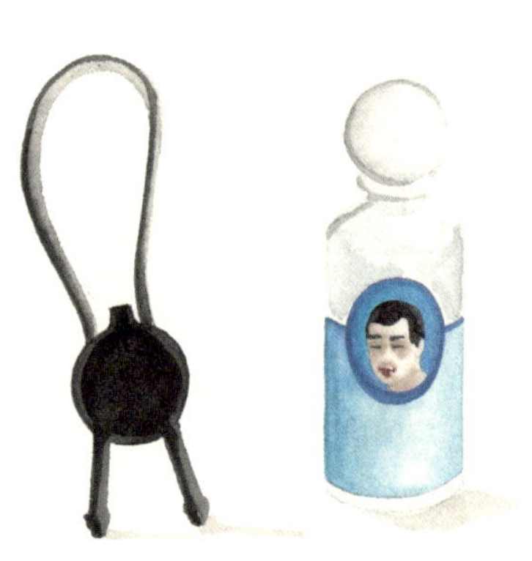

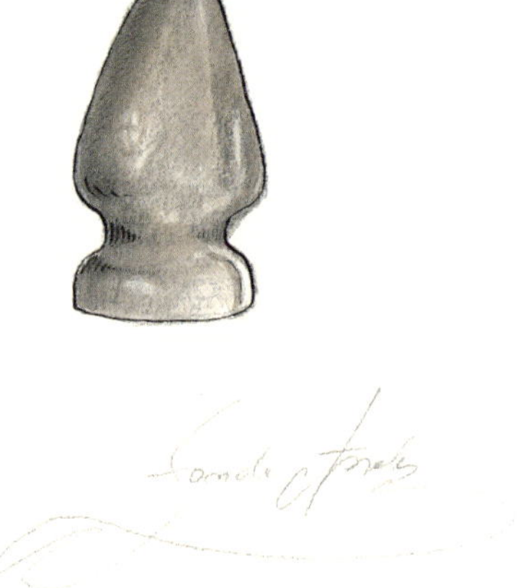

1.81 —

Sketch of a testicle restraint and small bottle of spray liquid.

1.82 —

Sketch of solid anal dildo.

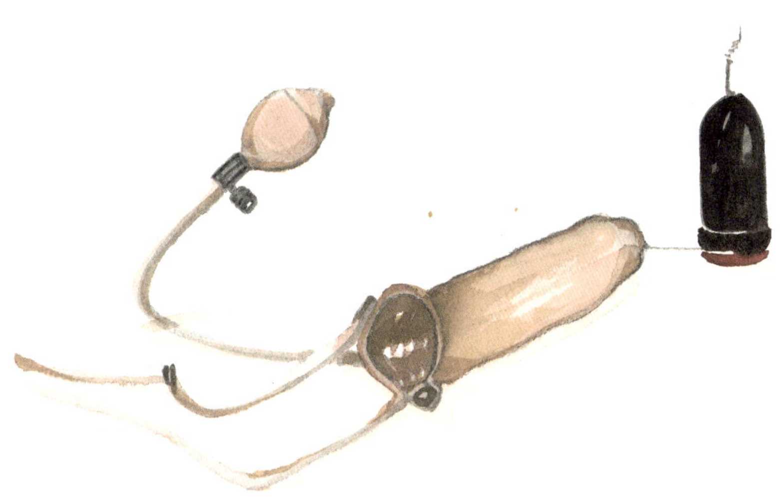

1.83 ——
Sketch of penis restraint, with double cap.

A VEDOVAMAZZEI FETISH

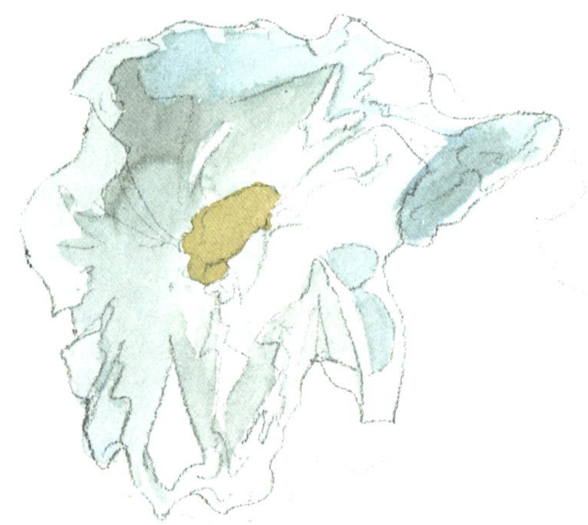

1.84 —

A souvenir of vedovamazzei's first sexual encounter. Beside the picture is written, 'screwed up tissue full of sperm. Hurrah for vedovamazzei.'

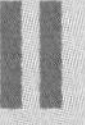

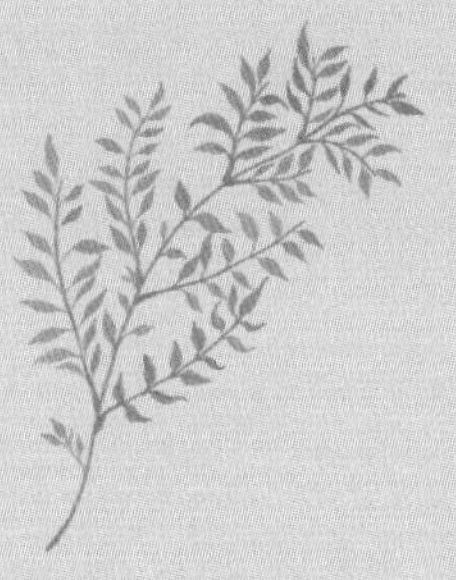

II

Organisational Basis for the Corpus of Vedovamazzei's Pictures

The basis for the organisation of the corpus of vedovamazzei's pictures combines a series of five different sets of pictures, which are divided either according to their external form or to their internal organisation. It includes a travel memorandum which originated with the idea to document the work for this *Natural History* in a compendium. There are also various loose leaves with mere hints of ideas, noted in vedovamazzei's typical style of exchange and transmission. It also contains an early study for *Time Without Example,* inspired by a conversation about studying the different number of colours perceived by people in a coma.

EXTERNAL FORM OF THE CORPUS OF VEDOVAMAZZEI PICTURES

TRAVEL MEMORANDUM

Sketches for Various Projects and Other Pissing About

This set groups a series of ideas from one of Simeone's diaries. They are watercolours vedovamazzei did to document their *Natural History,* with brief, comic-strip style comments referring to many ideas which are developed later. Others are simply undeveloped ideas which they never used afterwards.

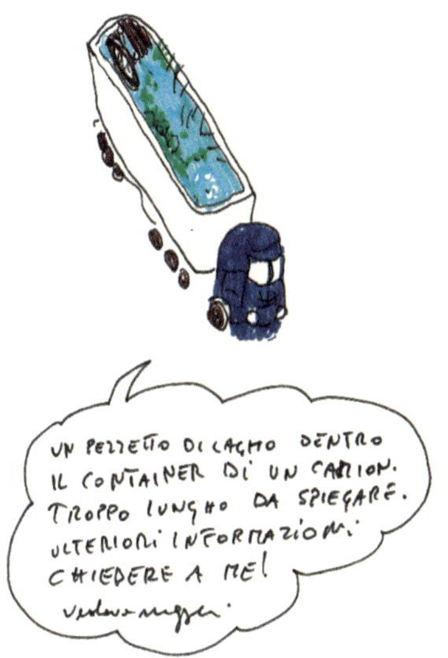

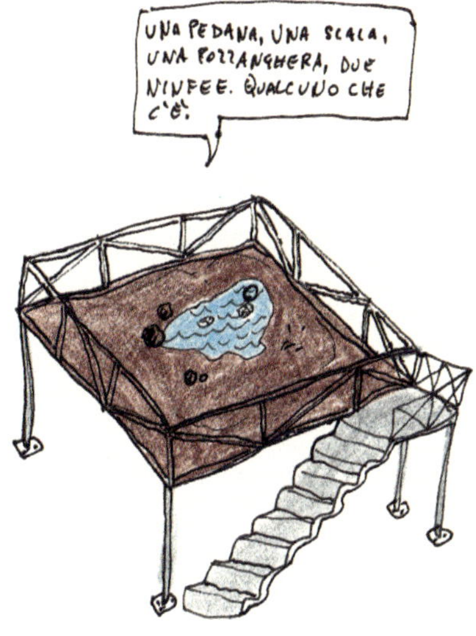

2.01 ——

An overhead view of the lorry in *Go Wherever You Want, Bring Me Whatever You Wish* presented by vedovamazzei in Hann Münden in 2000. The caption says, 'A bit of lake inside the trailer of a lorry. Too long to explain. For further information ask me! vedovamazzei.'

2.02 ——

The picture shows an idea for *Marvellous Harmony* that was not followed through. The speech balloon coming out of the installation says: 'A wooden board, steps, a puddle, two water lilies. Someone who's there.'

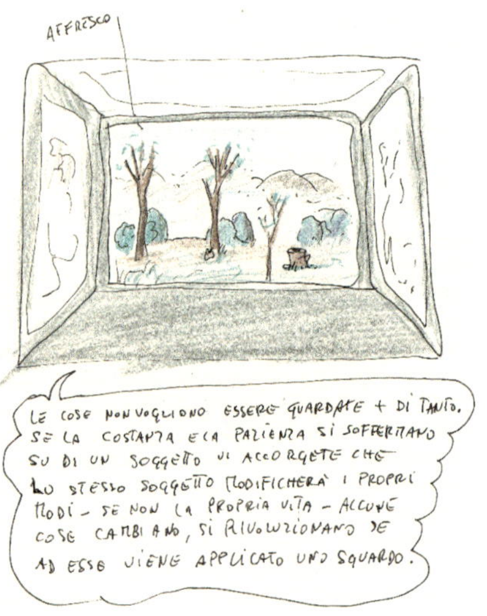

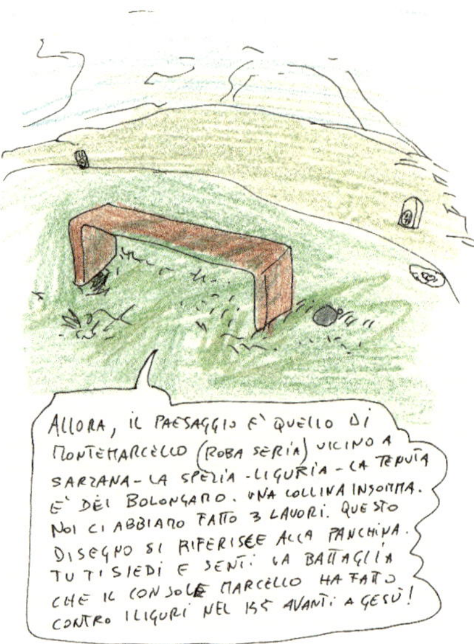

2.03 —

Picture of an idea for the video about Karl Vogt's story, which is conceptualised here as an animated fresco. This was not realised. The writing says, 'Things do not want to be looked at too much. If constancy and patience dwell on a subject, you will notice that the subject itself will change its behaviour. If not its whole life. Some things change, they are revolutionised if someone looks at them.'

2.04 —

The picture portrays the project entitled 155 BC, produced in Monte Marcello in 2001. A comic-strip style speech balloon comes out of the bench and says: 'So, the landscape is that of Monte Marcello (serious stuff) near Sarzana, La Spezia-Liguria. The farm belongs to the Bolongaro's. In a word, a hill. We did three pieces of work there. This picture refers to the bench. You sit down and listen to the battle which Consul Marcellus waged against the Ligurians in 155 before Jesus.'

2.05 —

The picture shows aspects of the geographical context featured in different vedovamazzei works and here put together. The speech bubble comments: 'Dawn. Two artificial satellites. The moon (looks like it's cold) The sun. The clouds and the rain. A tornado. The little flag at the South Pole and parallels of latitude and mathematics. From this perspective, Isaac Newton wouldn't have discovered gravity. From God's perspective, you don't discover anything at all.'

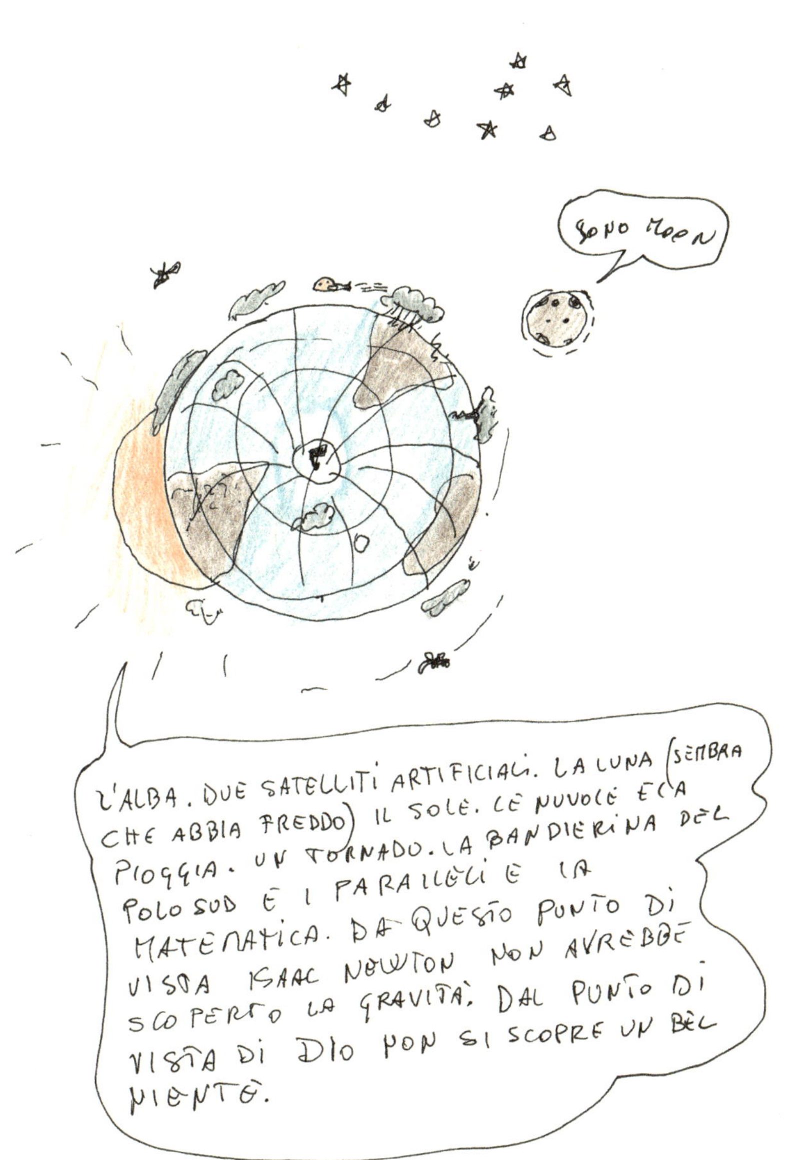
SONO MOON
L'ALBA. DUE SATELLITI ARTIFICIALI. LA LUNA (SEMBRA CHE ABBIA FREDDO) IL SOLE. LE NUVOLE E LA PIOGGIA. UN TORNADO. LA BANDIERINA DEL POLO SUD E I PARALLELI E LA MATEMATICA. DA QUESTO PUNTO DI VISTA ISAAC NEWTON NON AVREBBE SCOPERTO LA GRAVITÀ. DAL PUNTO DI VISTA DI DIO NON SI SCOPRE UN BEL NIENTE.

2.05—

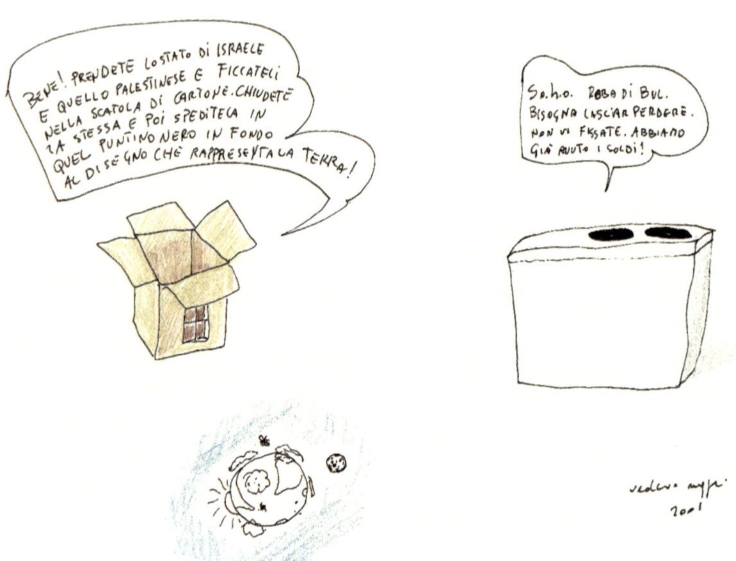

2.06 ——

The picture is a kind of impromptu inanity which was never followed up, a private raving which is typical of Simeone. It constitutes a kind of loose set of instructions. It combines a sketch of the world in miniature and a talking cardboard box with a speech balloon coming out of it which says: 'Fine! Take the state of Israel and the Palestinian state and stick them in the cardboard box. Close the box and then send it to that black dot representing the earth at the bottom of the picture!'

2.07 ——

The picture is of *Records,* a 2001 work consisting of a base for two LPs with sounds of the sun and earth. In the balloon, the title is *So.H.O. (Solar Heliospheric Observatory).* Both works are linked to the study of the solar system and to vedovamazzei's interest in sound as a residual memory of the universe: 'So.H.O. Bul stuff. Need to forget it. Don't insist! We've already had the money!'

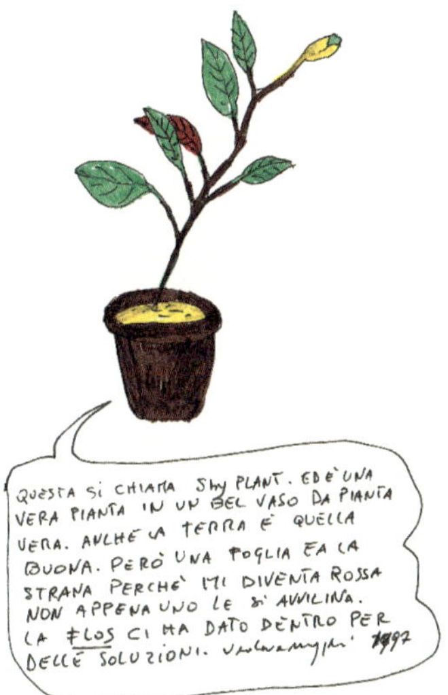

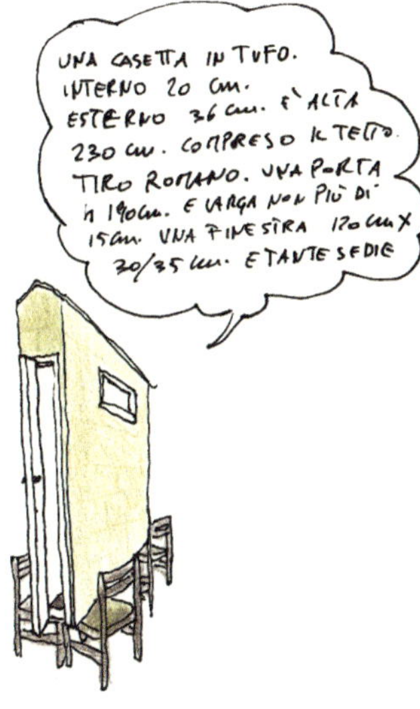

2.08 ——

The picture shows *Shy Plant* (1997). The speech bubble describes and comments: 'This is called Shy Plant. And it is a real plant in a nice pot for real plants. Even the earth is good stuff. But one leaf is being a bit strange. Because it goes red on me as soon as someone goes up to it. Flos really slogged away to sort it out. vedovamazzei 1997.'

2.09 ——

The picture shows an early version of the project with the reproduction of the house where L. F. Céline was born in Normandy, entitled *Novel*, done in 2003. The speech balloon says: 'A little tufa house. Interior 20cm. Exterior 36cm. It's 230cm tall. Including the roof. Roman style. A door, h. 190cm. It is no wider than 15cm. A window 120 x 30/35cm. And lots of chairs.' In the version produced in Rome, the house is not on the chairs and it is a different size.

CASSAFORTE CON DUE DISCHI IN VINILE CON SUONO DEL SOLE E DELLA TERRA. TUTTA LA CASS. E' IN FERRO, POI C'E' UNA MENSOLA DI PLEXGLASS E I DUE DISCHI APPUNTO. DIMENTICAVO IL GIRADISCHI. vedovamazzei 2001
SOLAR SOUND
SOLAR EART

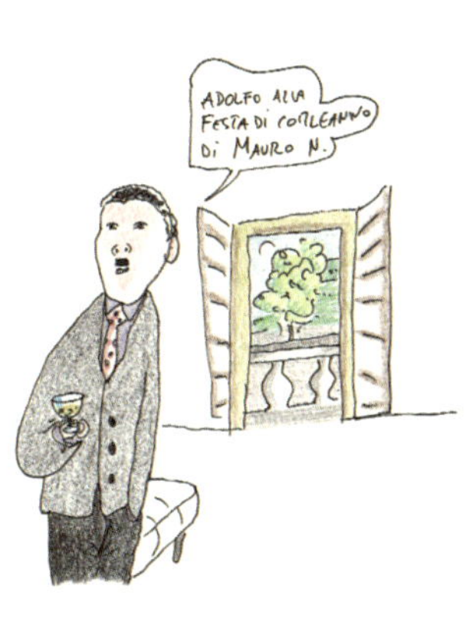

2.11 ——

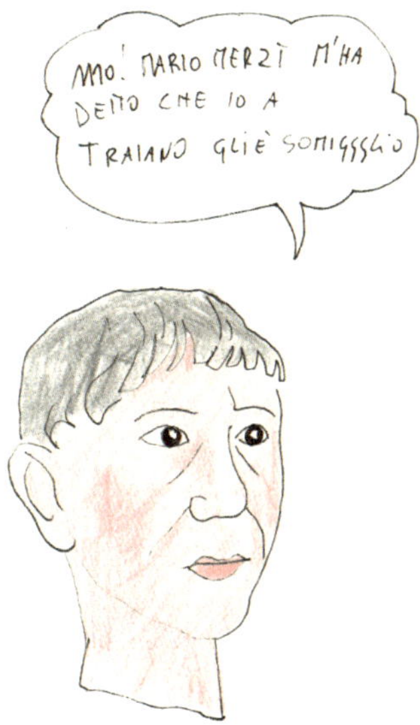

2.12 ——

2.10 ——

The picture describes *So.H.O (Solar Heliospheric Observatory)* (2001) with a strongroom to shut oneself in to listen to the sounds of the earth and the sun recorded on two vinyl records. The speech balloon comments: 'strongroom with two vinyl records with sounds of the sun and earth. The whole strongroom is made of iron. Then there's a Plexiglas shelf and the two records. I forgot the record player. vedovamazzei 2001.'

2.11 ——

The picture is a Hitler fantasy by vedovamazzei. The caption says 'A portrait of Adolph at Mauro N.'s birthday party.'

2.12 ——

The picture shows the self-portrait of Simeone as Trajan saying: 'Mario Merzi told me that I look like Trajan.'

SCRAPS

2.13 —

Study for snow dome. A stele inside the snow dome is inscribed with ideograms by vedovamazzei (1999). vedovamazzei began the snow dome series with *vedovamazzei You Don't Scare Us We've Got the Shot in the Barrel, Without the Safety Catch On!* (1994), a miniature protest demonstration against themselves. This one is a posthumous commemoration of them.

2.14 —

Football Pitch in Make-Up Bag. Study for the football pitch in a make-up bag in foundation cream or face-powder or blusher. Project not realised (1999).

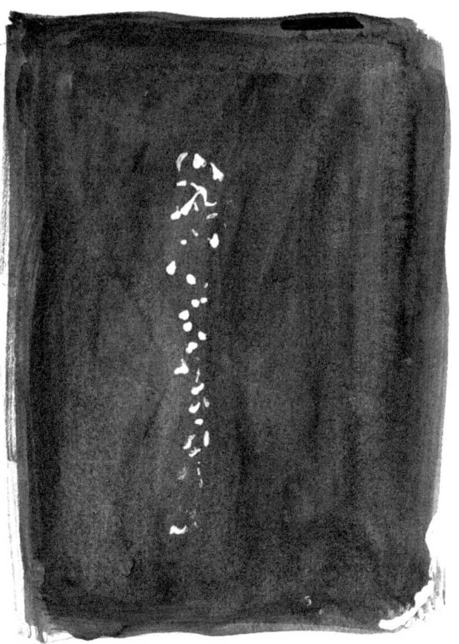

2.13 —

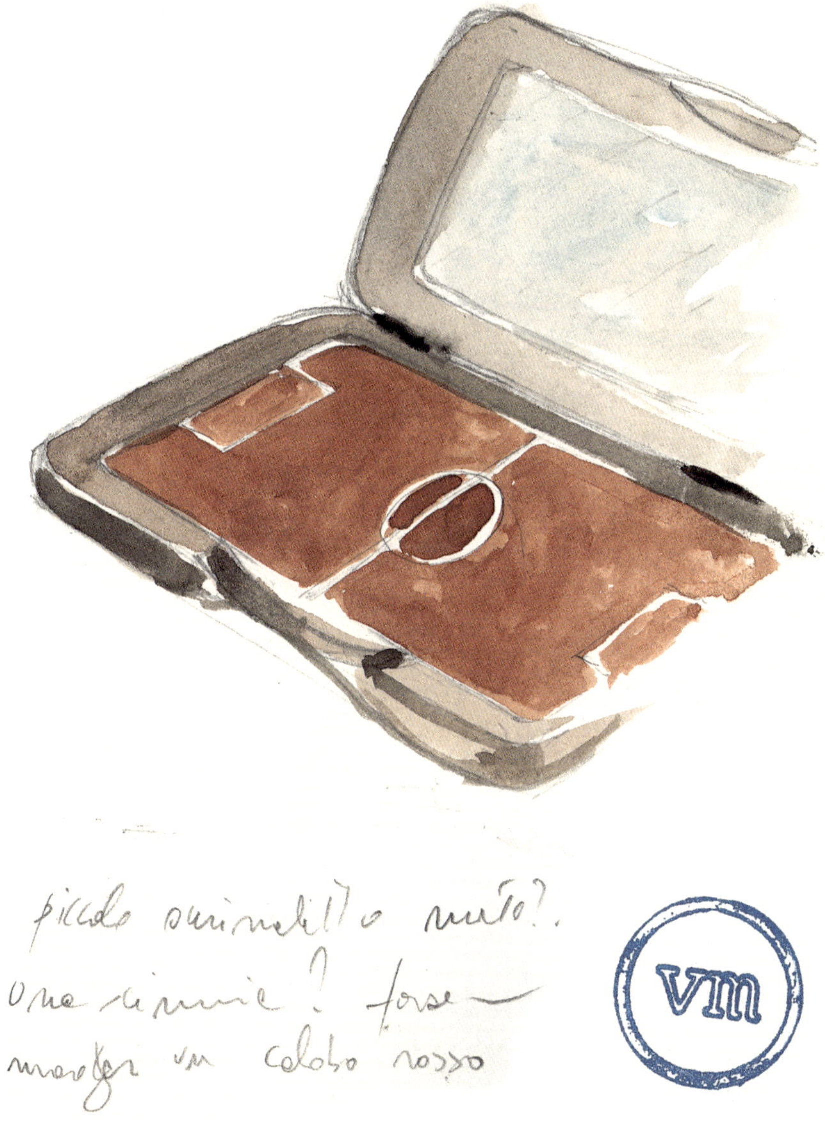

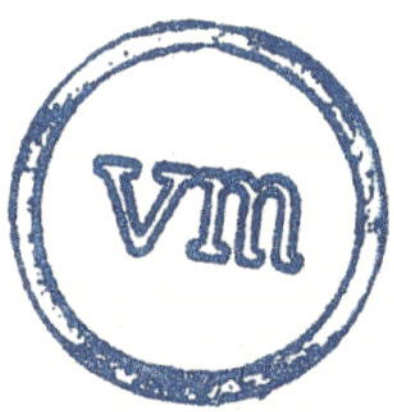

piccolo animaletto muto?.
una scimmie? forse —
mangia un coloro rosso

2.14 —

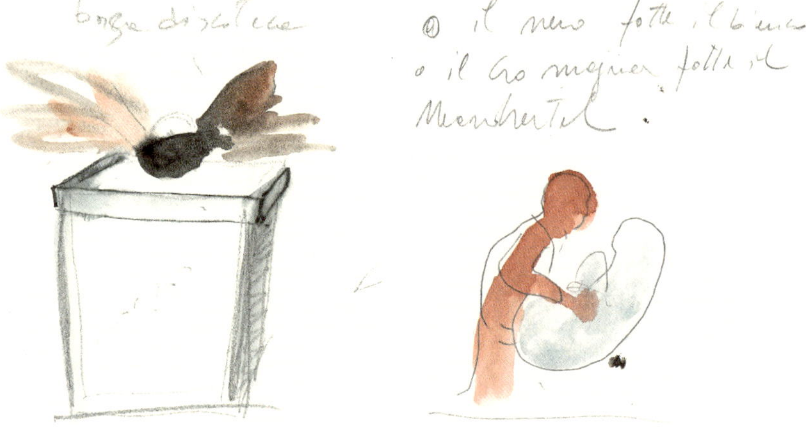

2.15 —

Portable Disco. Study for a bag with a portable disco inside, with flashing lights and music. An idea for an exhibition in Southampton, not realised (1995).

2.16 —

Ancient Fuck. The sketch depicts a sculptural group with two Dionysian, copulating figures; a demigod and a goat. The writing says: 'black fucks white or Cro-Magnon man fucks Neanderthal man.'

OTHER SCRAPS

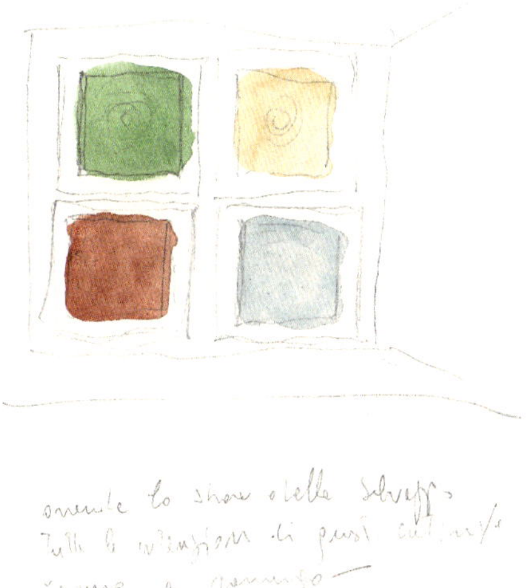

2.17 —

Study for *Time Without Example* (1999). The colours
hypothetically discerned by a person in a coma, in 16
photographic panels of video frames, were exhibited
in Milan and Genoa. The work was inspired by a
conversation vedovamazzei had in Milan with a doctor
studying what remains of the senses in a coma.

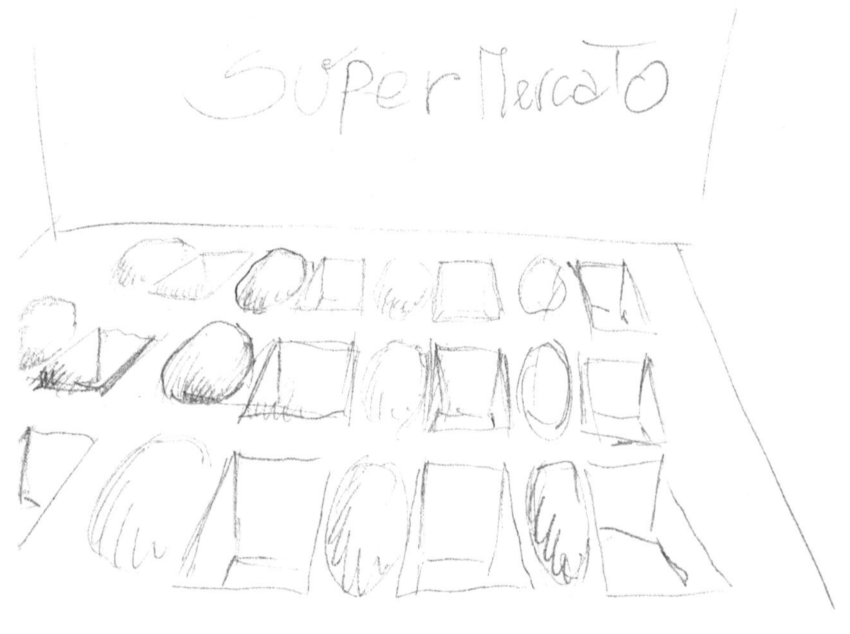

2.18 —

Study for a supermarket display as a cemetery.

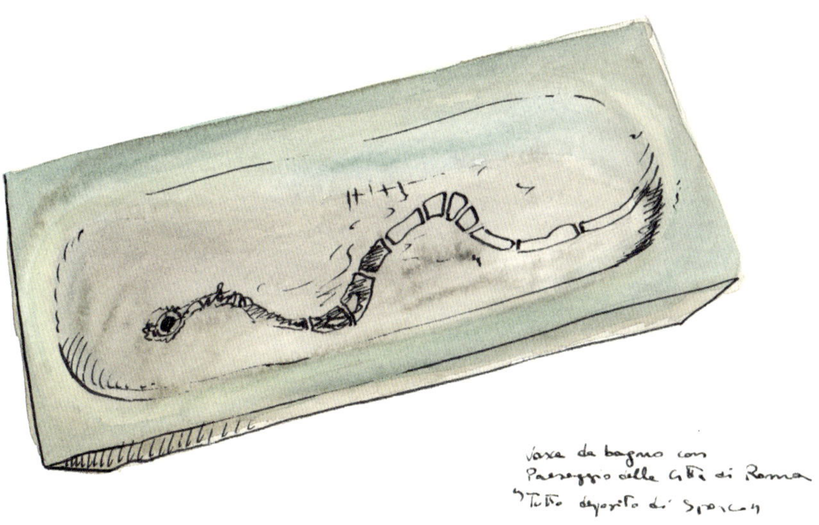

2.19 —

Bathtub project. The writing says: 'Bathtub with view
of the city of Rome. The whole lot is scum.'

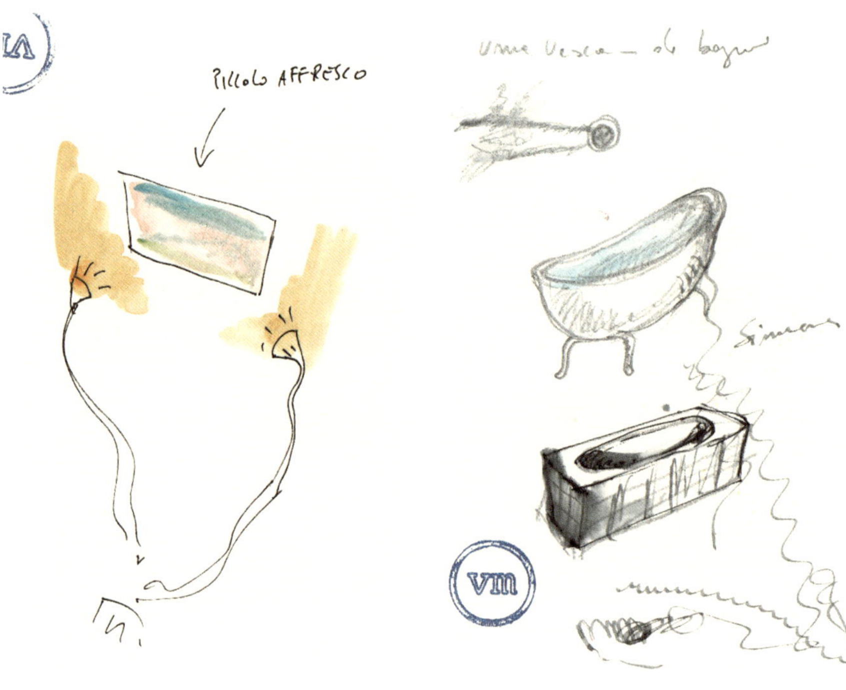

2.20 —

Watercolour study for a small fresco to put in a corner of a wall (2001).

2.21 —

Variation for the bathtub project, with the course of the Tiber or the Ganges traced in the dirty trickle left behind by the waste bathwater going down the plughole (2001). Project not realised.

2.22 —

Further variation.

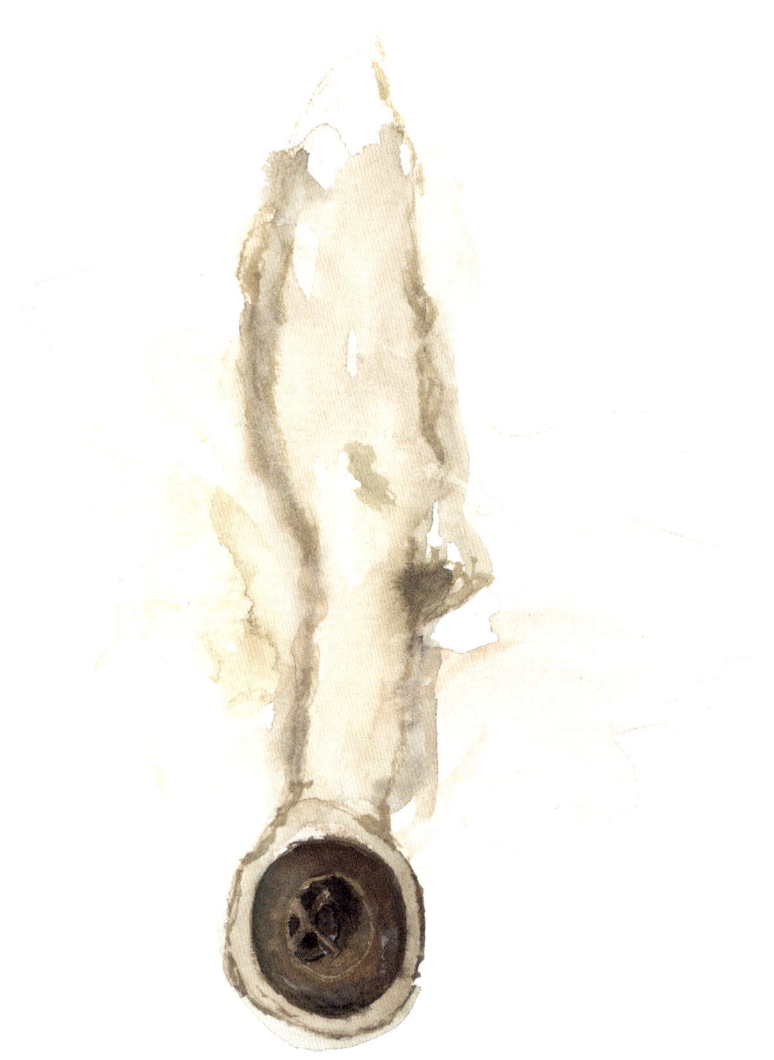

—— 2.22

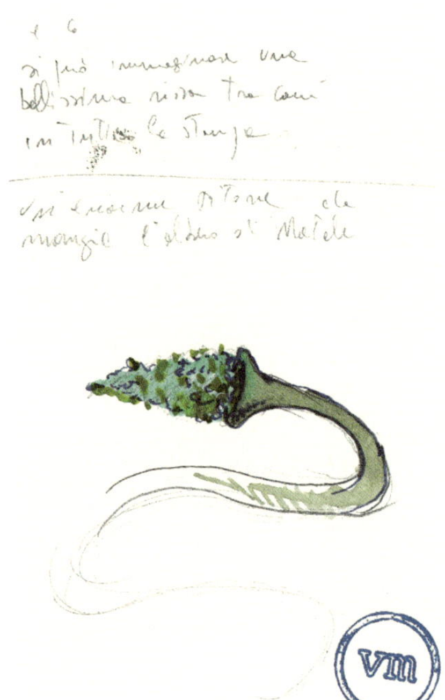

2.23 —

Study for *Snake Eating a Christmas Tree* (1994–1995).
Project not realised.

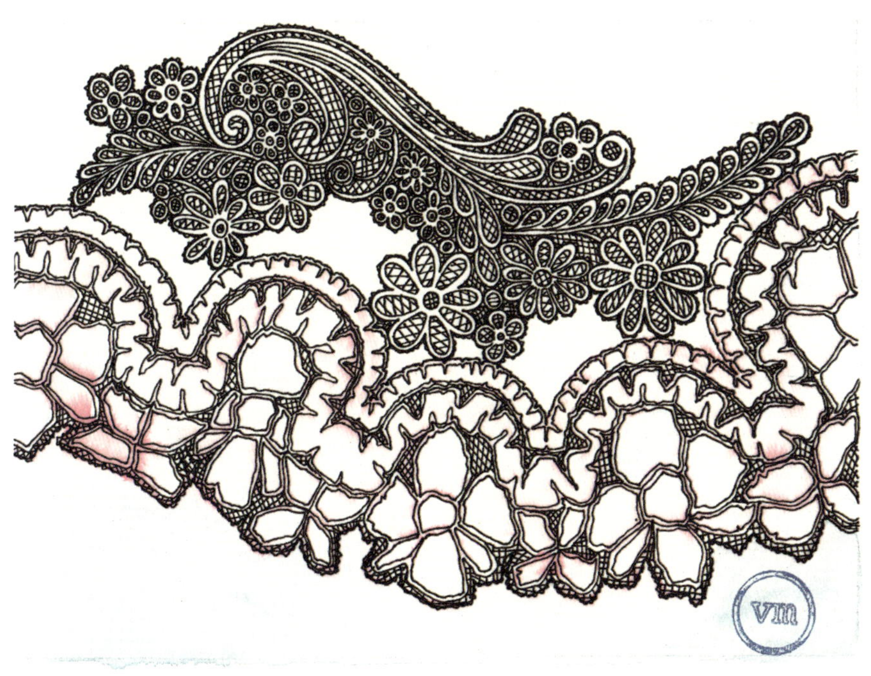

2.24—

Study for embroidery done in heroin (1998).
Project not realised.

**INTERNAL ORGANISATION OF THE VEDOVAMAZZEI
CORPUS OF DRAWINGS**

THE VEDOVAMAZZEI STUDIO JOURNAL (1991–2002)

The Desire For Mutual Violence
The vedovamazzei studio journal collates their sketches
and projects in a more systematic way and shows how
the couple organise their ideas together. Indeed, the
Mutual Violence watercolours take us to the heart of
vedovamazzei's confidential diary in which pictures
and quotations are pooled freely. Over the years,
sketches and ideas for many projects are put down and
stored in it. The only common denominator which
helps to define their otherwise extremely varied forms
and structures would seem to be the inspiration derived
from observing both the conscious and unconscious
desire for mutual violence. This inherent feature in both
nature and man is a driving force in life around us and
an expression of the universe's perpetual activity and,
therefore, unreprehrehensible.

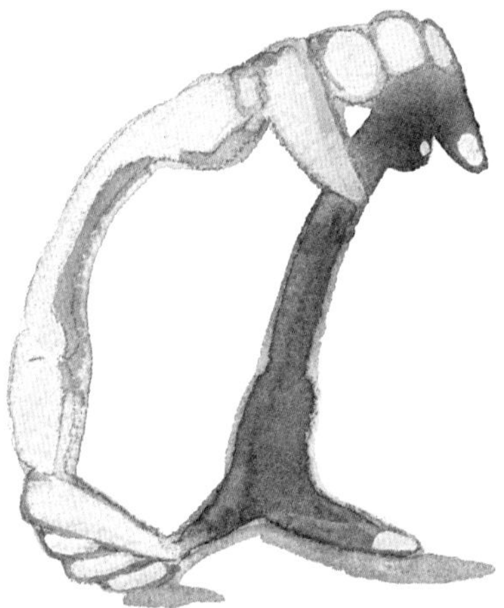

La dignità di una persona si può valutare dalla prima impressione che dà.
C'è dignità nello sforzo e nell'assiduità, nella SERENITÀ e nella DISCREZIONE.
C'è dignità nell'OSSERVAZIONE, nella RETTITUDINE.
C'è anche NELLO STRINGERE I DENTI e mantenere gl'OCCHI APERTI.
L'avidità, la rabbia e la stupidità vanno sempre INSIEME (quando il mondo va male)
Se guardiamo ciò che vi è di buono, ci accorgeremo che non manca di SAGGEZZA,
UMANITÀ E CORAGGIO.

2.25 —

Study of plastic set of false vampire teeth. Note the contrast between the apparently jokey triteness of the picture and the tone in the comment: 'A person's dignity can be assessed from the first impression they make. There is dignity in effort and in assiduity, in composure and in discretion. There is dignity in observation and in rectitude. It is also found in gritting teeth and keeping your eyes peeled. Greed, anger and stupidity always go together (when the world goes wrong). If we look at what is good we will realise that there is no lack of wisdom, humanity or courage.'

2.26 ——

Study of forearm and hand with slashed, bleeding
wrist. In Catholic tradition, *ex-voto* images are usually
offered in thanks for a grace received for the limb
depicted. Here, the ambiguity of the image has a
paradoxical significance as it is linked to the text which
states: 'Without denying a certain morbid curiosity to
know how the scalping was carried out. I do not
believe it was a cruel practice in itself. We are aware
that some tribes must not die out unless through
natural causes. As if men's actions were not natural.
Even if the reasons for them are among the most
barbaric. I believe there is a natural condition that
mixes up the natural causes.'

Non nascendo una certa
morbosa curiosità nel sapere
come veniva effettuato lo scalpo.
Non credo fosse in sé una pratica
crudele. Abbiamo la consapevolezza
che alcuni tabù non debbono
scomparire, se non ad opera di
effetti naturali. Come se le
azioni naturali degli uomini
non fossero azioni naturali.
Anche se le reazioni sono tra le
più barbare. Credo vi sia una
naturale condizione ad accogliere
gli effetti naturali

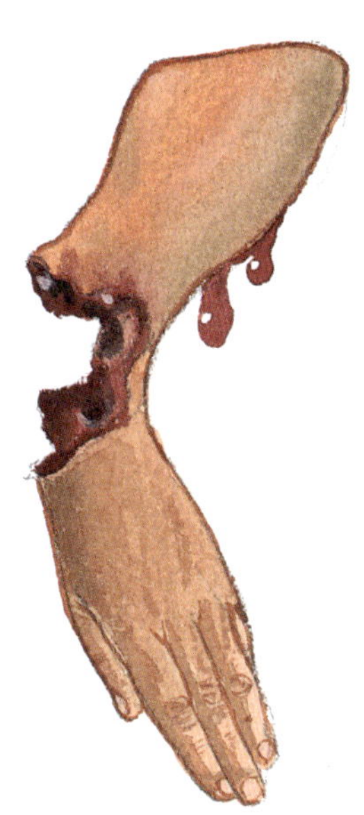

2.27 —

Study for *A Liver Isle* (1999). The idea will be developed
in the installation of a porcelain sculpture laid on the
ground like an island in the shape of a liver which is
perforated and filled with red wine, entitled *Fat In The
Land* (2000).

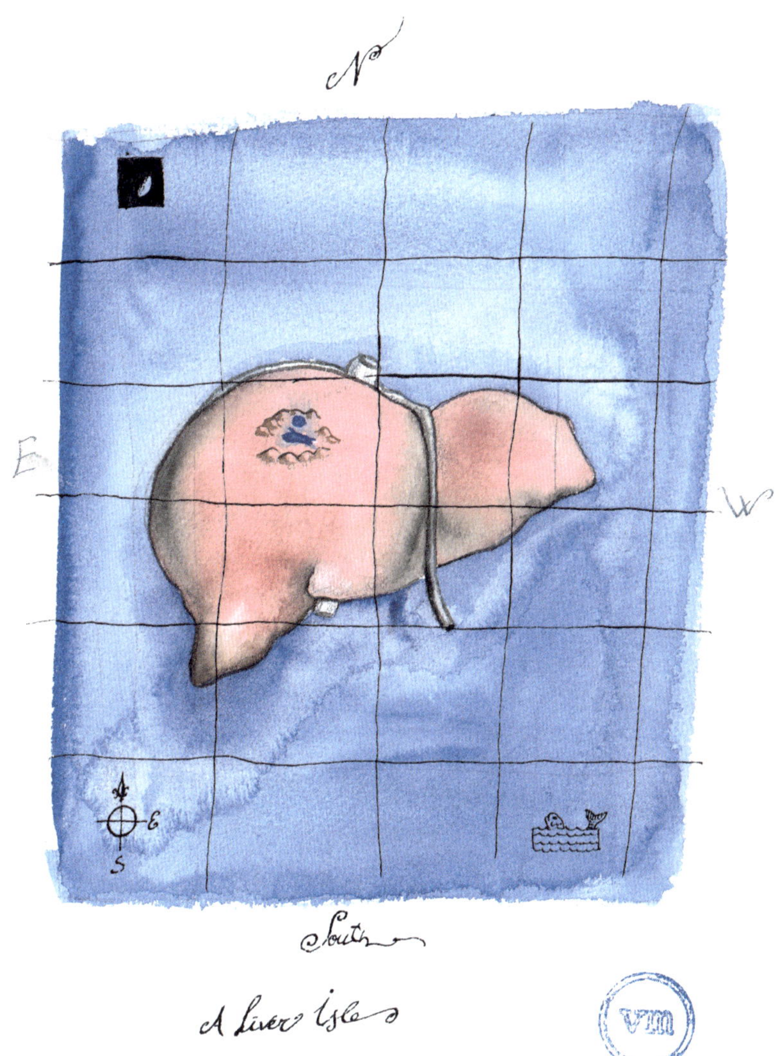
N
E
W
S
A Liver Isle

2.28 ——

Study for *Shy Plant* (1997). The project, dedicated to the memory of Lady D., is accompanied by a short text in China ink which states: 'At the time of the advance towards the Tricholia Spectabilis, the single leaf goes red. Is it embarrassed?'

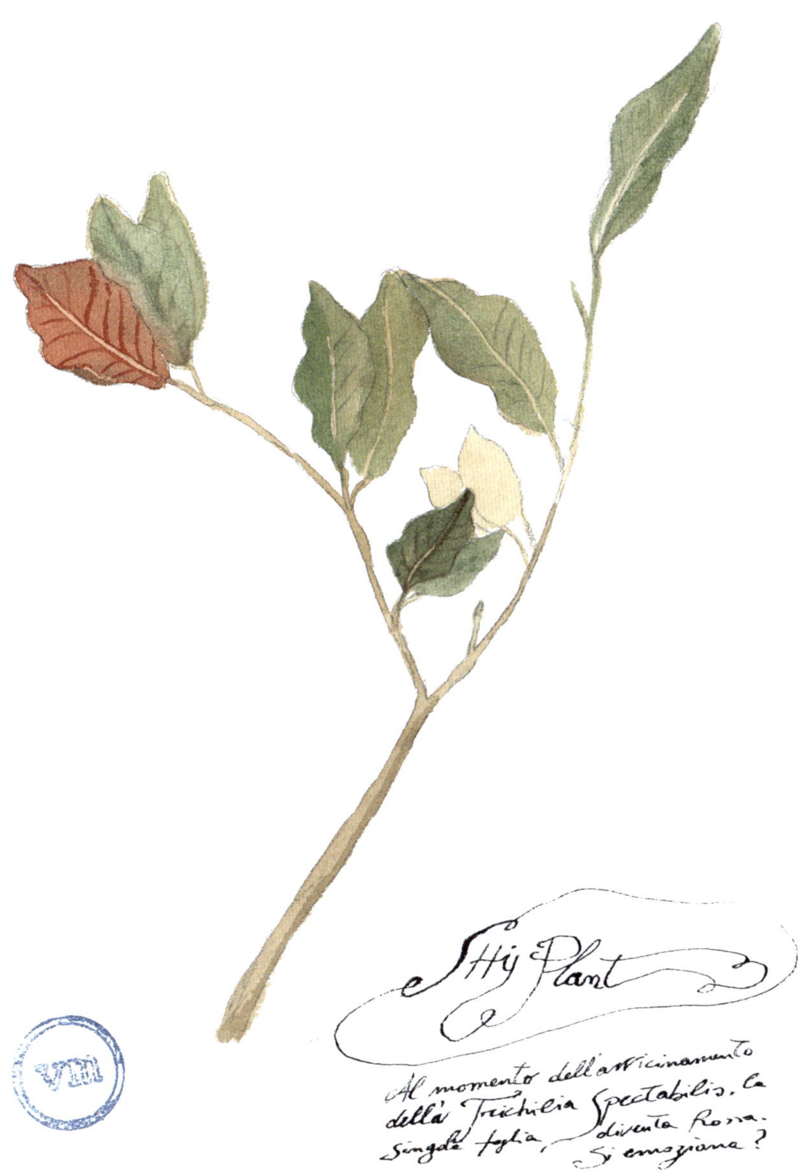

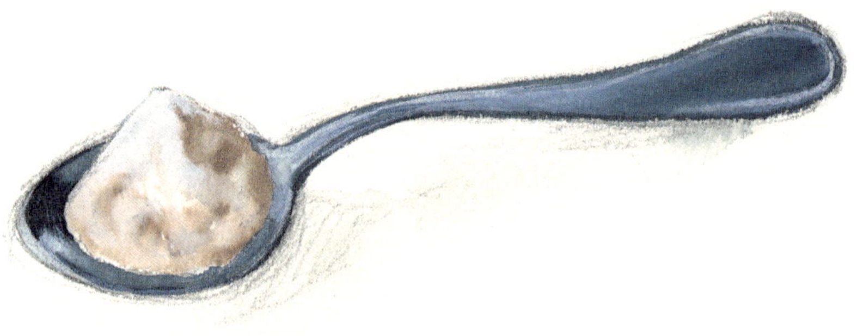

2.29 ——

Study for *Monviso 2000* carved in a spoon of heroin
(1998). Unrealised project for an exhibition in Turin.

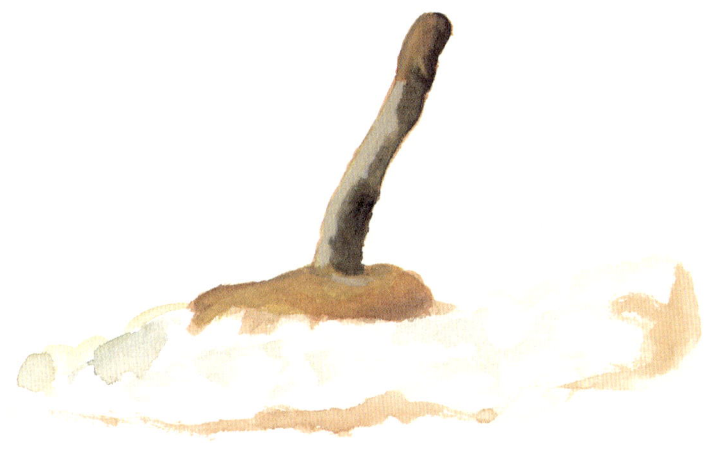

2.30 —

Study of a cigarette extinguished in a fried egg for
Monument (1994), dedicated to Hitchcock. Copies were
produced in Capodimonte ceramic as presents for
guests at the Arcella-Silvestro wedding, held at Santa
Chiara Church, Naples, where vedovamazzei were
the witnesses.

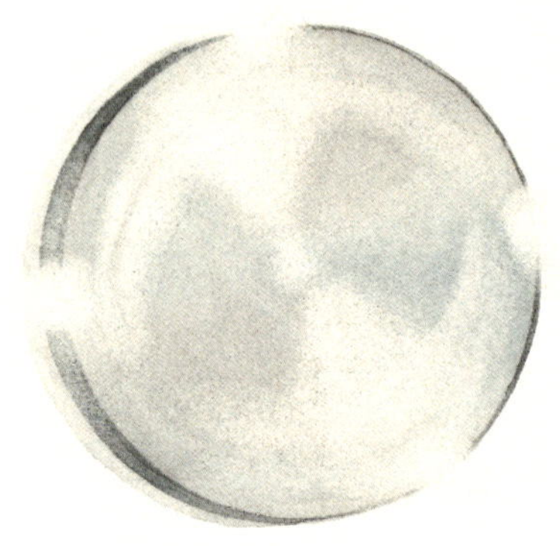

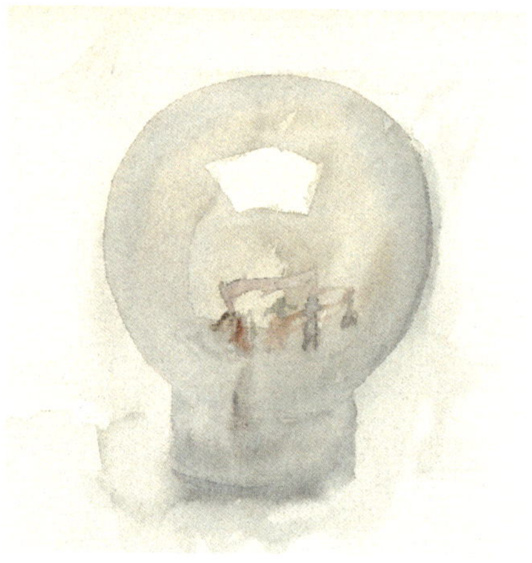

2.31 —

Watercolour study for *Myopic Mirror* (2002).

2.32 —

Study for *vedovamazzei You Don't Scare Us We've Got the Shot in the Barrel, Without the Safety Catch On!* Snow storm with a demonstration for workers' independence in opposition to vedovamazzei (1993).

2.33 —

Watercolour study of two stuffed birds as an idea for a mid-air collision between two birds (1994). Later realised in the photographic work *Untitled* (1995).

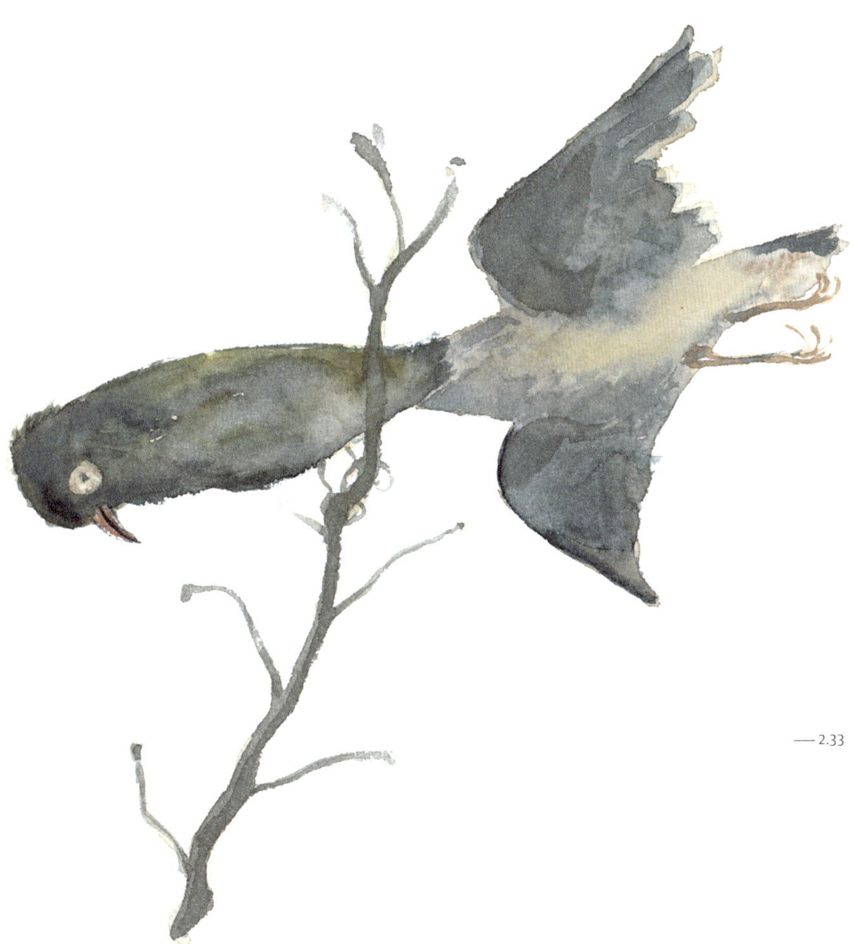

— 2.33

2.34 —

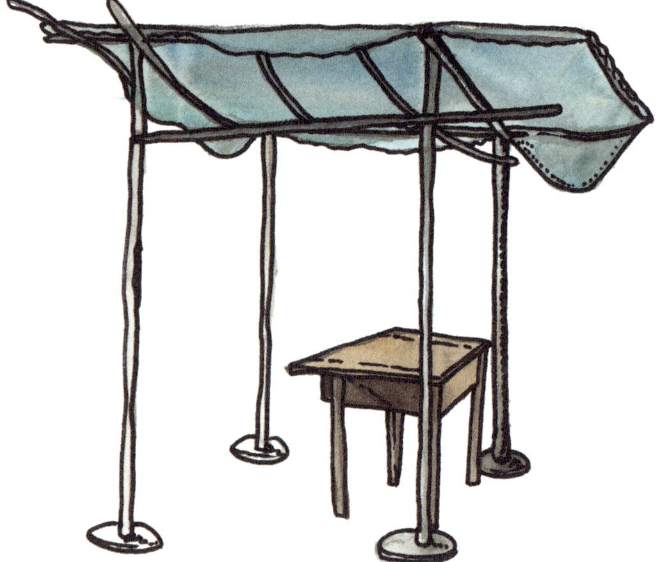

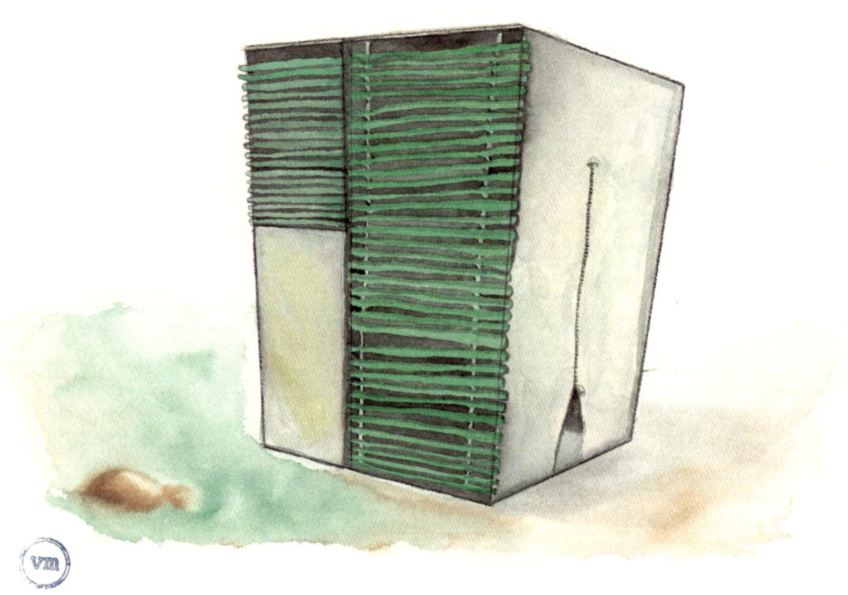

2.35 ——

2.34 ——

Study for sheet embroidery of a mobile kiosk from
Southern Italy. The project was realised, with a
variation, as a fresco for a city building with a drawing
and embroidery beneath the roof of a kiosk (2003).

2.35 ——

Study for a nineteenth century confessional with
Venetian blinds. Project for an installation in Monte
Marcello (2000).

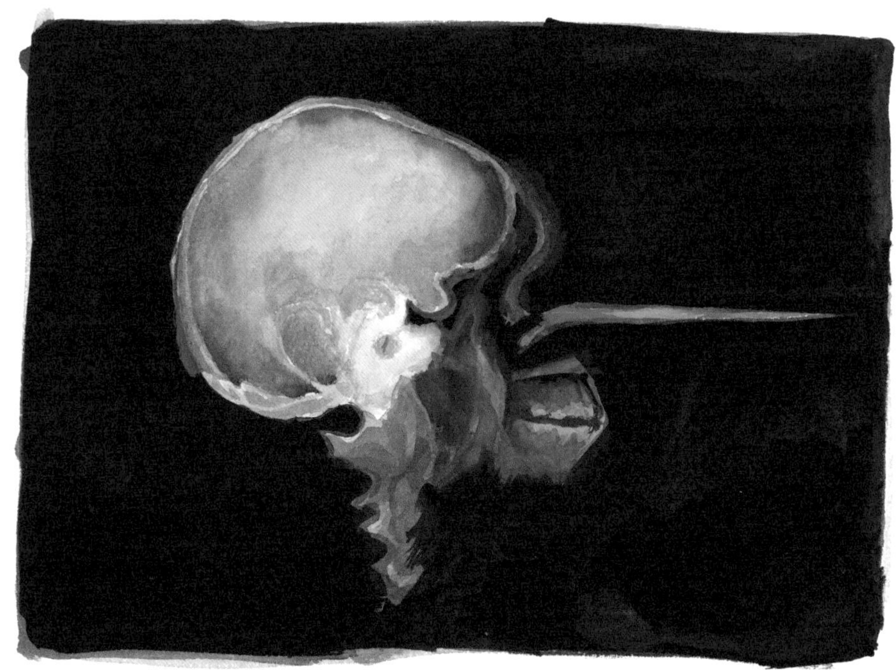

radiografia di "Pinocchio"

—2.36

2.36 —

Study for Pinocchio's x-ray (1991). The picture belongs
to the series of x-rays of icons of Italian popular
culture in which the idea of deformity, caused by the
disease itself, is instead reflected back into the symbol.
It consists of nine big oils on canvas in the style of
Mattia Preti: *Pinocchio, Lucignolo, Carabiniere, Bud
Simpson, Queen, Werewolf, 18th-Century Wig* and
The Saint (1992). Pinocchio is the only study in the
series, which vedovamazzei otherwise painted directly
onto canvas.

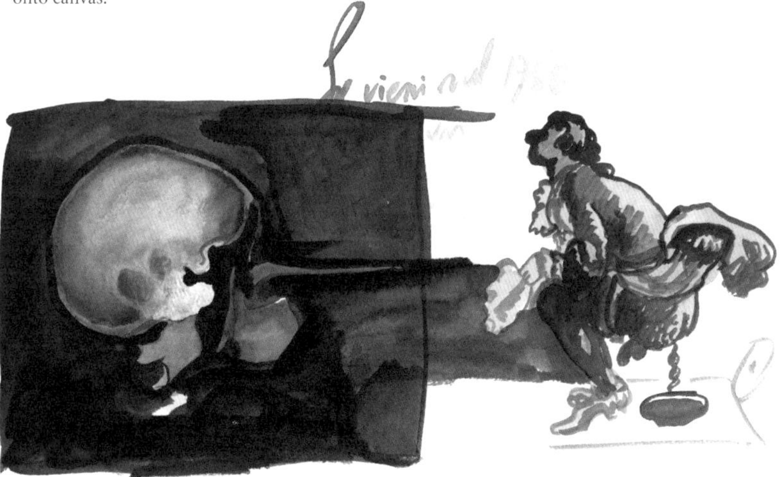

2.37 —

Study for Pinocchio who appears before Rembrandt
while he defecates (2000).

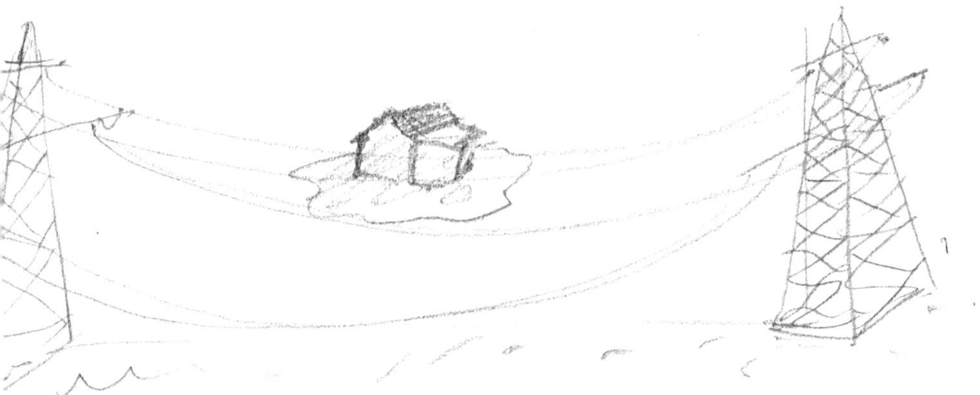

2.38 —
Sketch for *Nest* (2001), the house in search of a nest.
Model of a small building caught up in electrical cables
between two pylons.

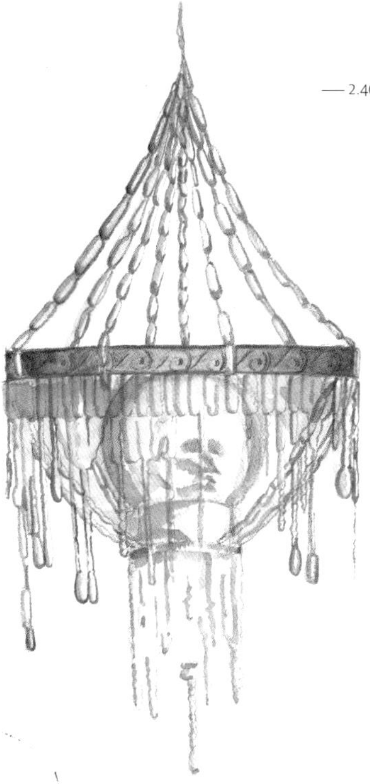

2.39 & 2.40 ——

Study and details for *Ho Chi Minh* (2002), a chandelier
with Ho Chi Minh's skull, which can only be seen
when the chandelier is switched on. The work draws
its inspiration from the recollection of a phrase used
in Vietnam war reports. On an evening when the
Americans did not expect to be attacked by Ho Chi
Minh, an American journalist mistook the flashes from
Vietcong bombardments for fireworks. The project
was first presented together with *Marvellous Harmony*
in Rome (2000).

2.39 ——

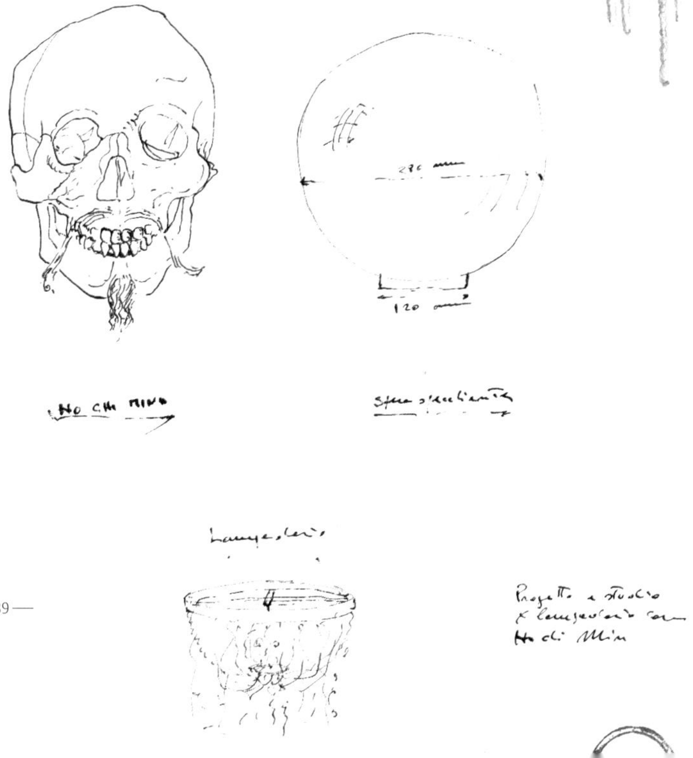

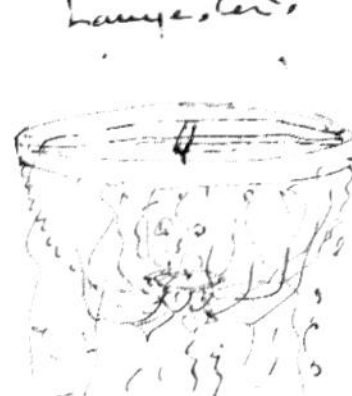

2.41 ——

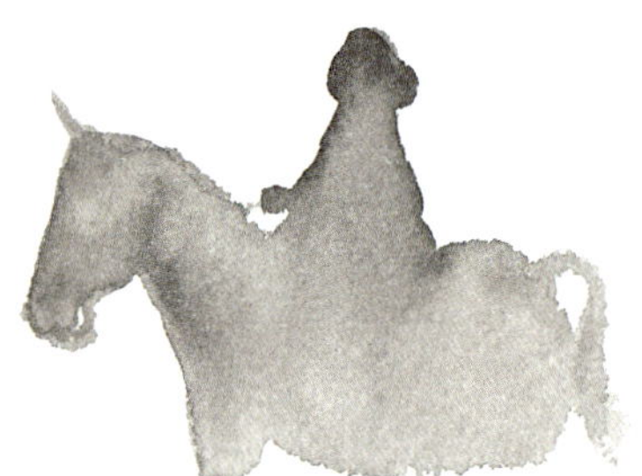

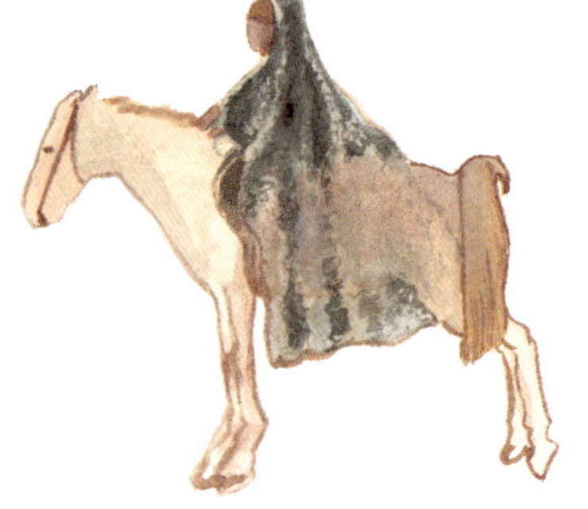

2.41 & 2.42 ——

Study and detail of the shadow of Queen Victoria on horseback for the video *A Modest Proposal* (1998), taken from the pamphlet of the same name by J. Swift (1729). In vedovamazzei's video, Queen Victoria and King Edward recite the whole text of the satirical pamphlet in which Swift suggests eating Irish children as a solution to the problems of famine and poverty in Ireland.

2.42 ——

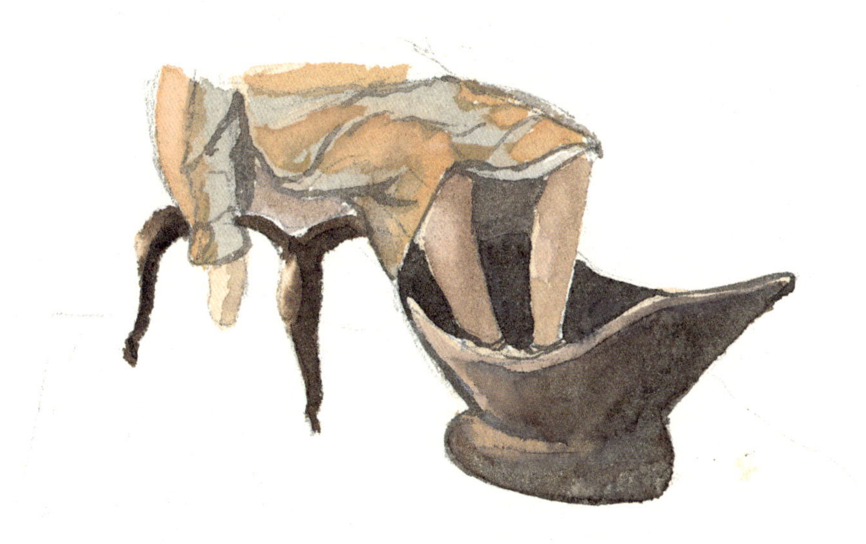

2.43 —

Study and detail of King Edward soaking his feet in a
bath, for the video *A Modest Proposal* (1998).

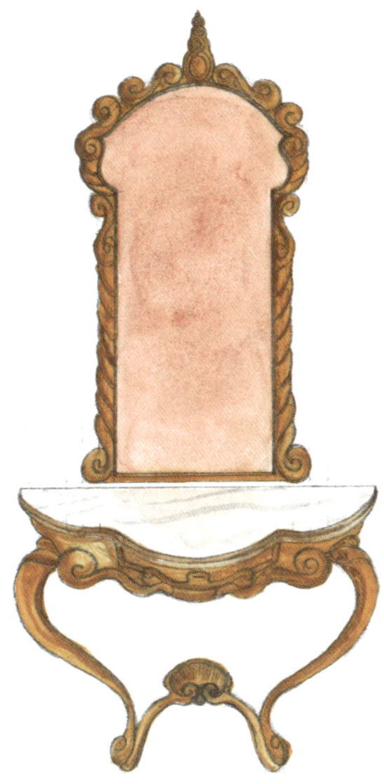

2.44 & 2.45 —
Study and detail for a Louis xv console table with a
burning mirror. The idea was that on approaching the
mirror the spectator could be burnt by a white-hot
steel plate (1990). Project not realised.

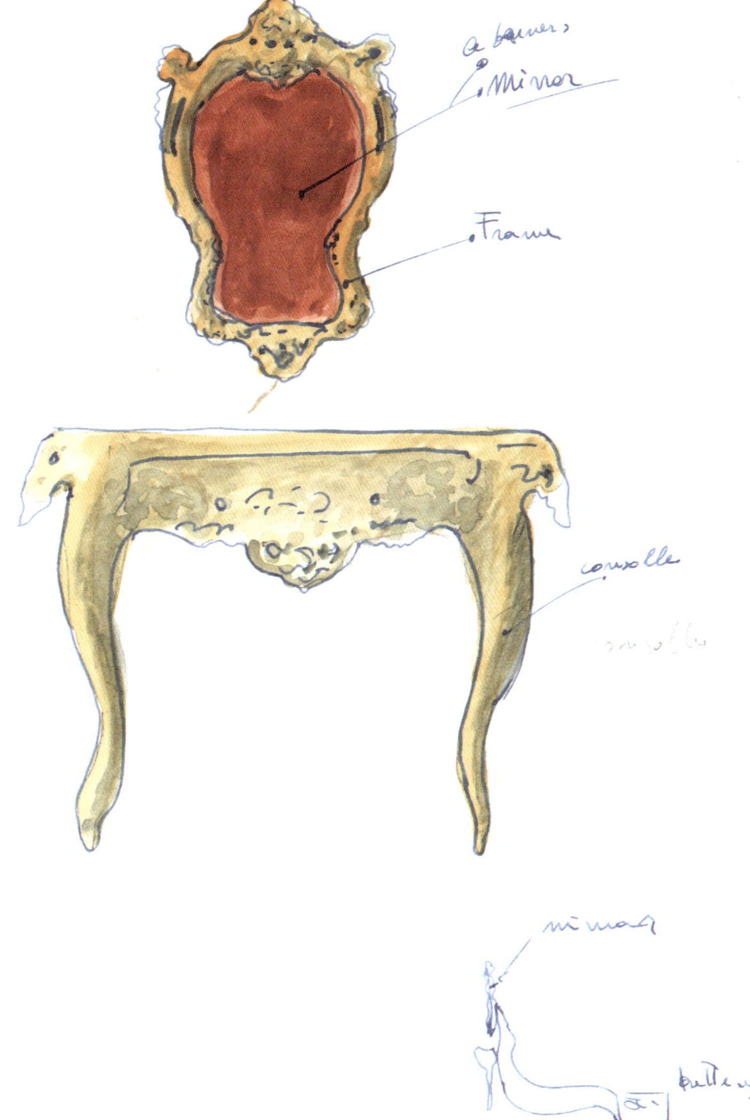
Mirror
Frame
consolle

2.46 & 2.47 ——

Study and details of memory association from one of
Stella's dreams about Rembrandt's bathroom. A detail of
the inside for an installation (2000). Project not realised.

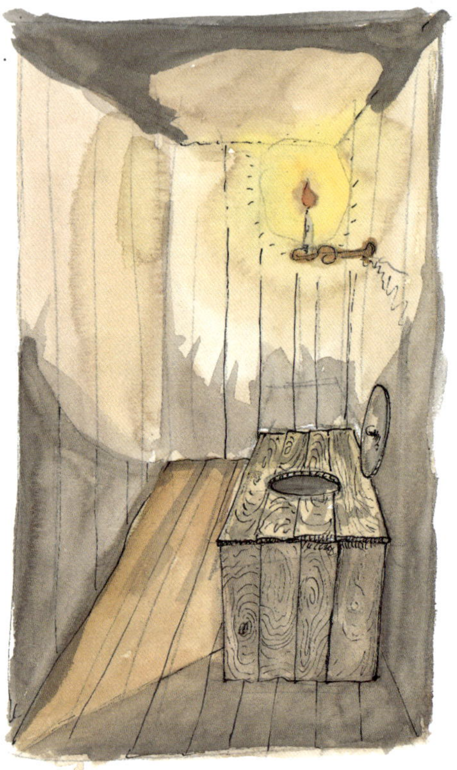

2.46 ——

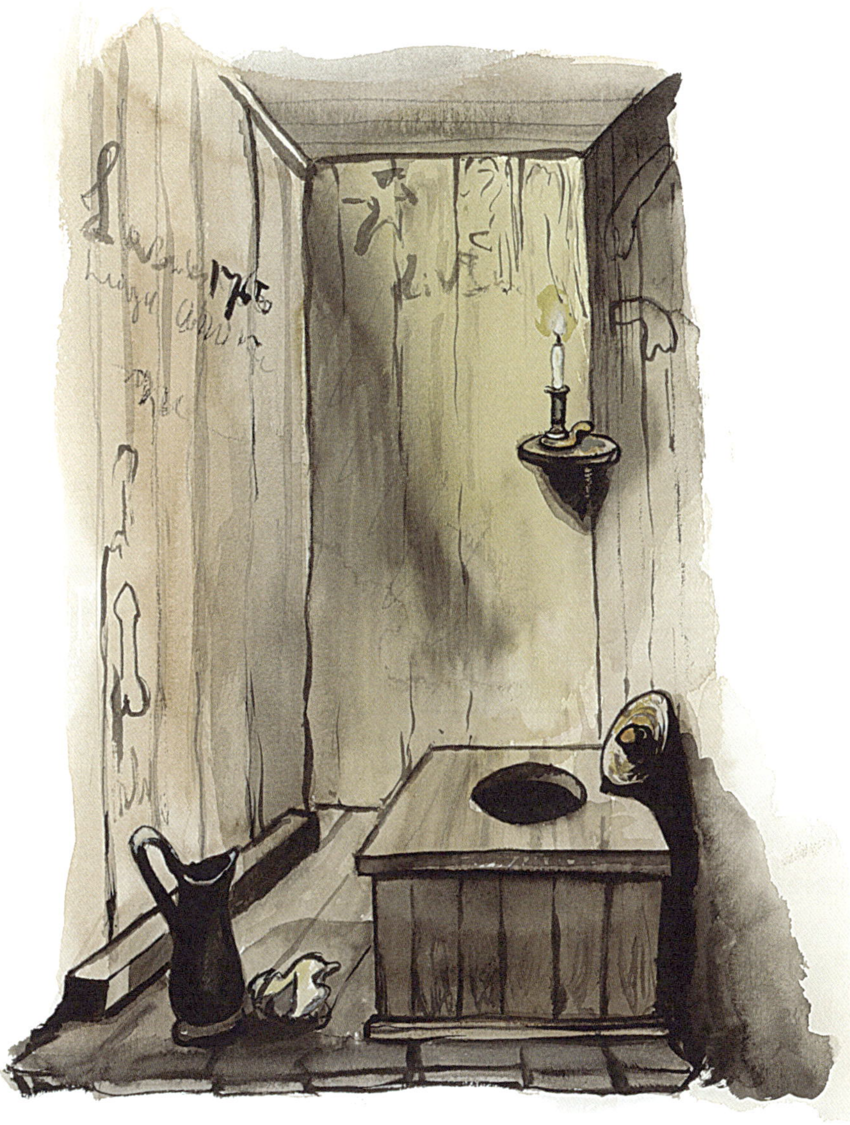

2.47 —

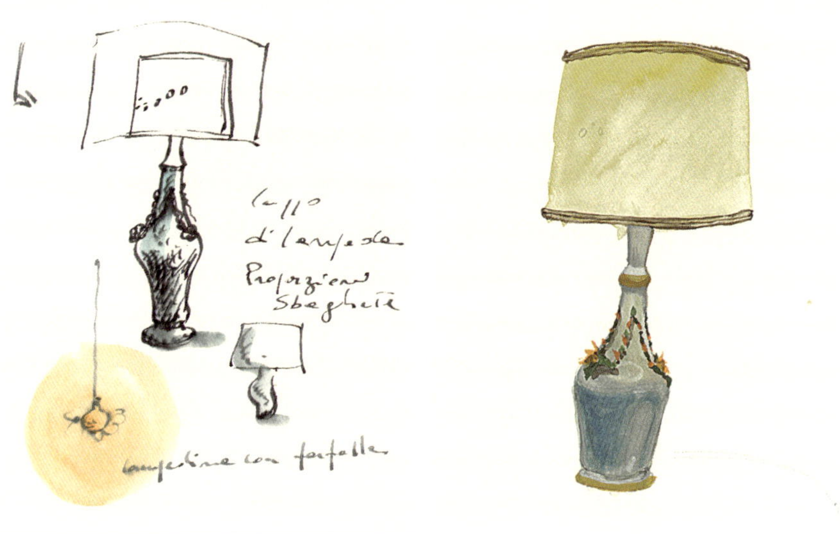

2.48 ——

Study for a lamp with a shade containing holes like sunspots. The project is linked to the study of sunspots painted in coffee and watercolour on paper from the same period. Beside it, a sketch of the idea of the lightbulb with a moth (2000).

2.49 ——

Detail of the lampholder with a blue base which vedovamazzei bought to carry out the previous work of sunspots on a lampshade. Project not realised (2000).

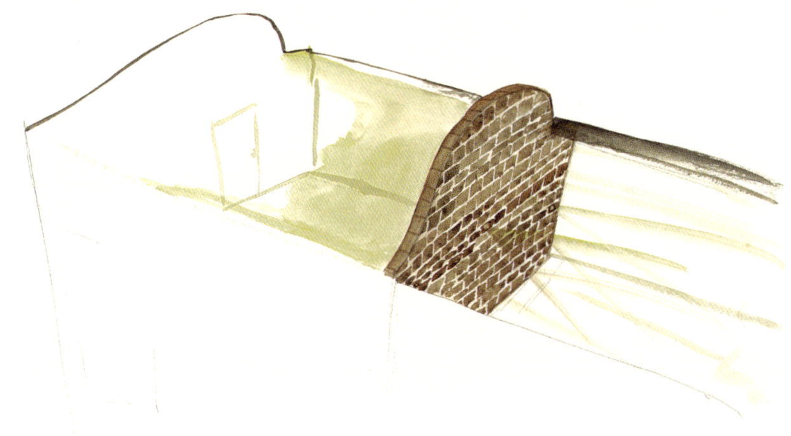

2.50 ——

Sketch of the wall built for the *Sun Dumm* project
(2001). The wall appeared filled with light as if it were
on the verge of exploding.

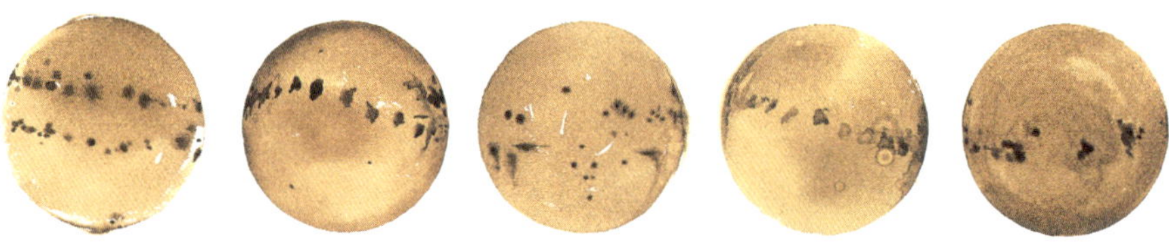

2.51 —

Detail and study of the sun with sunspots which
Galileo saw with a *d'après*, in coffee and watercolour.

2.52 —

Study of the sun for an oil on canvas. The China ink
text states: 'On this side of the earth the sun bemoans
our deafness...'

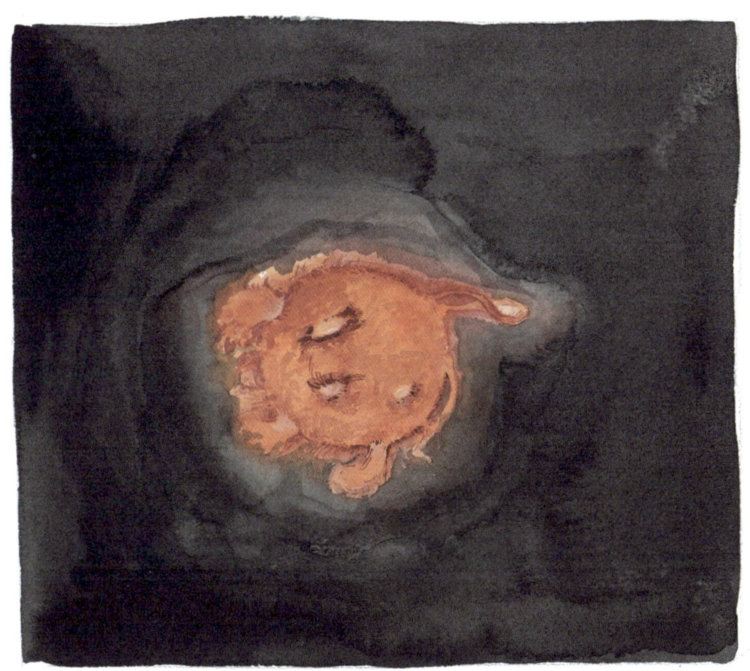

2.52 —

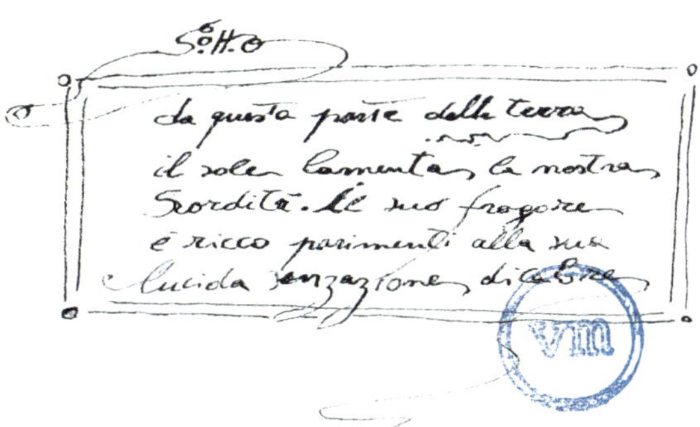

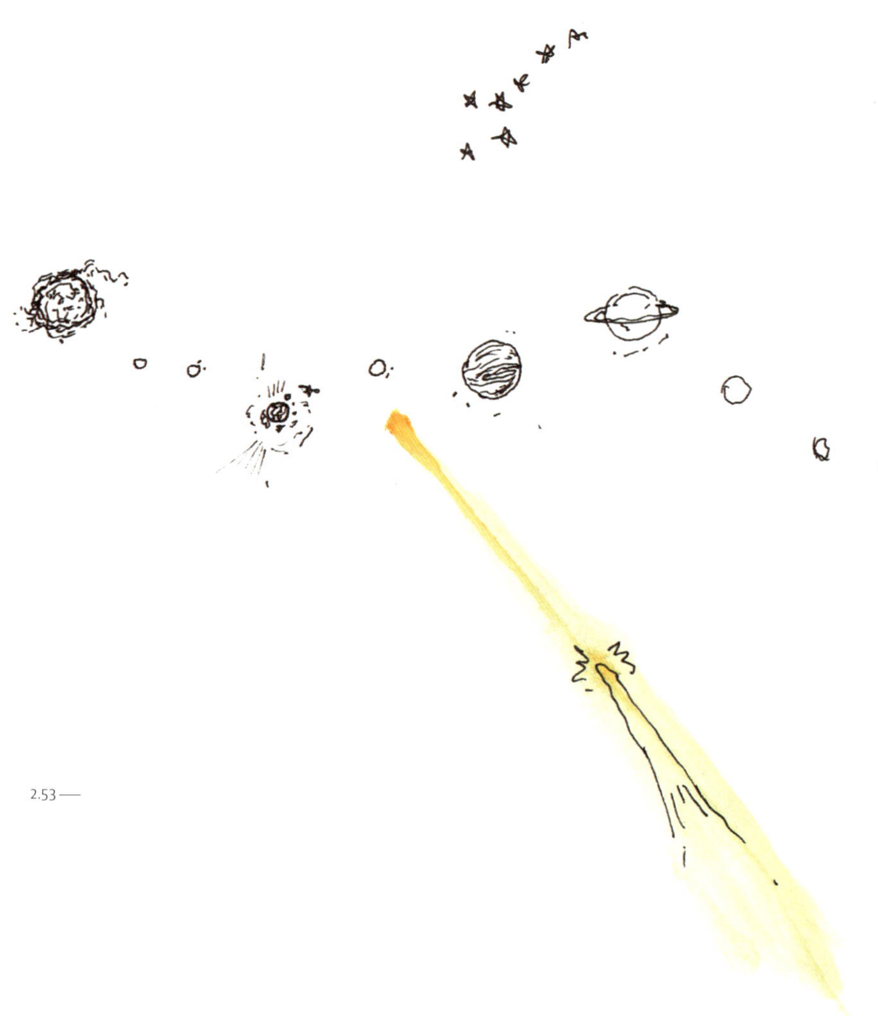

2.53 —

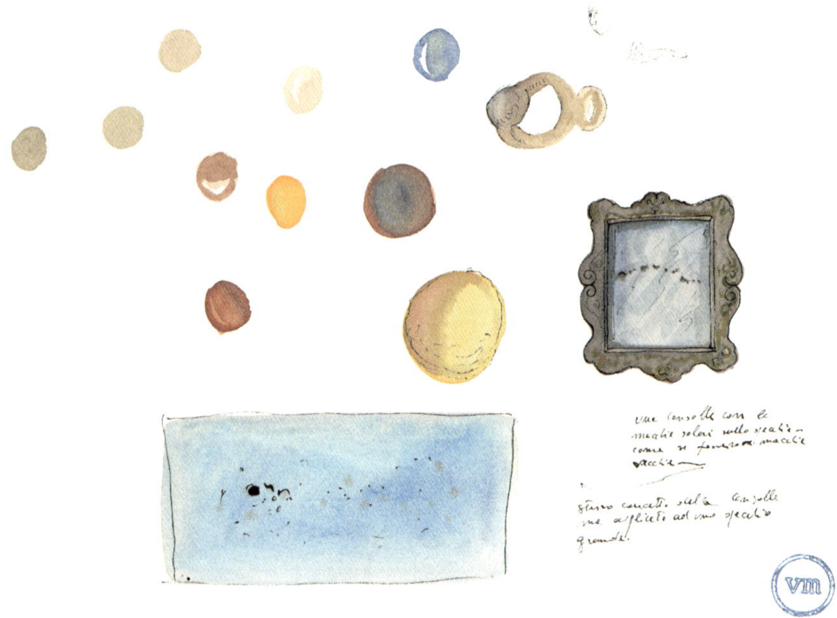

2.54 ——

2.53 ——

Study of a solar flare (2000). The picture *Sun Dumm* (2001) is the project for the wall built in Bergamo, which was broken and lit up using 1000-watt lights, simulating a solar flare.

2.54 ——

Study for a console table with mirror and sunspots. Detail of a big mirror with sunspots. The notes in China ink say: 'a console table with sunspots as if they were real spots' and 'same concept as the console table, but applied to a big mirror.' Like the previous pieces, this belongs to the period of the study of the sun and earth, together with the various works labelled *So.H.O (Solar Heliospheric Observatory)* (2001), as does the strongroom and vinyl records piece.

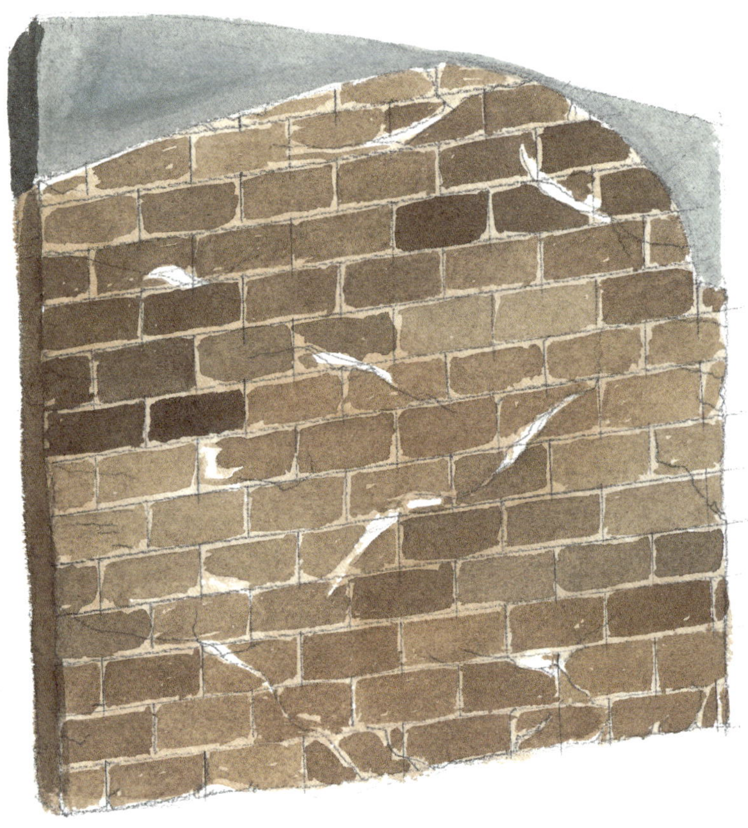

2.55 —
Study for the wall in *Sun Dumm*.

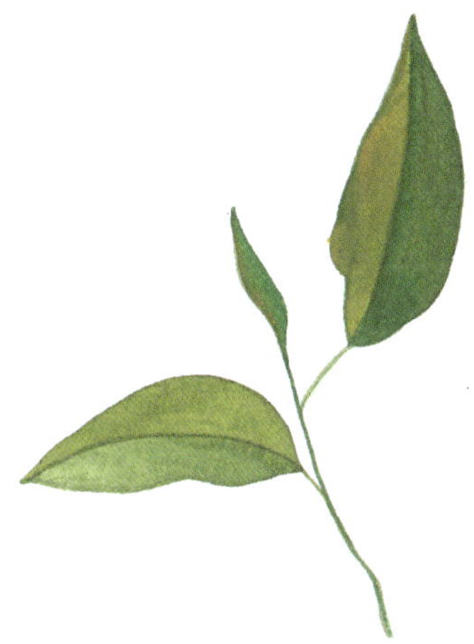

BOTANICAL TABLES
Tribute to a friend who has to lose weight

2.56 — 2.72 —

The invention of a miraculous herb diet, with plants
reproduced in tables with botanical illustrations taken
from an imaginary, ancient herbal, invented by
vedovamazzei as a tribute to and present for a friend
who had to lose weight.

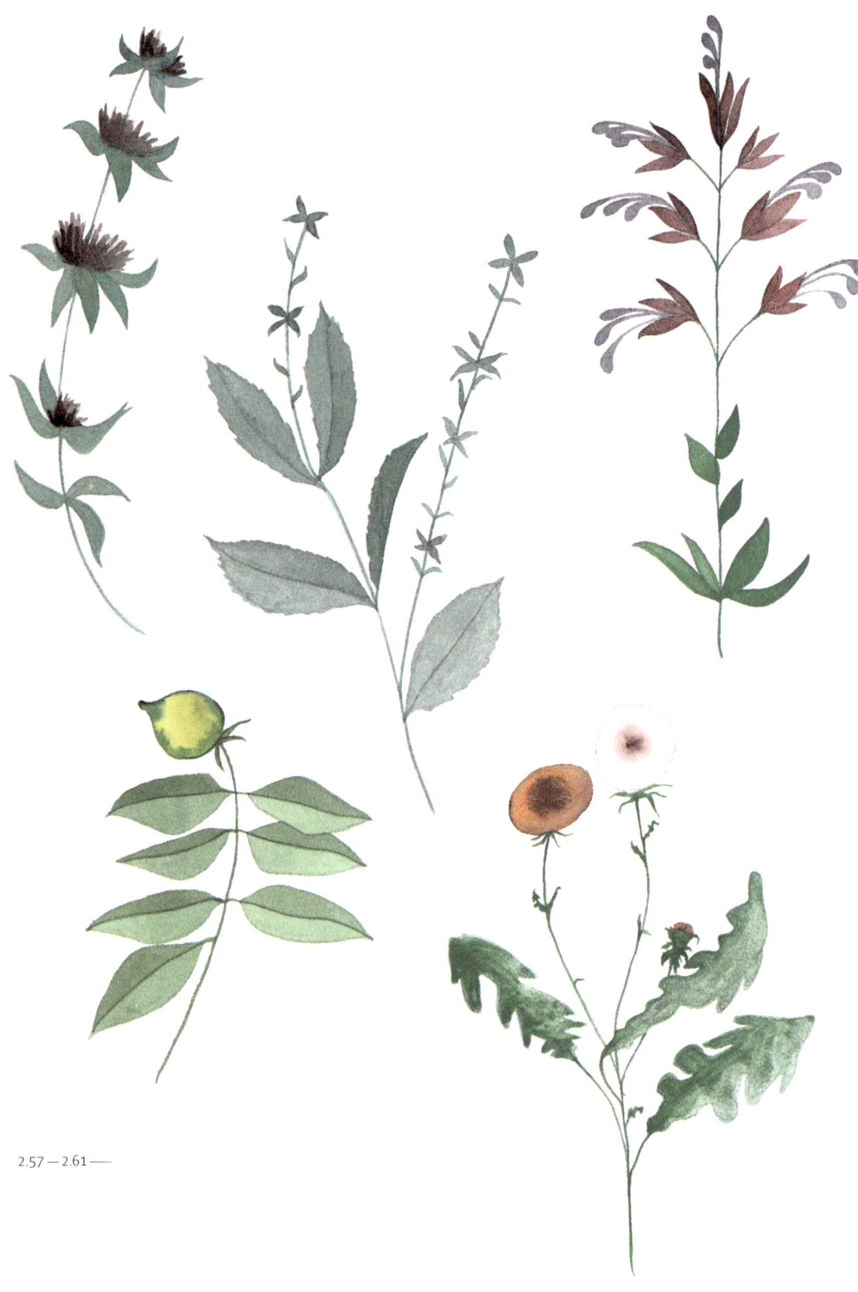

2.57 — 2.61 ——

2.62 — 2.66 —

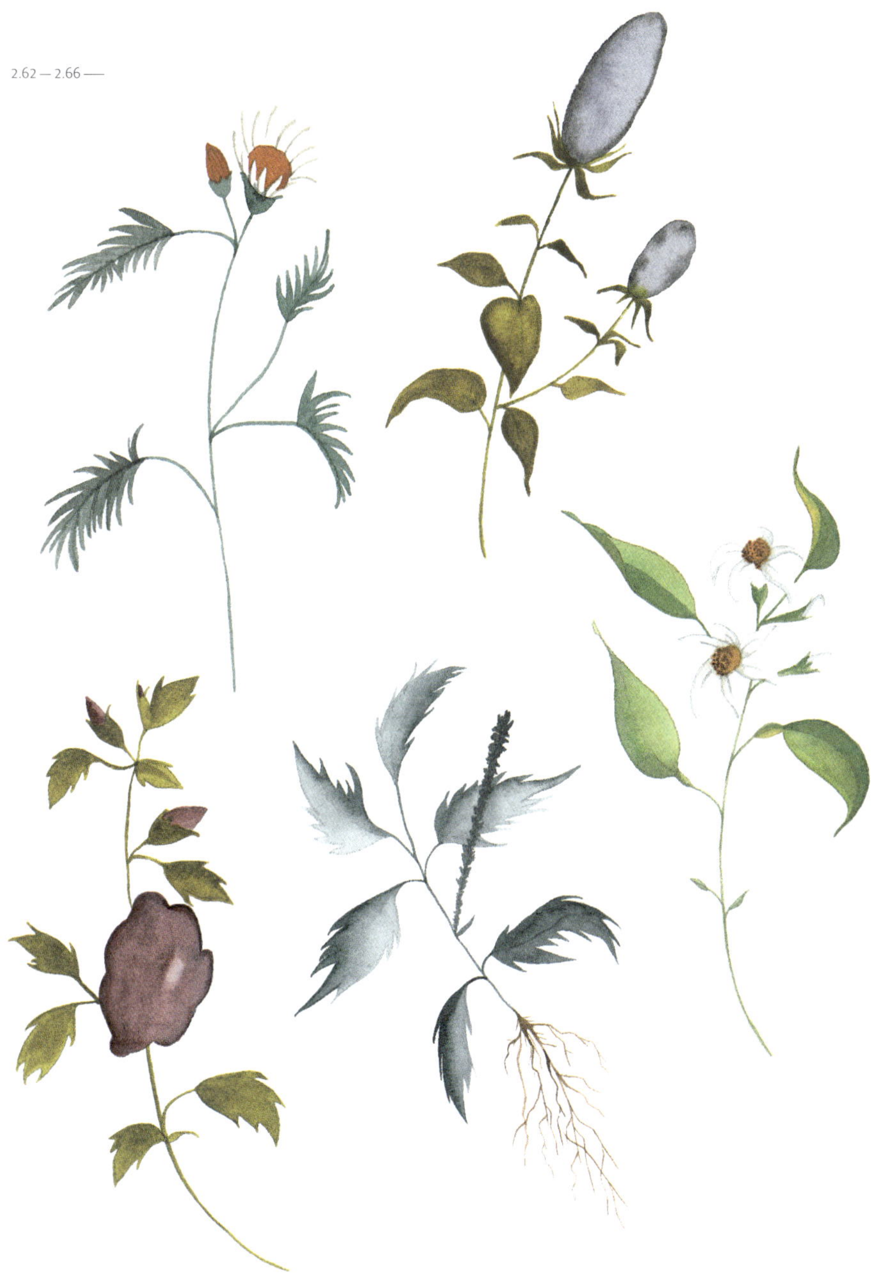

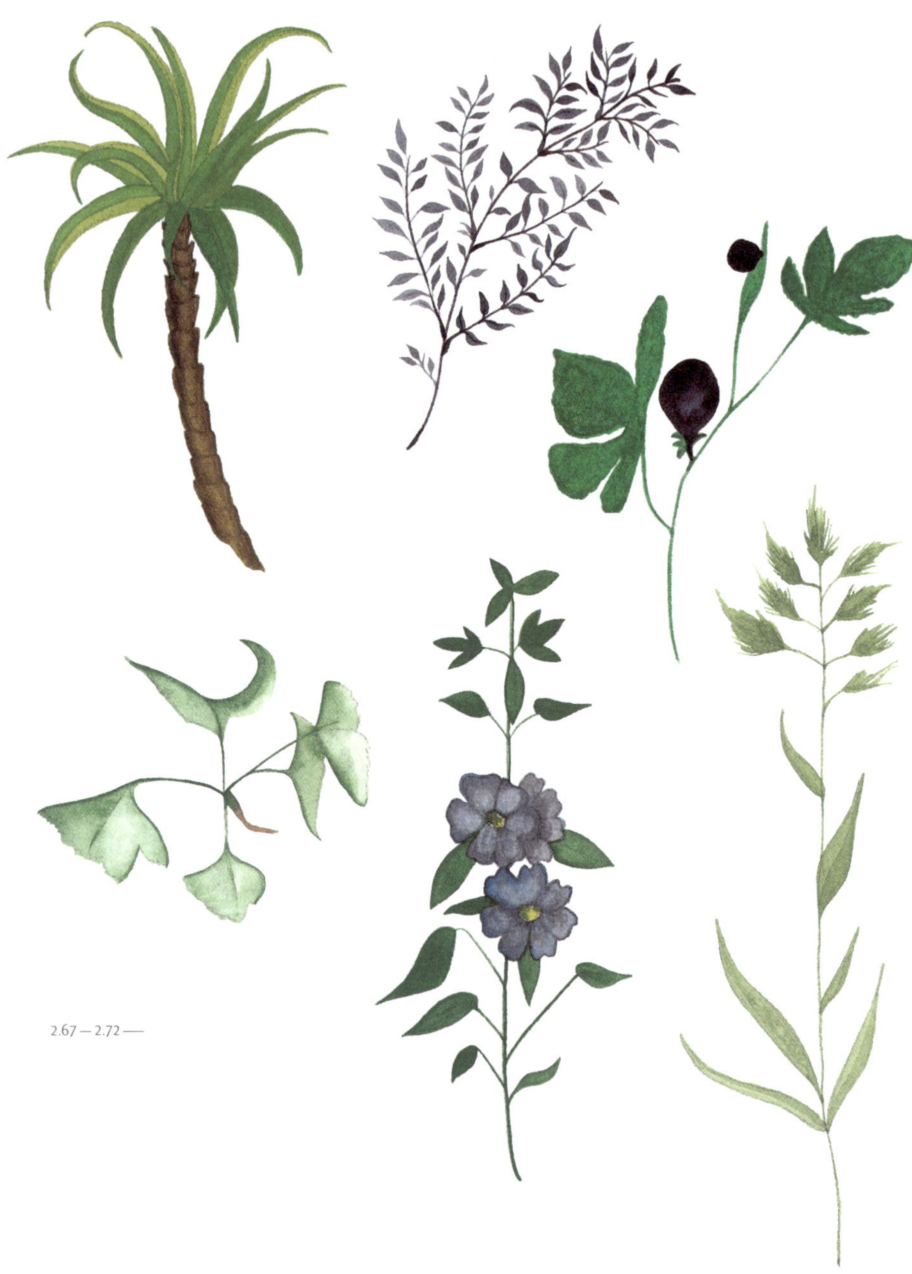

2.67 — 2.72 —

III

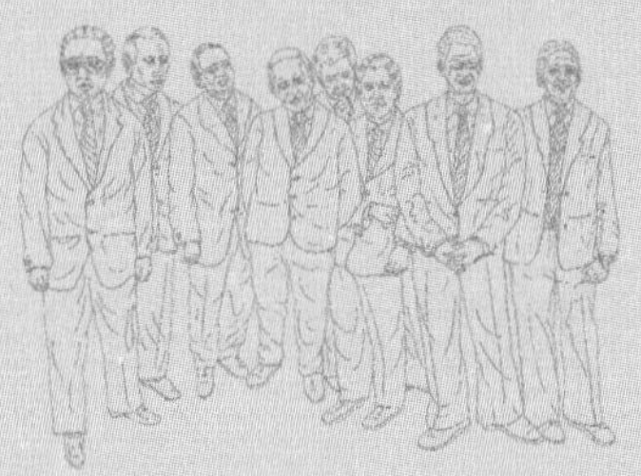

Morphology of a Project and Its Offshoots
(Ghent 1999–2000)

Throughout the evolution of its form and structure, this project provides a typical example of how the artists work. It forms part of that current of as yet unrealised ideas whose undercurrent, like the river-god Alpheus, acts as a constant drip, feeding the sea of vedovamazzei's work.

Here, three ideas for Ghent are presented. The first two were very different from each other but were both rejected as impracticable. Finally, the third idea will be realised with its 'unfinished' cement structure.

vedovamazzei first got the idea from a real tornado, Tornado Jarrell, which devastated Texas in 1997. They chose and studied it and then developed various hypotheses, with the help of CNR, Rome, and the University of Oklahoma City. The idea of reproducing a real tornado in scale or in a box was subsequently abandoned (*Tornado* 1999–2000). However, vedovamazzei continued to make an in-depth examination of potential models for reproducing the tornado, again with the collaboration of various different scientists.

The end result was not the physical production of the tornado. Instead, an allegorical image was created in our imagination, reflecting the strength vedovamazzei draw from the visionary ingenuousness of pre-Renaissance Italian artists. The fascination with this image has continued to flourish in vedovamazzei's mind and indeed they have recently used the *Tornado* idea again in a 2003 installation. Here, the most rudimentary wire model inside cardboard, and illuminated dramatically, returns once again to the idea of the scourge of nature.

ATMOSPHERIC SCIENCES,
UNIVERSITY OF OKLAHOMA CITY

3.01 ——

Study of Tornado Jarrell and its effects in Texas, with
vedovamazzei's notes on the advice received for
carrying out the project.

3.02 ——

Study of Tornado Jarrell, taken from a scientific
journal, with the addition of the little man and text in
China ink: 'Jarrell starts on 27 May 1997. A raging rope
tornado appears in the sky, the unpredictable tornado
which moves unusually slowly, breaks up into different
vertices to then merge back into a ravenous funnel
with winds filmed at over 226km/h.' Initially,
vedovamazzei wanted to recreate a real tornado in a
box in a scale of 10 x 5 x 5m. John Snow, Professor of
Atmospheric Sciences at the University of Oklahoma
City, provided advice on the theory for this and the
Belgian CNR built a box in the laboratory, at
vedovamazzei's request. The idea turned out to be
impracticable because, in Physics, what happens at
one metre does not occur at ten metres.

BREAKING-UP OF TORNADO JARRELL

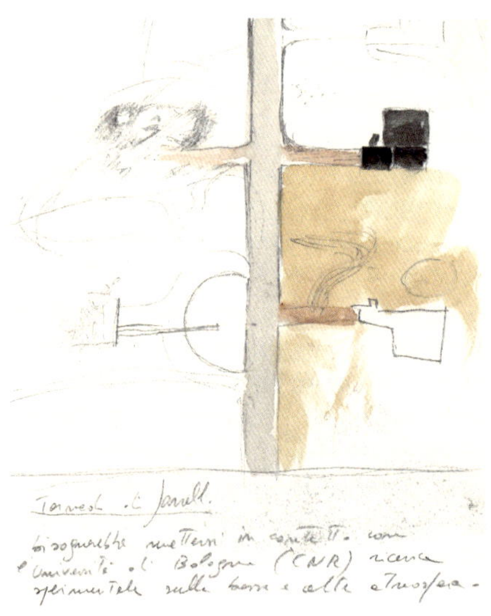

3.01 ——

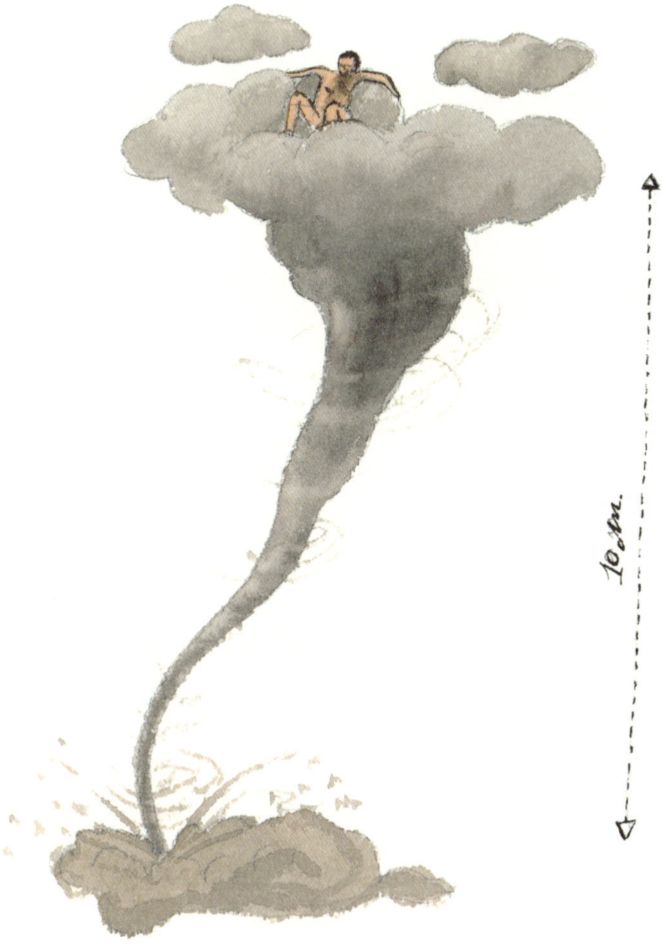

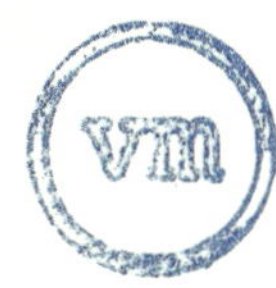

Jarrell, inizia il 27 maggio 1997. Nel cielo appare un sinuoso cordone, il tornado. Imprevedibile, si muove con inconsueta lentezza, si divide in più vortici, per poi fondersi di nuovo in un famelico crabuto, con venti stimati a oltre 320 Km/h.

3.02 —

THE BODY OF THE TORNADO IN THE CORNER OF
THE CHURCH OF ST. MICHAEL IN GHENT

3.03 ——

Study and detail from above of the tornado which
they considered to put on the side of the Church of
St. Michael in Ghent. This drawing represents the
first stage of an idea to produce a free tornado, to be
recreated ideally on the side of the church.

3.04 ——

Study for the tornado in a box, the second idea, to put
on the side of the Church of St. Michael of Ghent.

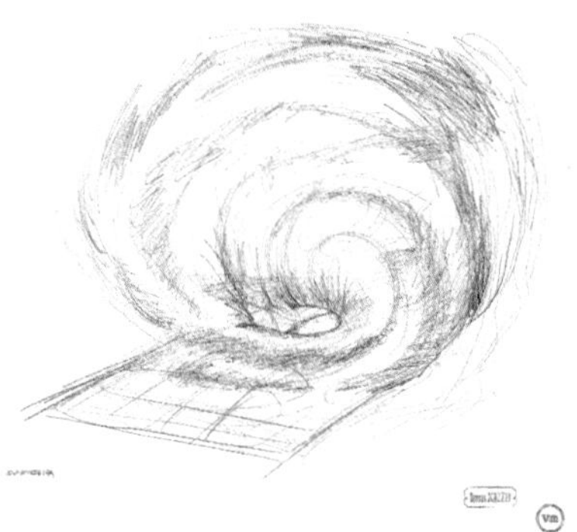

3.03 ——

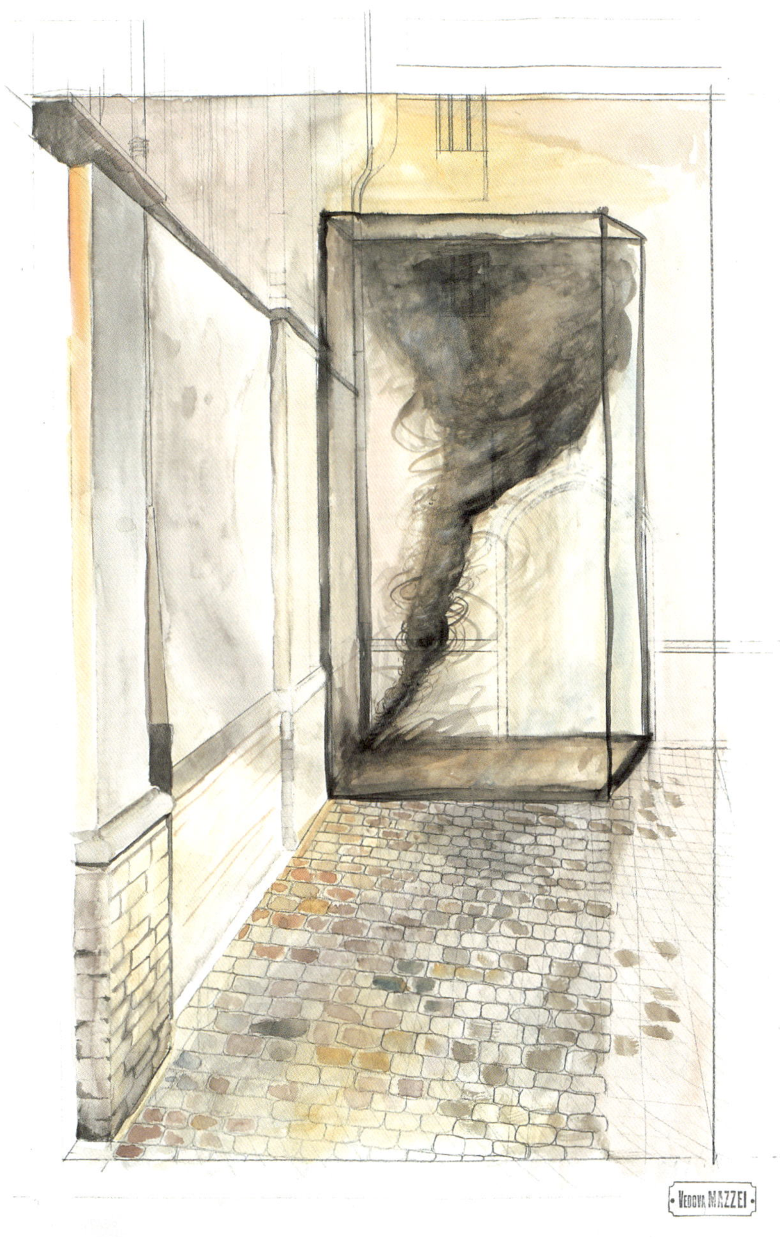

3.04 —

3.05 ——

Study for the tornado in a box, the second idea, to put on the side of the Church of St. Michael in Ghent.

3.06 ——

China ink study of Tornado Jarrell with variation (1999–2000). Here the text, with a slight change from the previous illustration, states, 'Jarrell, Texas, starts on the 27 May 1997. A sinuous rope tornado appears in the sky, the unpredictable tornado, which moves unusually slowly, divides into many vertices to then merge back into a ravenous funnel with winds estimated to be over 320km/h.'

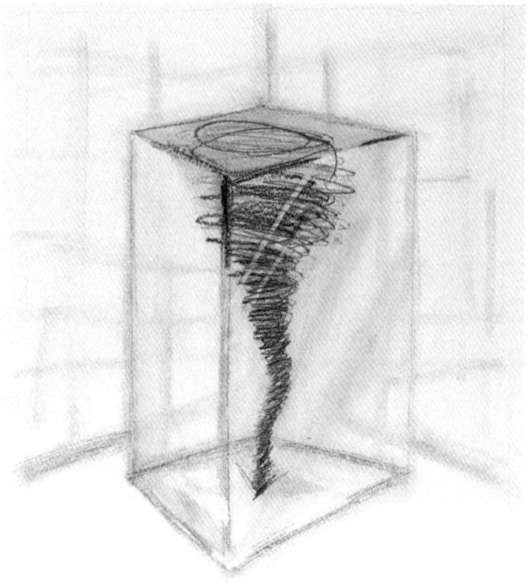

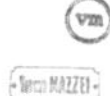

3.05 ——

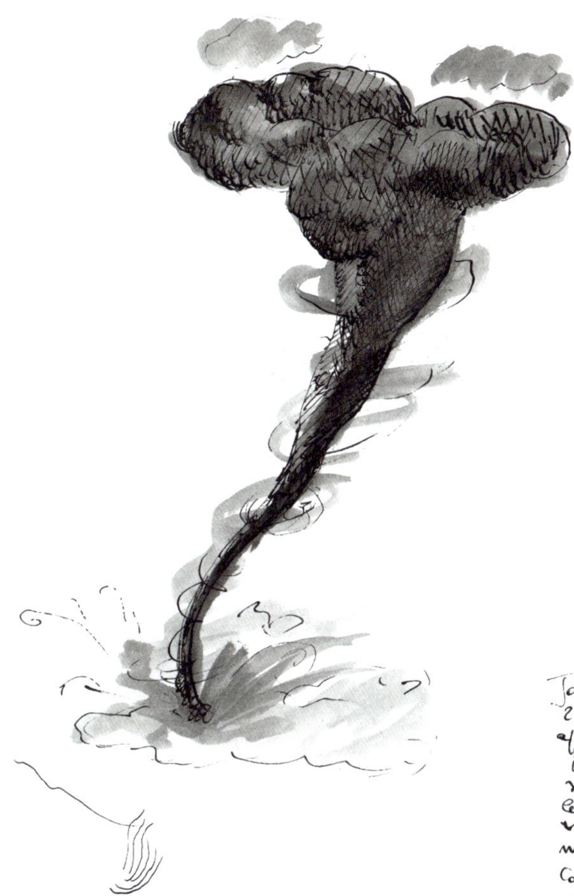
Jarrell, Texas, inizia il
27 maggio 1997. Nel cielo
appare un rimoso cumulone.
Il Tornado. Imprevedibile
si muove con incoerente
lentezza. Si divide in getti
vortici per poi tornare a
muoversi in un tunnel coinvolto,
con venti schiumati a
oltre 320 Km/h.

Progetto 199 — 2000

3.06 —

THE STRATIFICATION OF G8. STUDY FOR A SUMMIT

This second project is for an hypothetical virtual simulation of the G8 summit held in Ghent on 8 June 1999. It makes a detailed study of all the summit's real features as if they were epithelial layers which are analysed separately and then reconstructed to produce a scientific explanation. They even envisaged being able to find doubles to impersonate the political leaders. This project was not realised either.

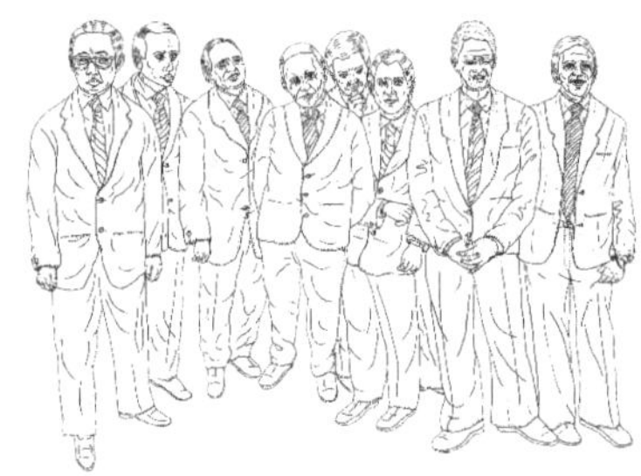

3.07 ——

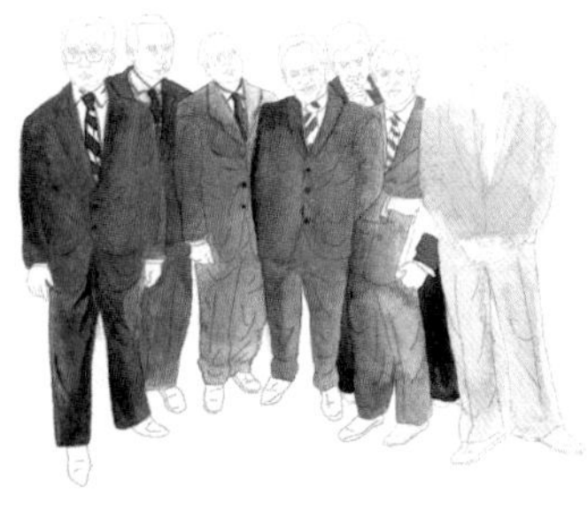

3.08 ——

CATALOGUING OF THE G8 LEADERS' MEMBRANES

3.07 — 3.09 ——
Details of the Cuticles. The leaders pose in front of the Church of St. Michael in Ghent for the commemorative photo shoot. Watercolour study of the G8 leaders' clothes.

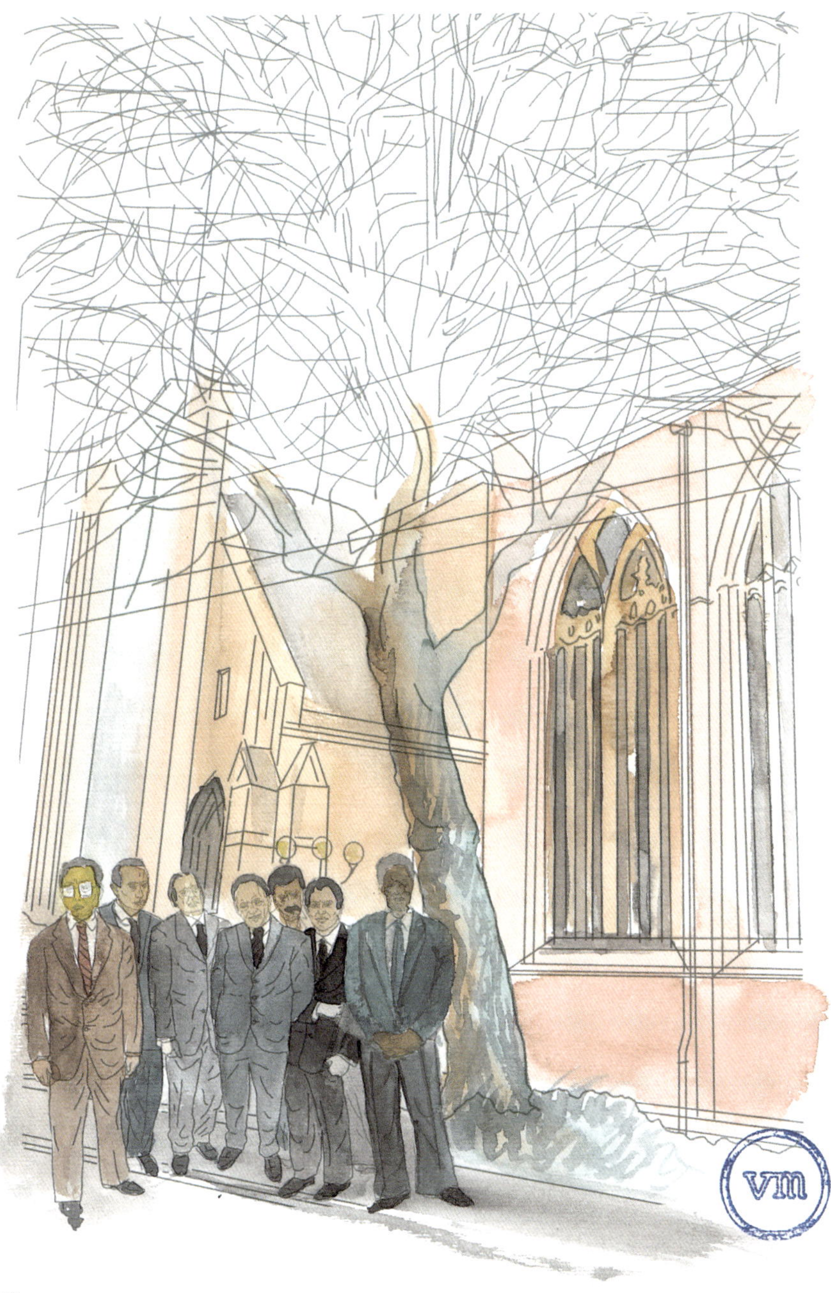

3.09 —

CRYING REINFORCED CONCRETE
Dew Drops

COMPOSITION OF THE UNFINISHED BUILDING

3.10 — 3.14 —
Preliminary studies of the 'unfinished' building in reinforced concrete crying real tears, *Dew Drops* (2001), produced in Ghent. In this case, the Michaelangelo-style 'unfinished' piece is an ironic reference to illegal construction. Such a practice is particularly common in Southern Italy where many buildings are left incomplete, with the concrete still visible, and yet are lived in.

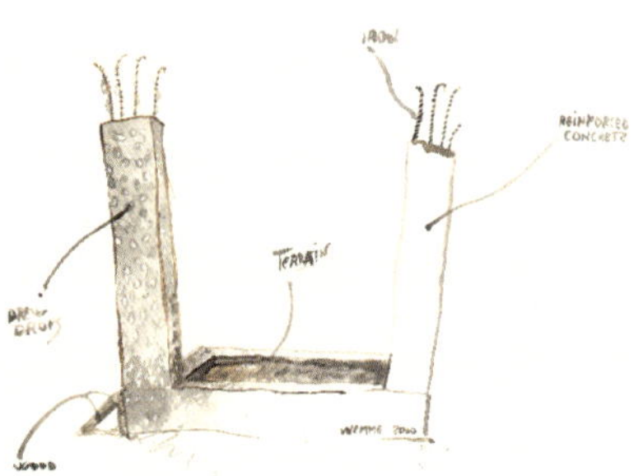

3.10 —

PAT GARRET AND BILLY THE KID
FROM SAM PECKINPAH

THE GRAVE'S OF OF SAM
PAT & BILLY

Tra : REINFORCED CONCRETE
ANNO : 96/2000

HEIGT : cm 220
WIDTH : cm 40
DEEP : cm 40

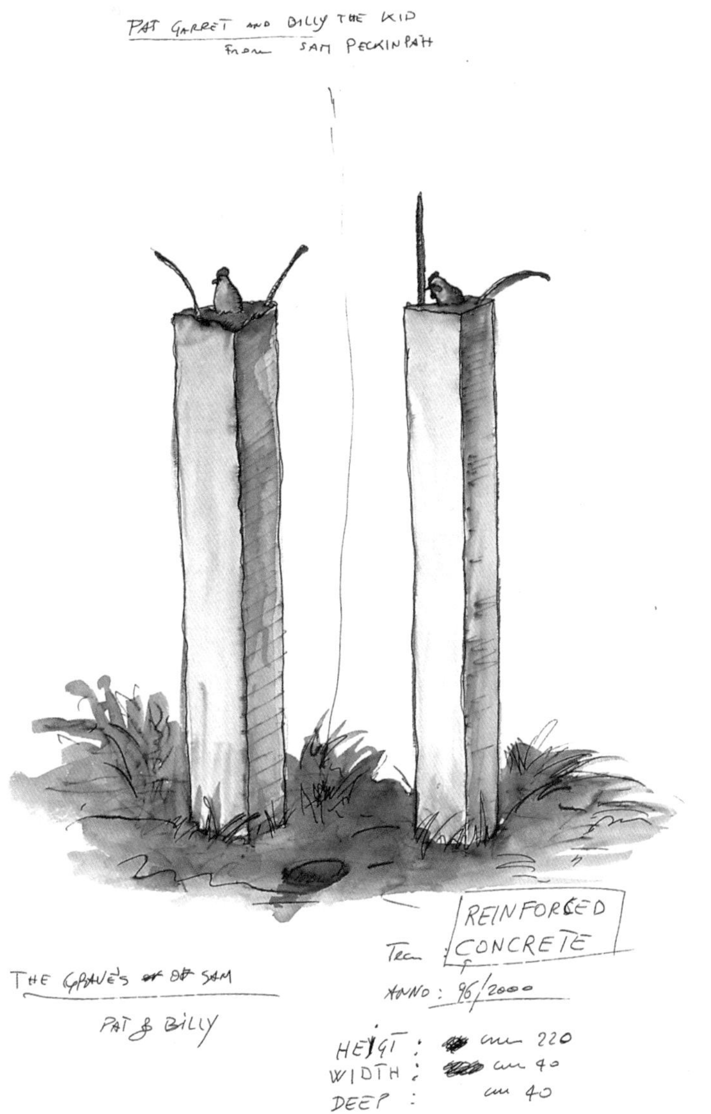

3.11 —

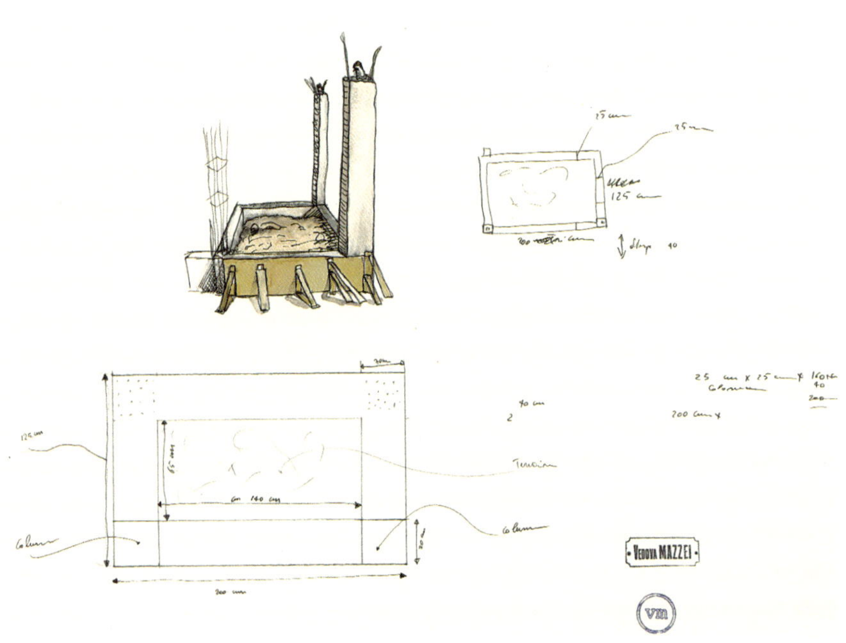

3.12 ——

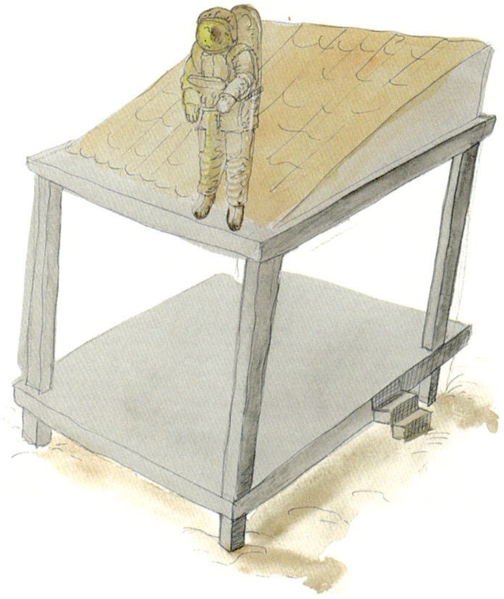

3.13 —

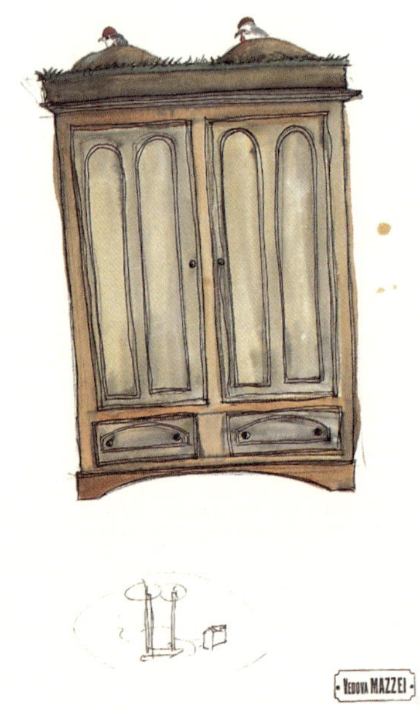

3.14 ——

IV

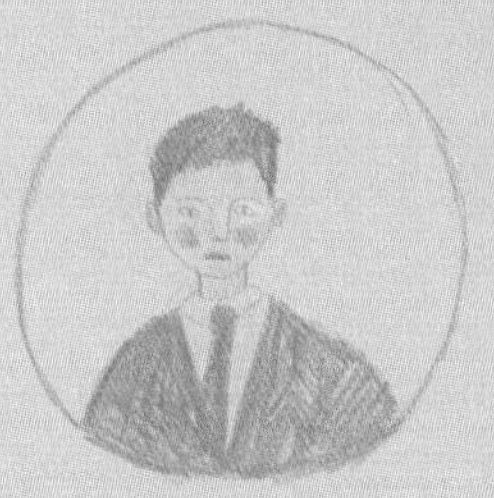

Artists' Reproductive Organs and Their Functions

The Natural History of vedovamazzei, described in drawings and watercolours, would not be complete without one of vedovamazzei's first works making use of the device of childhood drawings *d'après.* Here, masterpieces by great artists are used to make a half-serious analysis of the tool itself as well as of the propensity for art expressed at an exceptionally early age by great artists and their unmistakable style. Despite the apparent ingenuousness in their ideal gallery, which goes from Pisanello up to Koons, vedovamazzei in fact investigate fundamental issues in Art History. They take part in a debate first started off by Vasari, who located the basis of art precisely in the practice of 'Drawing'.

DRAWING

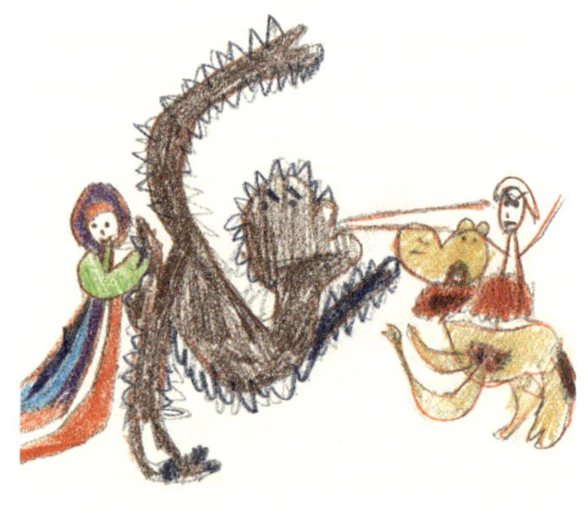

4.01 ———

BRIEF HISTORY OF ART LIMITED TO CHILDHOOD

These drawings constitute the study for a series of real
and metaphorical self-portraits of famous artists as
children. vedovamazzei then used them to produce ten
big cartoons entitled *Self-Portraits* (1992), which have
since been dispersed, to bear witness to a brief and
personal History of Art limited to childhood. The
whole series was done in 1992; vedovamazzei's and
Velazquez's pictures in 2001.

4.01 ———
Paolo Uccello at eight years old. Self-portrait as
St. George and the Dragon.

4.02 ———
Sandro Botticelli at four years old. *The Birth of Venus.*

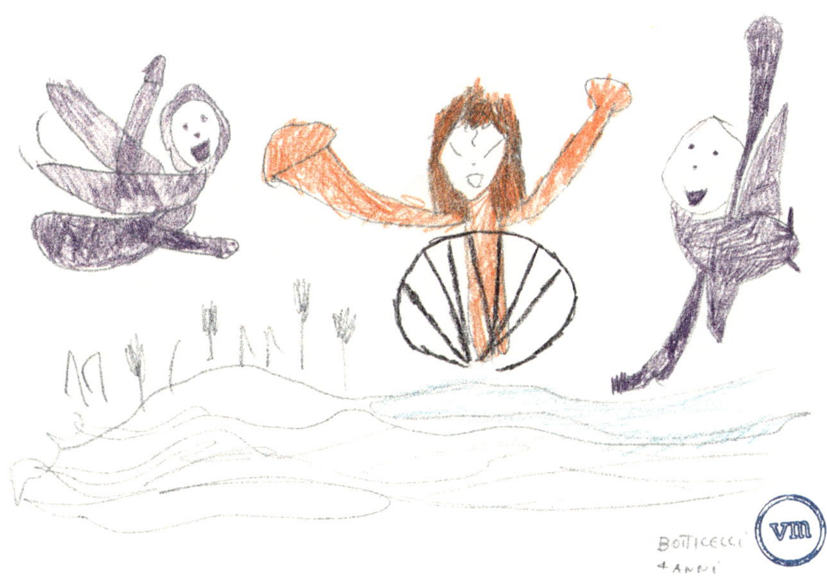

4.02 —

4.03 —
Piero di Cosimo at two and a half years old.
Mythological self-portrait with friends and animals.

4.04 —
Giulio Paolini at eleven years old. Portrait of a
classmate.

4.05 —
Rembrandt Van Rhijn at eight years old. Self-portrait
when an adult.

4.06 —
Gian Lorenzo Bernini at three years old. Drawn from
the cardinal window in front of the Basilica of Santa
Maria Maggiore.

4.07 —
Pisanello at five years old. Self-portrait as a horse.

4.08 —
Jeff Koons at eight years old. Self-portrait as a bear.

4.09 —
Piero Manzoni at eleven years old. Self-portrait.

4.10 —
Diego Velazquez at two years old. Self-portrait with
Las Meninas.

4.11 —
The Bronzetti brothers at four years old. Four-handed
landscape. A fabrication of history by vedovamazzei.

4.12 —
Leonardo da Vinci at eight years old. Portrait of an aunt.

4.13 —
vedovamazzei at six years old. Four-handed landscape.

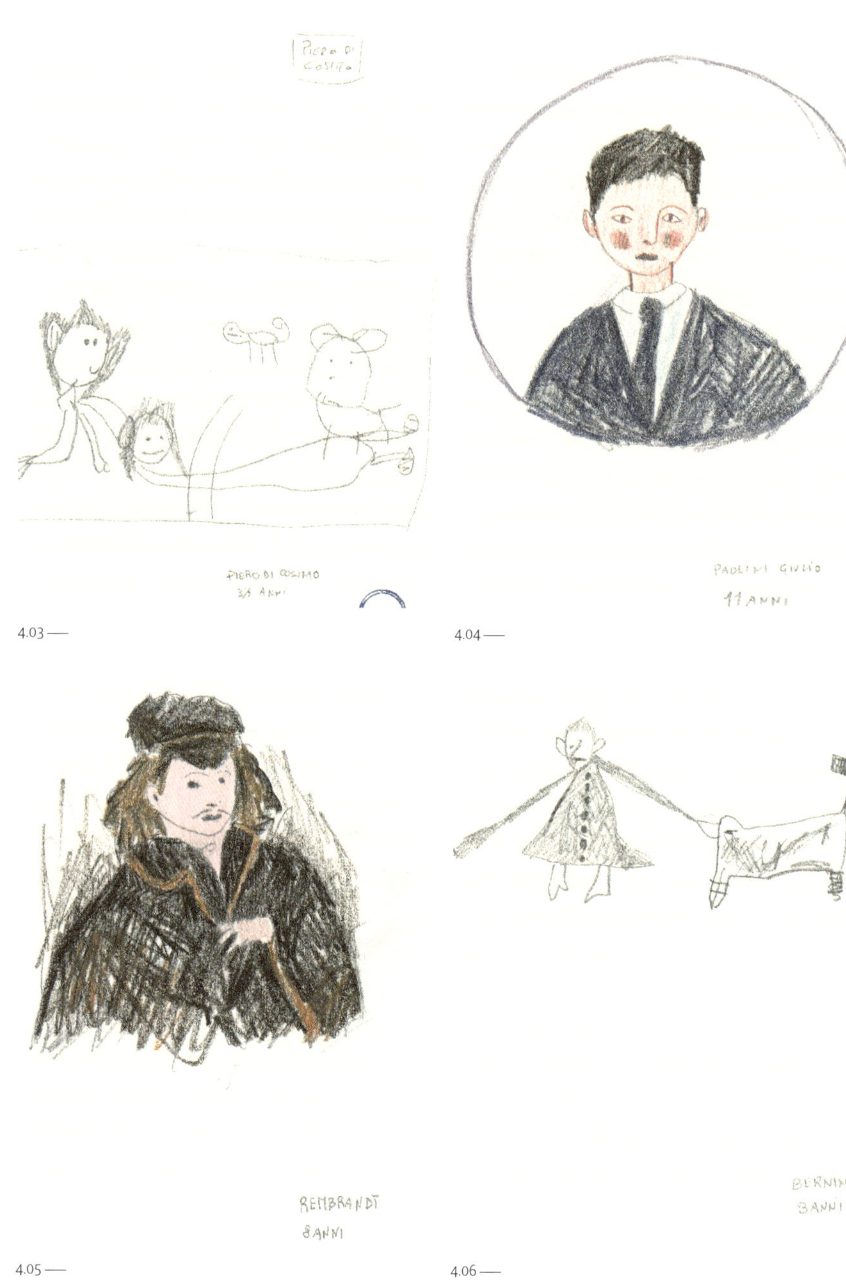

PIERO DI COSIMO
3/4 ANNI

PAOLINI GIULIO
11 ANNI

4.03 ——

4.04 ——

REMBRANDT
8 ANNI

BERNINI
8 ANNI

4.05 ——

4.06 ——

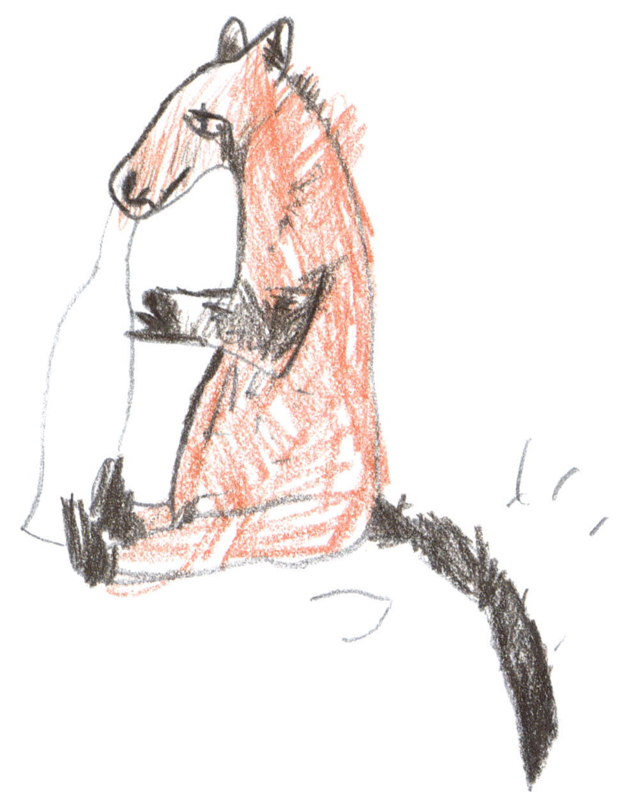

4.07 —

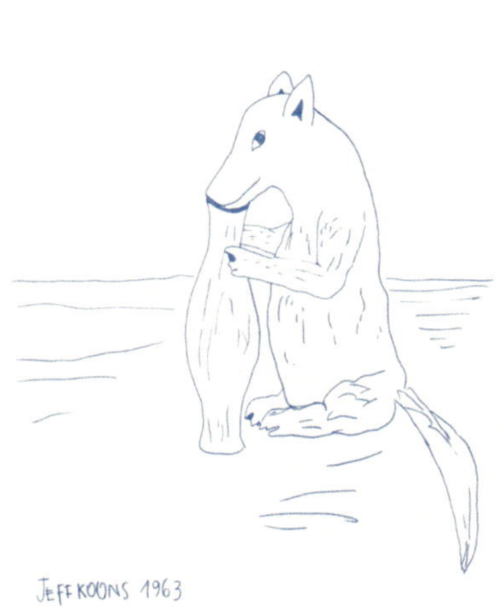

4.08 ——

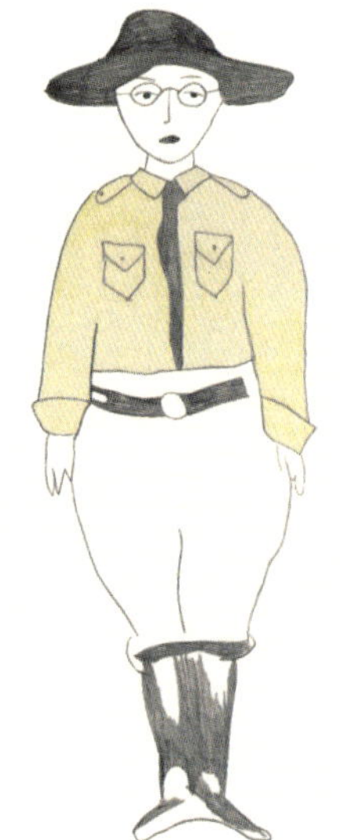

4.09 ——

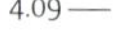
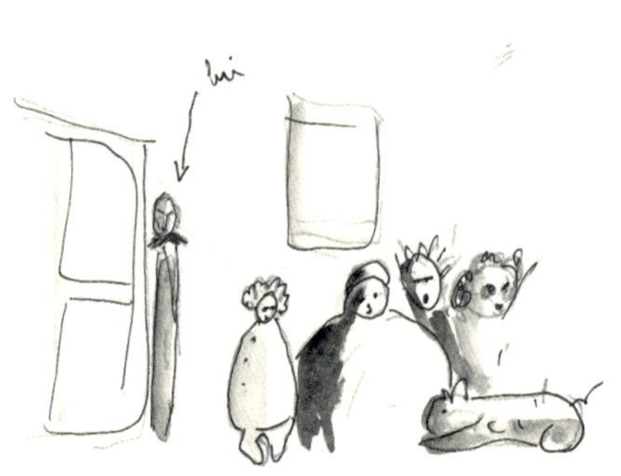

4.10 ——

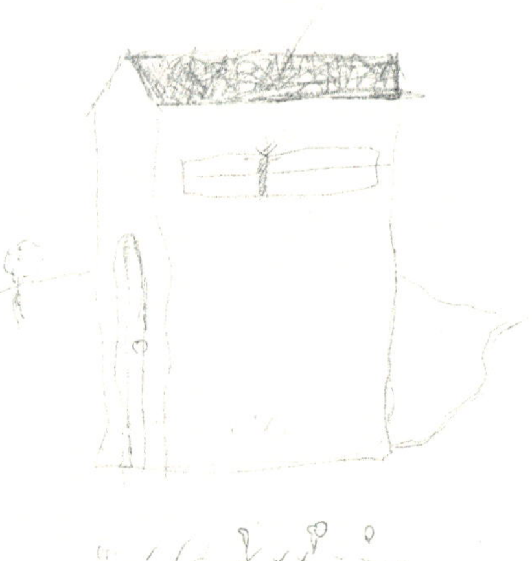

4.11 ——

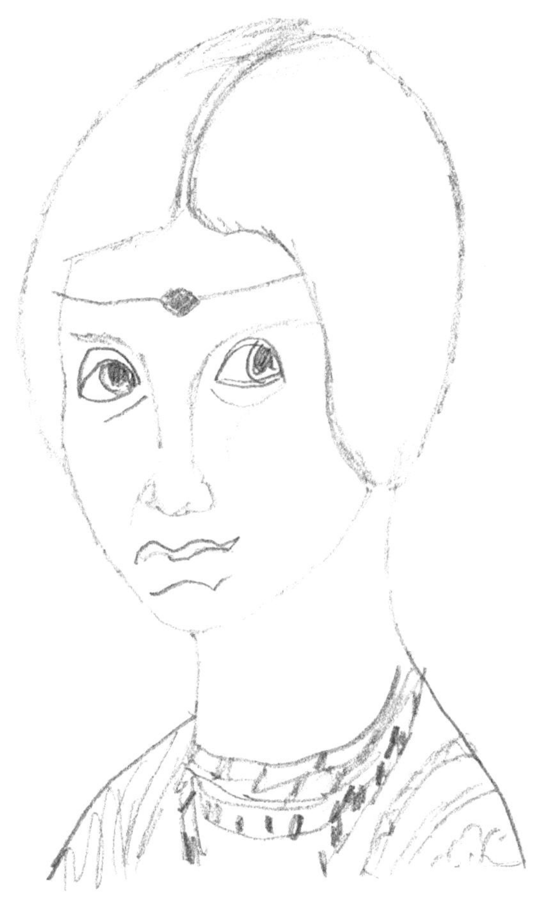

4.12 —

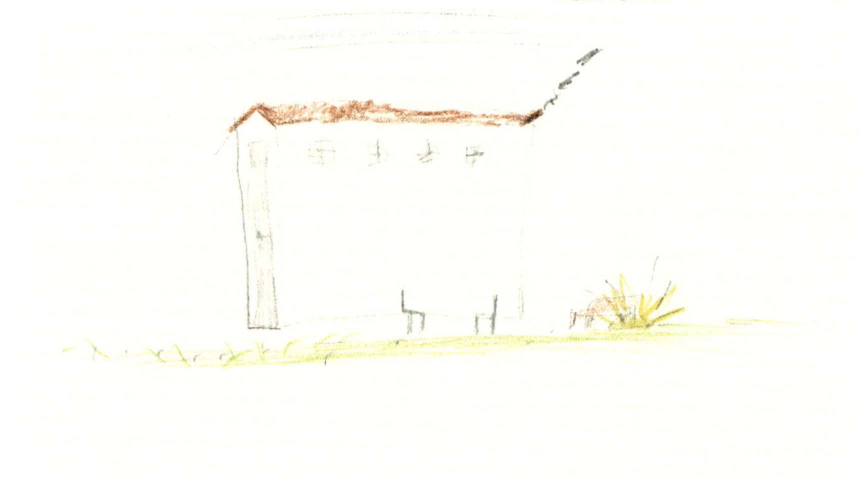

4.13 —

V

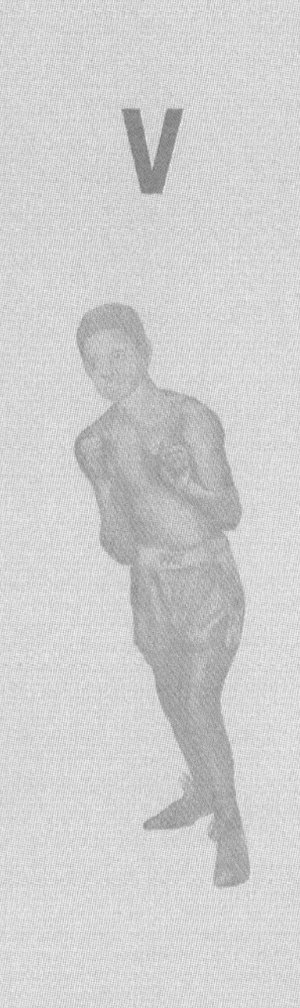

Habitat, Typology and Number of Portraits

vedovamazzei are interested in strangers, in anonymous people, as real subjects for portraits. People without any definable features, like the portrait Gogol draws at the beginning of *Dead Souls* of a featureless man who arrives in a city which is indicated only by the letter 'N'. vedovamazzei look for faces expressing an absence of historical memory, like Bulger James's, the identikit of a serial killer who disappeared without trace in the 1970s. This analysis of the portrait, whether in terms of depersonalisation or identification, originates in numerous early self-portraits which produce works like *Pupa quae etiam…* and the series of *X-rays*. The investigation into portraiture questions the ideology of the subject-object and places friends, clients and deities at the same level in the hierarchy. The study of the *Jesus Christ as a Bearskin Rug* (1999) expresses vedovamazzei's well-known desecrating indifference towards the most deeply-rooted values of Catholic religious tradition. It is well known that the Holy Shroud is preserved in Turin. vedovamazzei do not repudiate the tradition as such. Indeed, they are fascinated by it deeply. But they consider themselves free to interpret this tradition from positions which differ radically from those enshrined in canon law. They transform the idea of the relic as developed by religion into a trophy displayed by a hunter. The result is obviously blasphemous, as in all the portraits on the subject presented here. But it represents an innocent desire to interpret that grows out of that childish need for exorcism of and identification with our needs and religious heroes. In the *Portrait of C.G,* next to the image vedovamazzei note 'two beautiful fireplaces in two different rooms, both with fires burning in them, with the skins of Simeone and Stella as beautiful bears or tigers or something else. only skins and heads.'

**PORTRAITS OF FRIENDS, ACQUAINTANCES, DEITIES
AND A SERIAL KILLER**

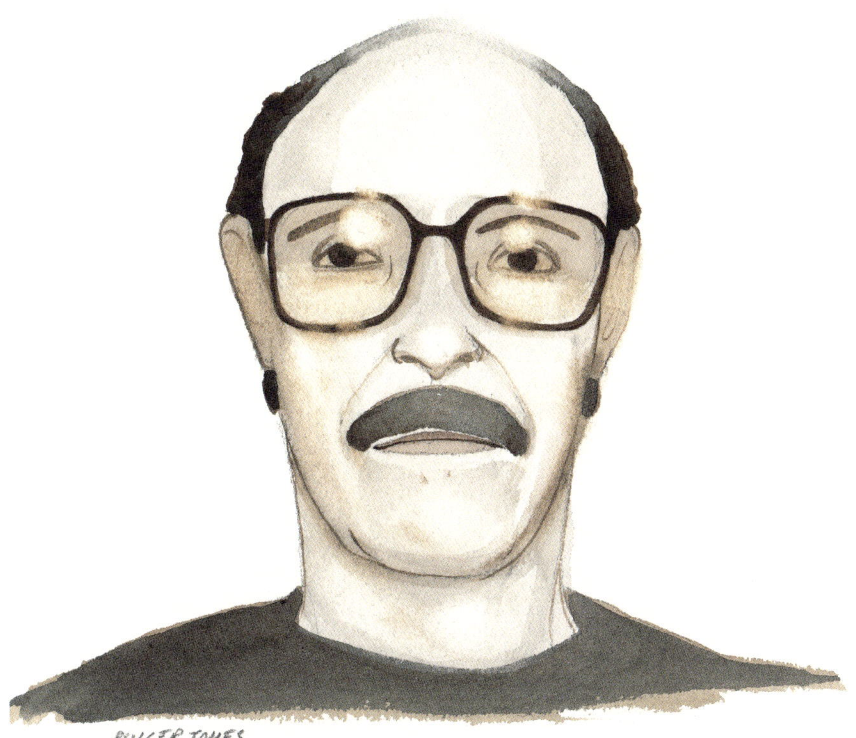

5.01 —

SERIAL KILLER
Portrait of Bulger James. From the serial killer's identikit
taken from the FBI's website (*www. fbi.gov/mostwant/
topten/fugitives/bulger.htm*). Bulger is still a fugitive and
appears on the FBI's list of ten most wanted men for
numerous murders he committed in the 1970s.

5.02 —

Study for a fax with a Hitler mask at M.N.'s birthday party.

5.03 —

Portrait of C.A. Carlo Alfano was Stella's mentor and is here depicted in honour of memory, a subject he investigated in his art. He worked in Naples at the beginning of the 1970s, gravitating towards the Lucio Amelio Gallery.

FRIENDS

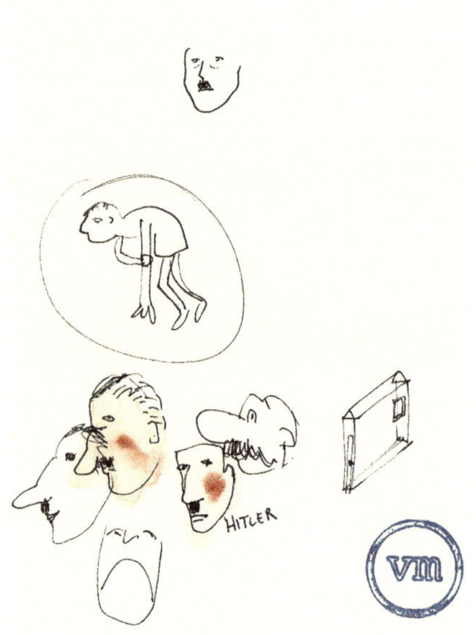

5.02 —

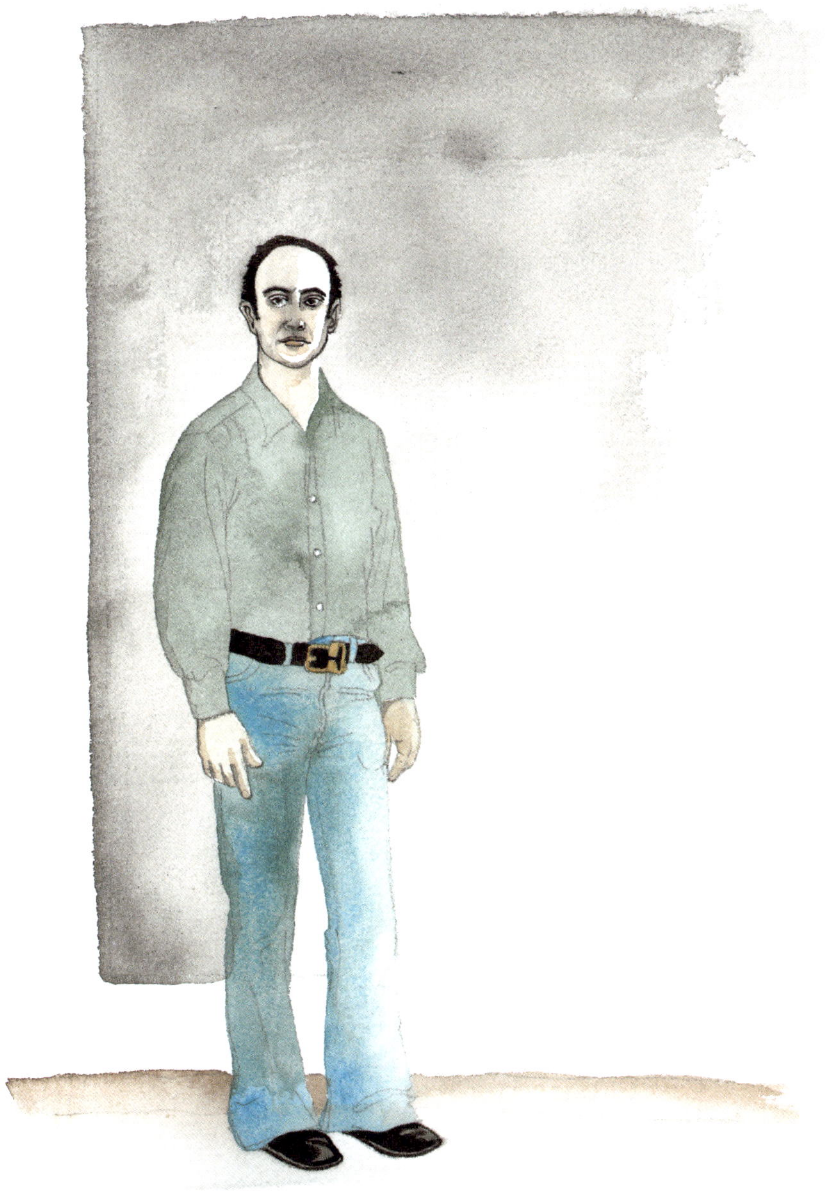

5.03 —

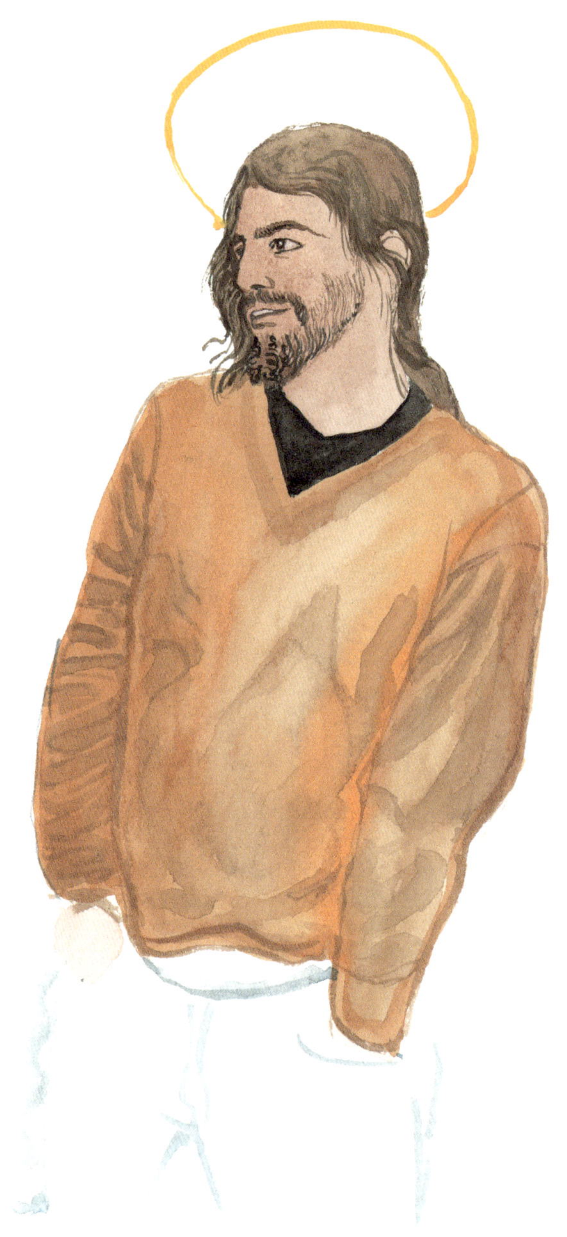

—— 5.04

5.04 —

Portrait of A.M. as Jesus Christ. Religious iconography returns as part of vedovamazzei's vernacular applied to the ordinary.

5.05 —

Portrait of C.G. In the note: 'two beautiful fireplaces in two different rooms, both with fires burning in them, with the skins of Simeone and Stella as beautiful bears or tigers or something else. only skins and heads.'

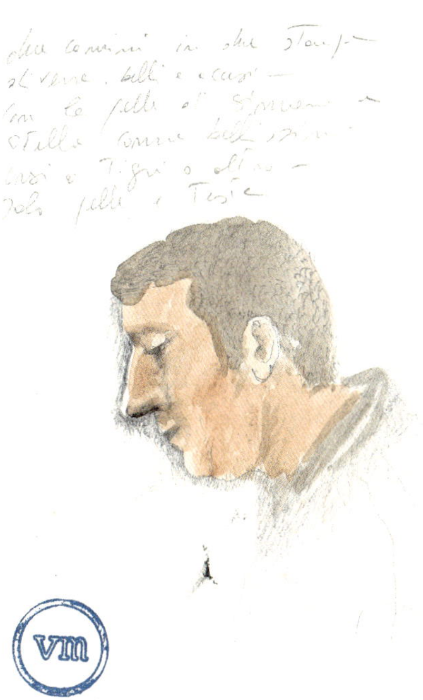

5.05 —

PORTRAITS WITHOUT A STYLE

The series of studies for large oils on canvas which the following portraits belong to are still being completed. Technically, the series originated with the possibility of using imaging software to abstract and manipulate any photographic image to obtain a portrait without a style. The image emerges out of a dark background and expresses the idea that culture has no taste. The watercolour is used not for aesthetic purposes but because this medium makes it possible to study the physical features to subtract and then acquire.

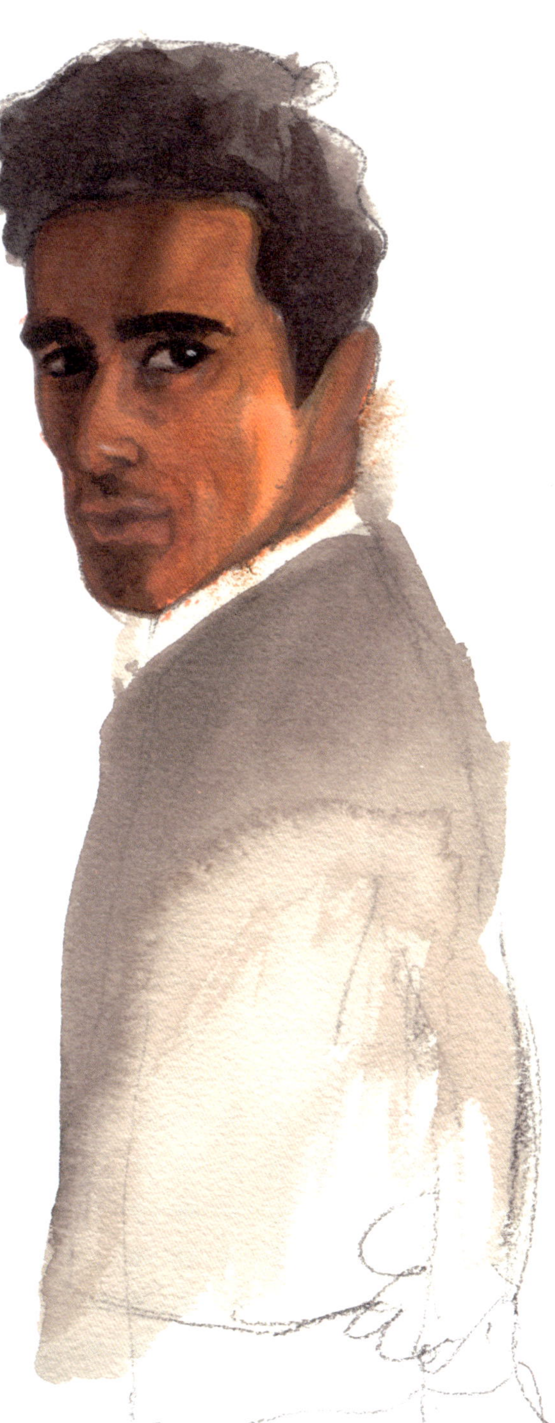

5.06 ——
Study for portrait of V.D.

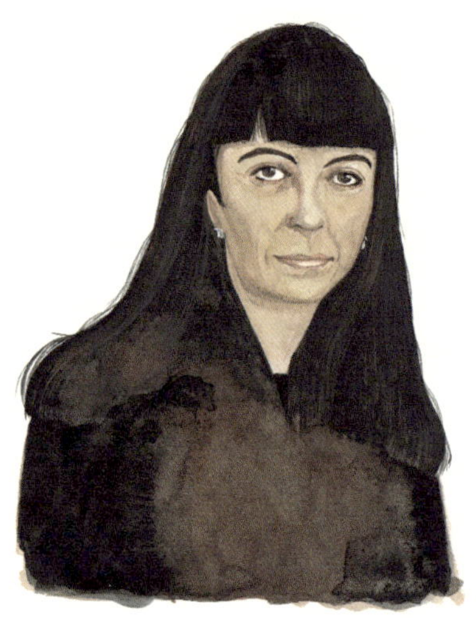

5.07 ——

Study for portrait of A.S.

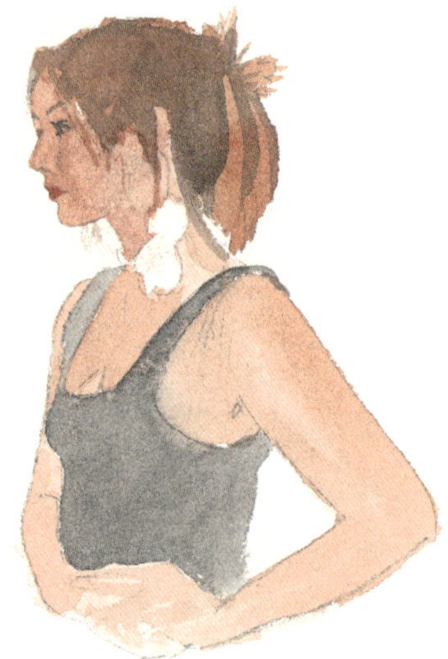

5.08 ——

Study for portrait of F.G.

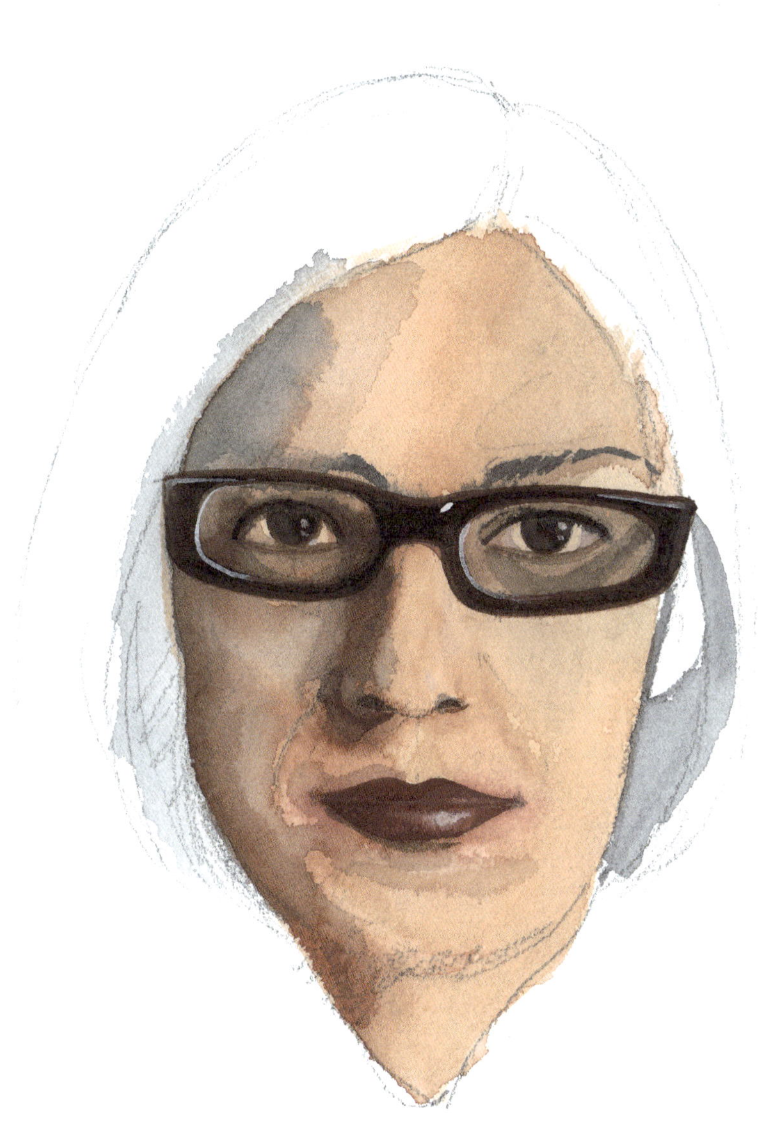

5.09 —

Study for portrait of A.V.

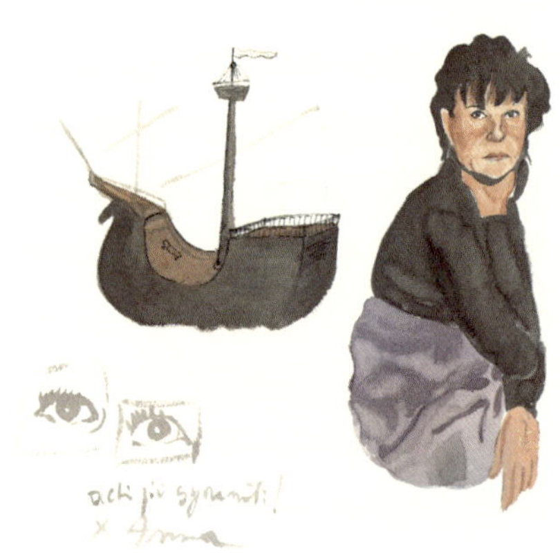

5.10 ——

Study for portrait of A.C.

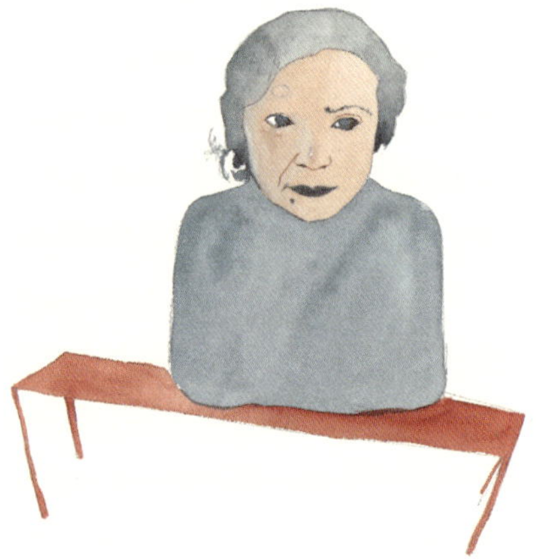

5.11 ——

Study for portrait of M.C.

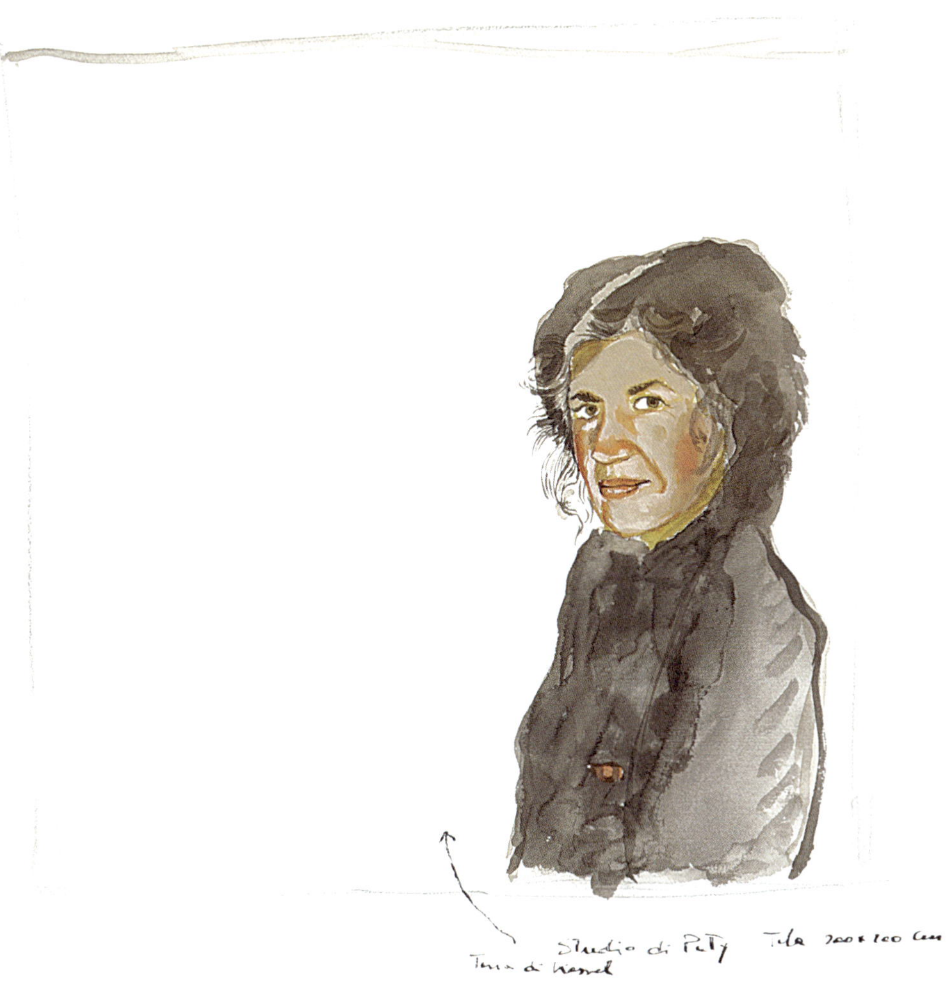

5.12 —
Study for portrait of P.O.

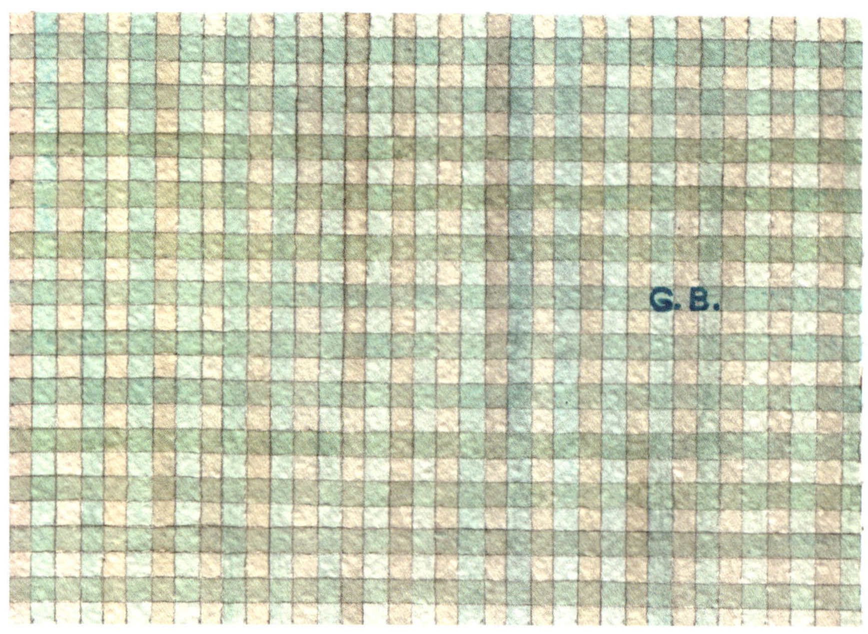

5.13 —
Study for portrait of G.B.

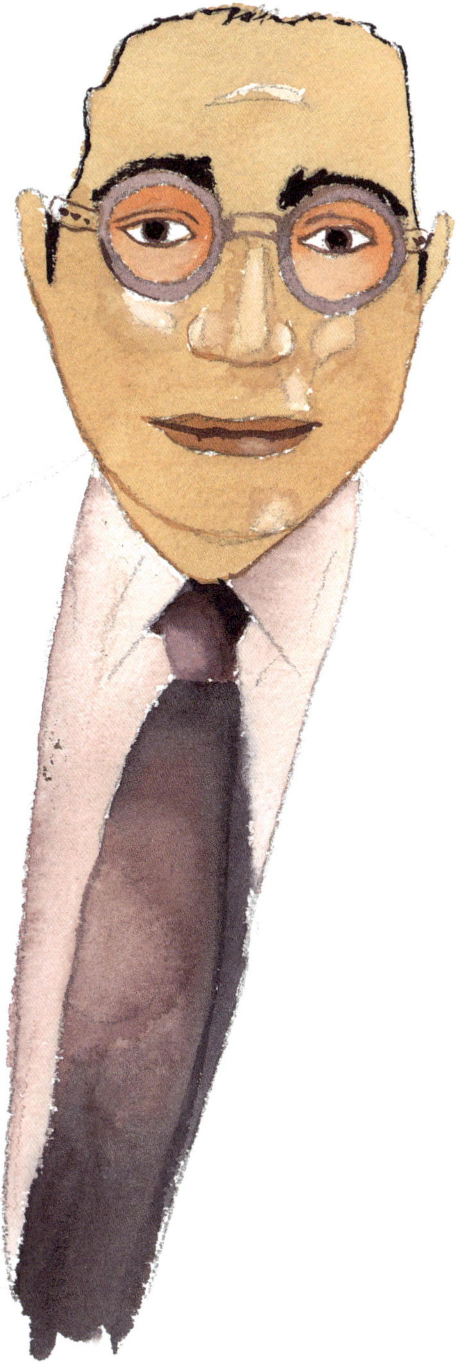

5.14 —
Study for portrait of J.D.

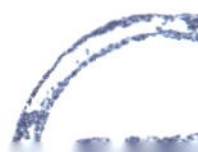

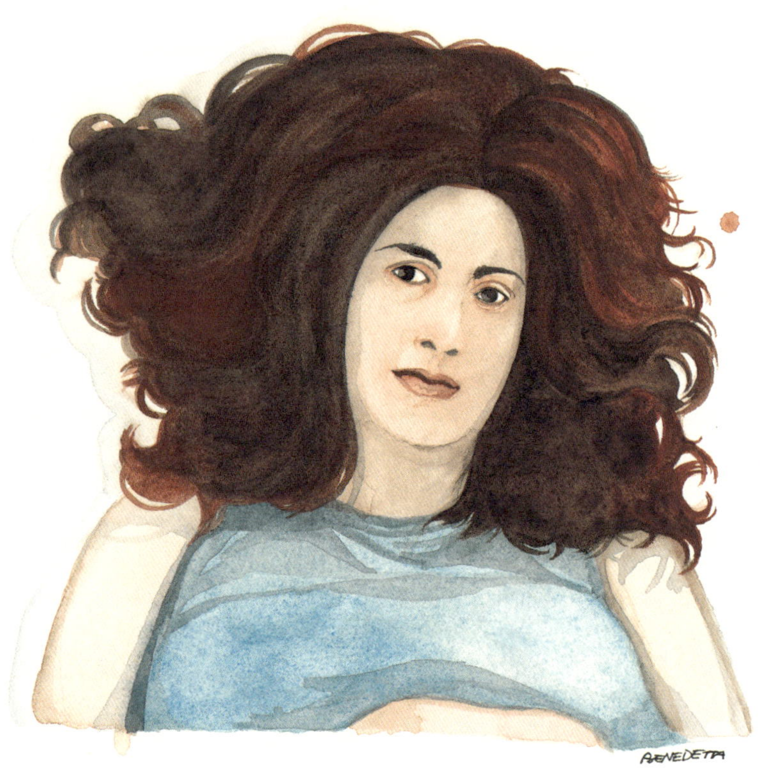

5.15 —
Study for portrait of B.S.

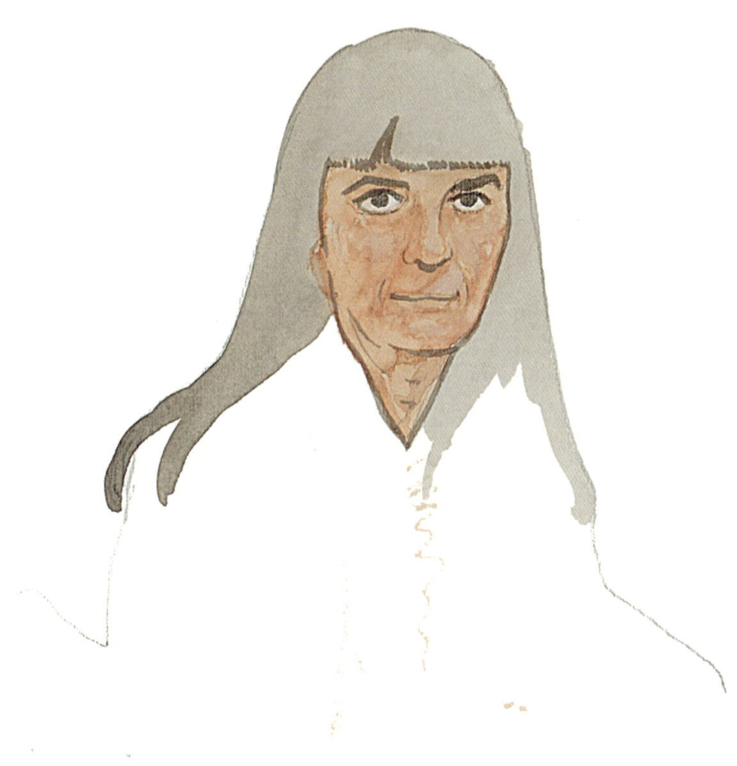

5.16 —

Second study for portrait of A.S.

DEITIES AND CHINESE SHADOWS

5.17 —

Picture of a hand producing Shakespeare's shadow. From a series of pictures inspired by eighteenth century etchings with Chinese shadows, from a 1991 project. The idea was to produce the hands in marble as sculptures whose shadows would be projected onto the wall. The project has not been completed.

5.18 —

Study in coffee for a bronze of Mohammed Ali as Cassius Clay. An unrealised project for a sculpture of present day idols.

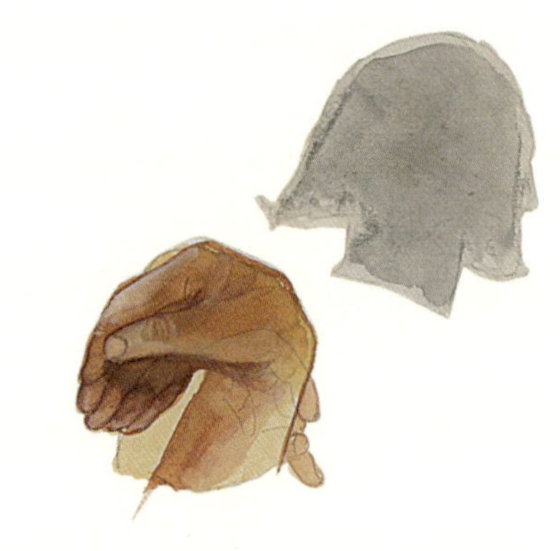

5.17 —

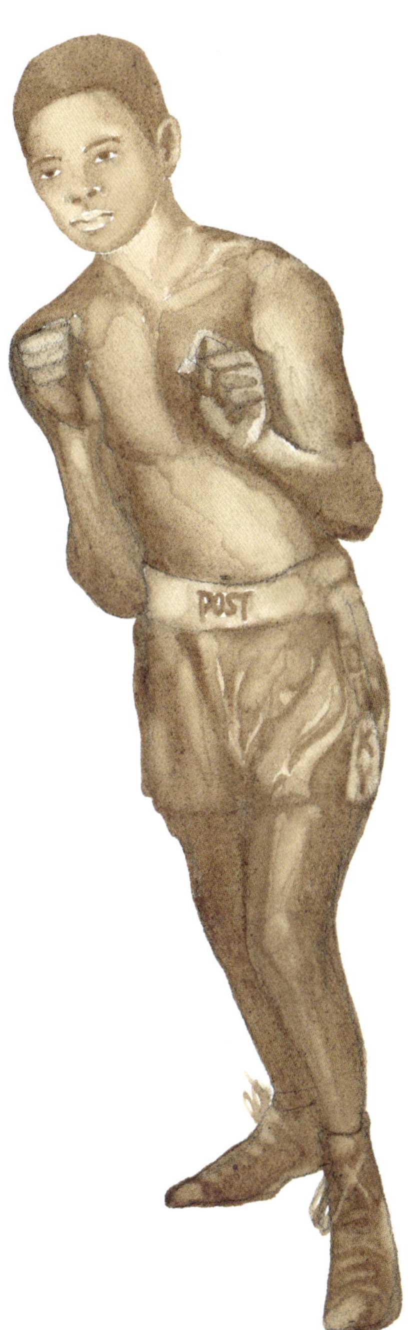

5.18 ——

5.19 ——

Detail of a study for *The Last Supper*. Jesus dresses
Helmut Lang.

5.20 ——

Study for *The Last Supper*.

5.21 ——

Study for *Jesus Christ as a Bearskin Rug* (1999).
The project was conceived for the city of Turin, to
be produced in latex, but was not realised.

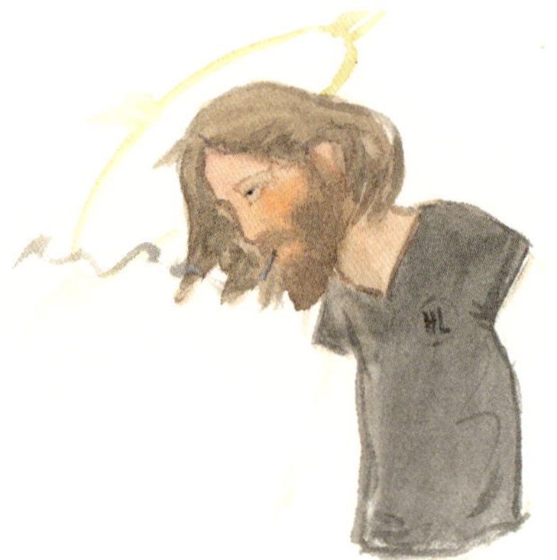

5.19 ——

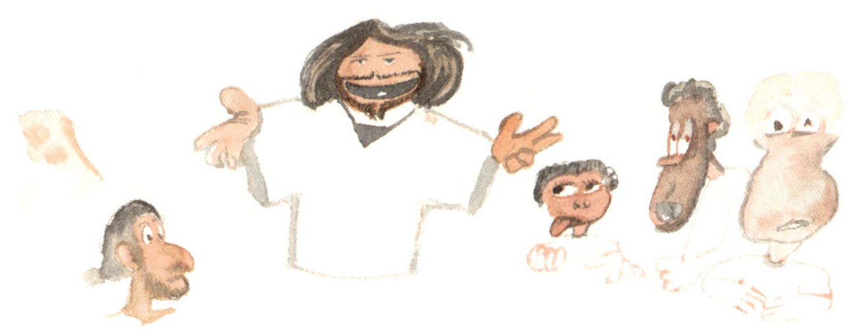

5.20 ——

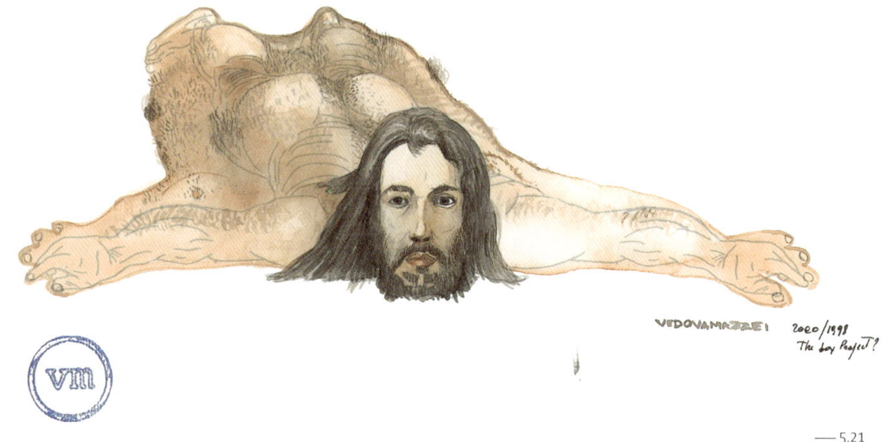

VI

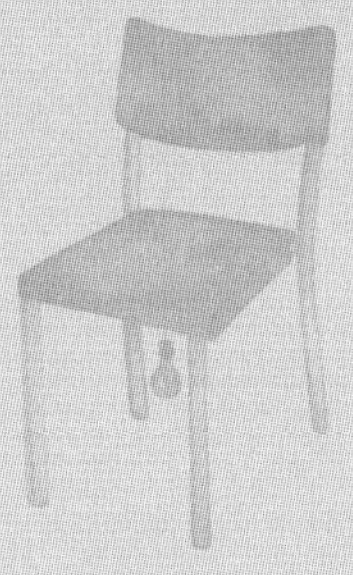

A System of Light, Shaking Projects and Related Installations

vedovamazzei also demonstrate a sense of childish astonishment at science, the real religion of our century. They adopt a contemplative stance, without any filtering, as the condition required for the artist as well as the scientist to make any discoveries. In this chapter, vedovamazzei's mind is filled with the development of ideas gleaned from a child's imagination. It contains studies and variations for illuminated spaces, tables, chairs and steps. The idea for Louis Ferdinand Céline's house in Normandy, later produced in *Novel*, also comes from a re-elaboration of a childhood, 'illuminated' idea. In the *After Love* installation (2003), the initial idea for the reconstruction of Buster Keaton's house is produced in neon light instead, as an architect's drawing board. The bent for parody and the love for the cinema are found again in the images conjured up from our childhood memory in flashes of light, as in *Neon Cloud*.

STUDIES FOR ILLUMINATED CHAIRS, STEPS AND TABLES

6.01 ——

Child's drawing of *Novel*. vedovamazzei recall a child's drawing where the sun on the horizon turned into a lightbulb. They wanted to create a space with a series of illuminated objects in which the light passes through the objects. In *Novel*, in L.F. Céline's house, just one illuminated element was created.

6.02 ——

Drawing for *Novel*. L.F. Céline kept a photograph of the house where he was born in Normandy on the bookshelves in his house of exile in Denmark. This kind of *mise en abyme* is visualised literally in the work. vedovamazzei's pencil notes also describe the work as a child's landscape at sunset. 'Children's lack of functionality is completely in favour of their egoism and extreme naughtiness. Their vision of life is equivalent to the absence of gravity. Does the absence of gravity makes things flat?'

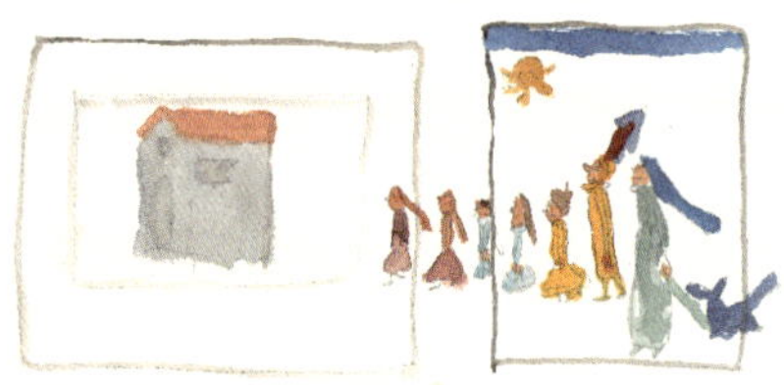

6.01 ——

CASETTA IN TUFO

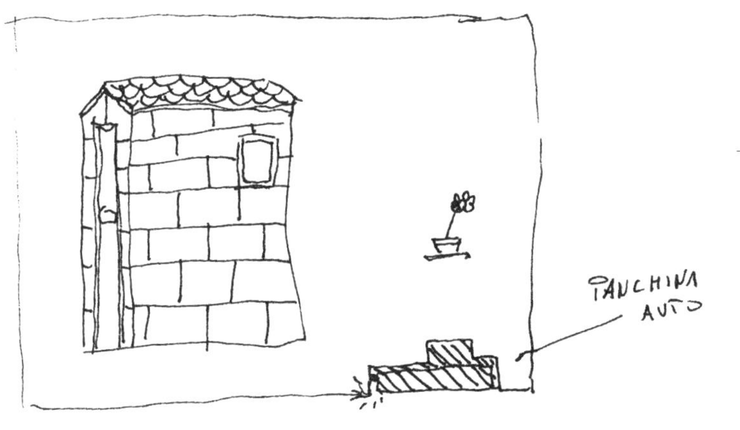

—6.02

DEFINITIVO AL MAGAZZINO

DI ROMA.

CASETTA DI BIMBO E LA MACCHININA
TIPO

LA MANCANZA DI FUNZIONALITÀ NEI BAMBINI
È TUTTO A FAVORE DEL PROPRIO EGOISMO E
PROFONDA CATTIVERIA — LA LORO VISIONE DELLA
VITA È L'EQUIVALENTE DELLA ASSENZA DI
GRAVITÀ — L'ASSENZA DI GRAVITÀ RENDE LE
COSE PIATTE?

PAESAGGIO DI BAMBINO AL TRAMONTO.

6.03 —

Study of the first idea for *Novel* and illuminated table.

6.04 —

Study of the first idea for *Novel* and illuminated chair.

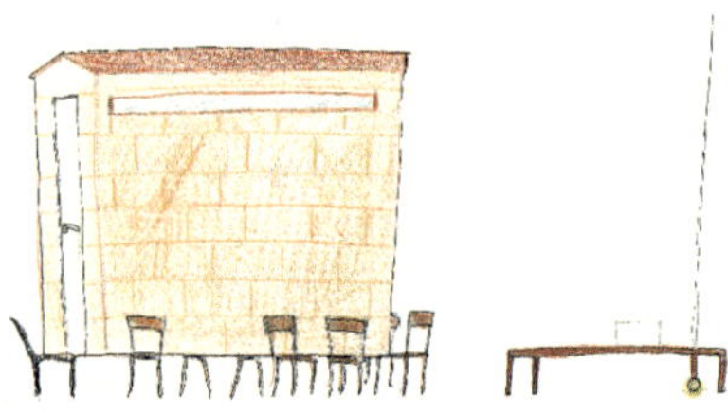

6.03 —

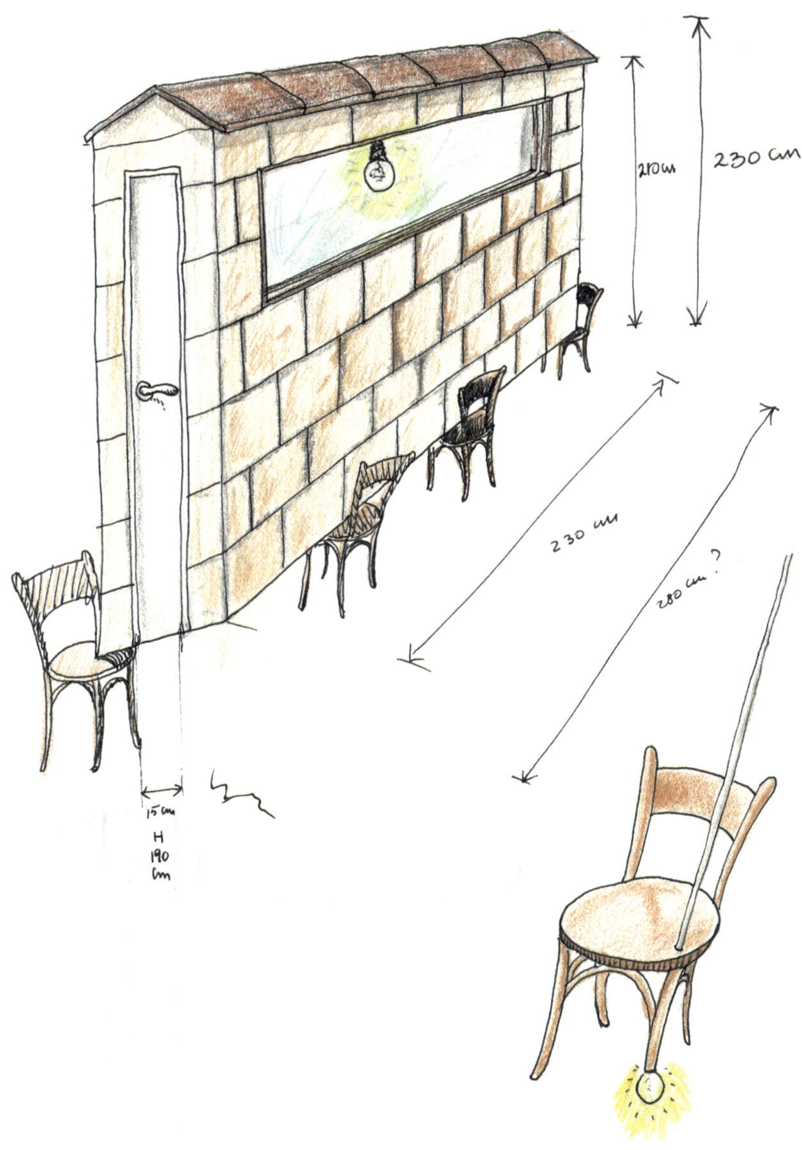

6.04 —

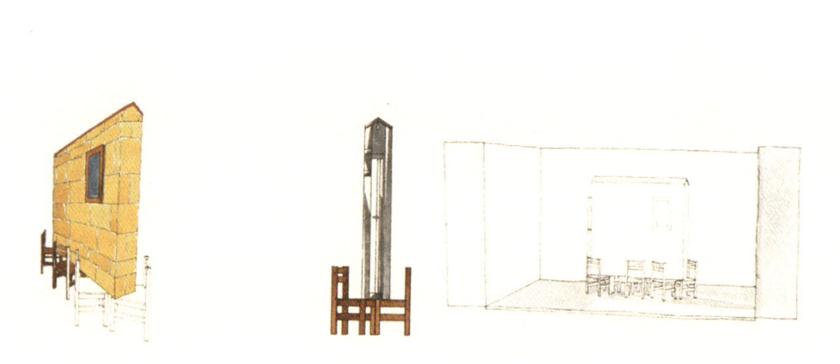

6.05 —
Study with perspective, section and space for the
Novel installation.

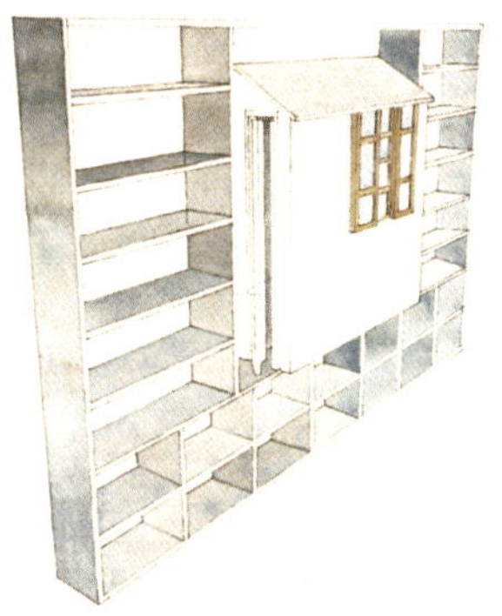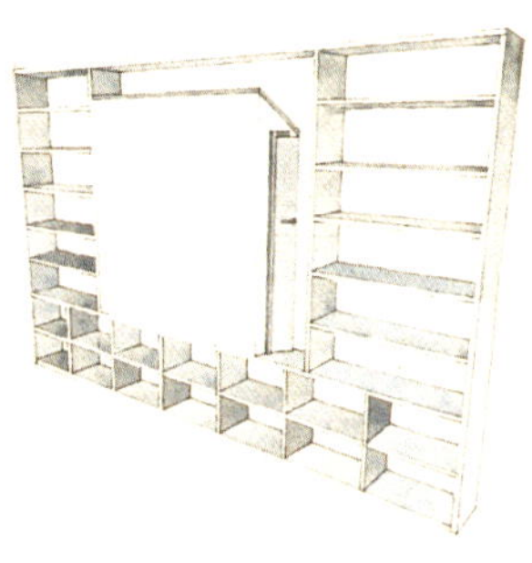

6.06 —

Definitive study for the bookcase in *Novel*. In the definitive version Céline's house no longer rests on the chairs but is set in a bookcase.

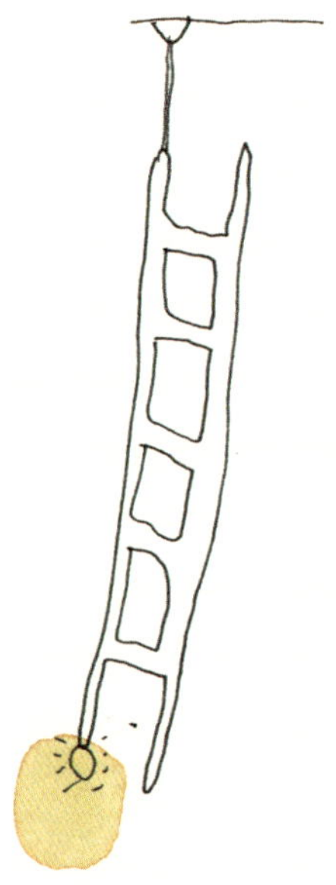

6.07 —

Study of illuminated steps.

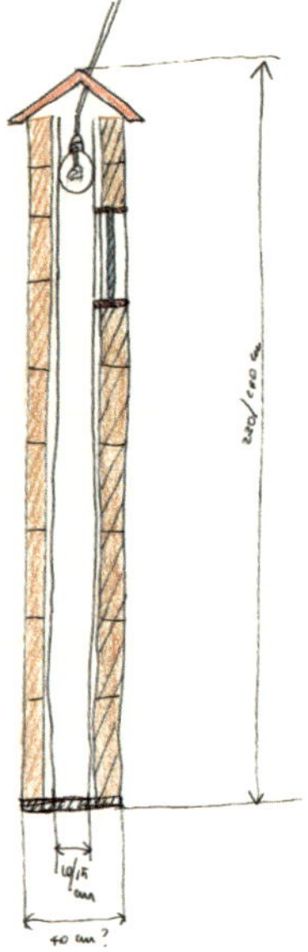

6.08 —

Section of *Novel*.

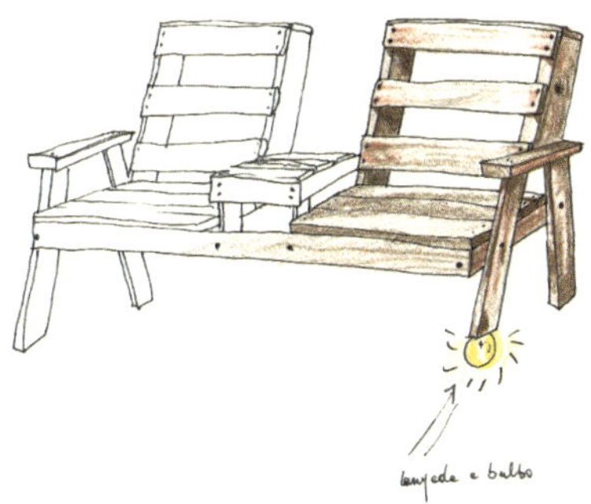

6.09 —

Study of illuminated bench.

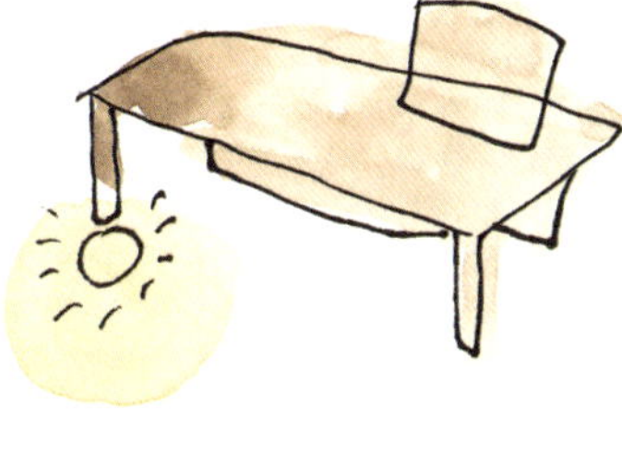

6.10 —

Study of illuminated desk.

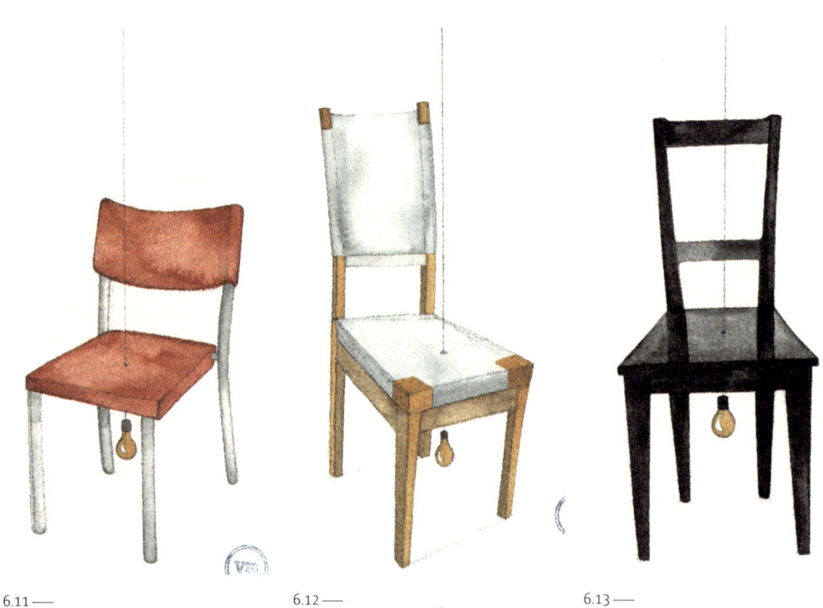

6.11 ——

6.12 ——

6.13 ——

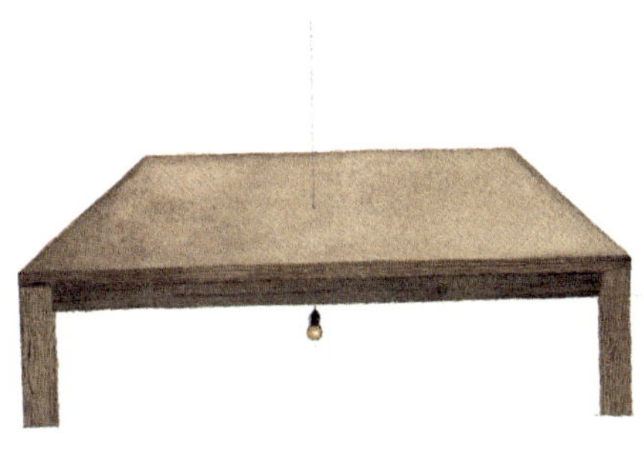

6.14 —

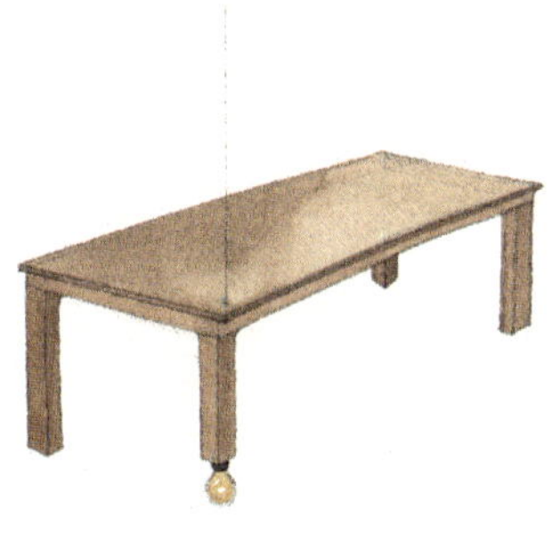

6.15 —

6.11 —
Study of illuminated red chair.

6.12 —
Study of illuminated wooden and fabric chair.

6.13 —
Study of illuminated black chair.

6.14 & 6.15 —
Study of illuminated table.

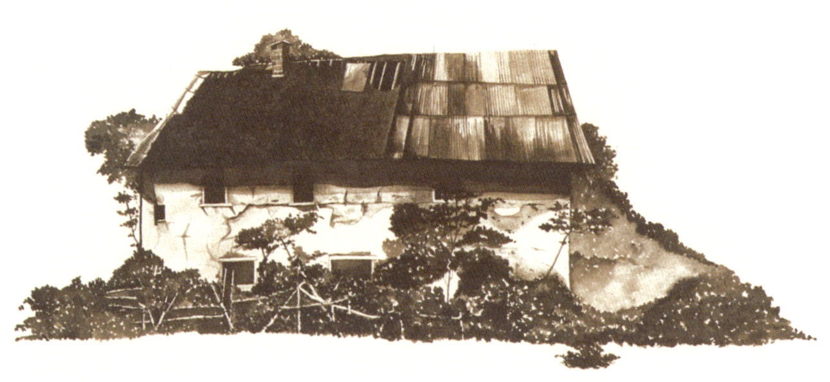

6.16 —

Study of the house in Normandy where L.F. Céline was
born, taken from a photograph the writer kept on his
bookshelves in Denmark.

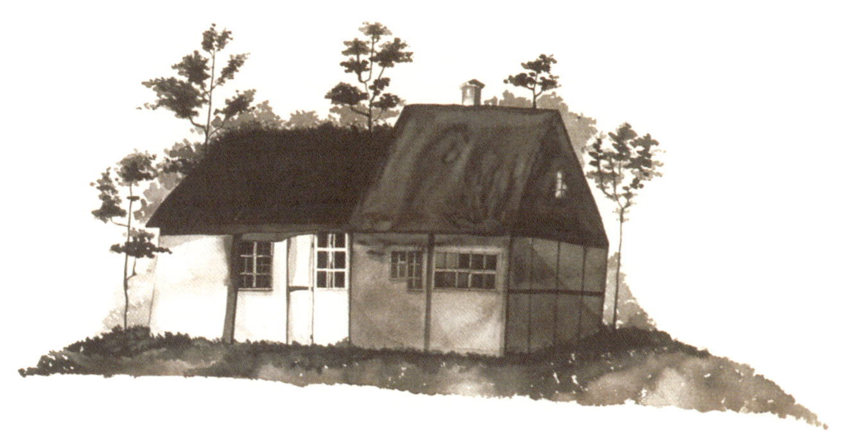

6.17 —
Study of L.F. Céline's house of exile in Denmark.

BUSTER KEATON'S HOUSE

6.18 —

Study for the *After Love* installation (2003), produced in Caraglio, with Buster Keaton's house, taken from the film *One Week* (1926). This short is a spoof on American building conventions. Out of spite, one of Buster Keaton's neighbours changes the instructions for putting up his prefab house. vedovamazzei initially produced a double, neon outline of it as an architect's drawing board.

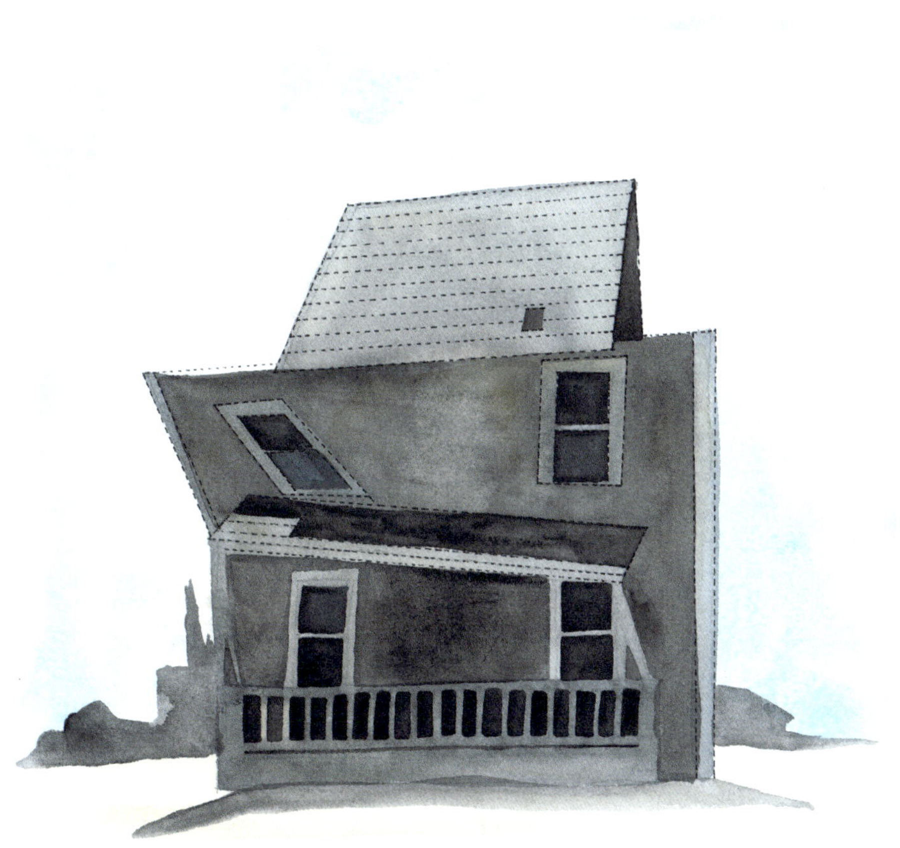

THE CLOUD ON THE HOTEL

6.19 —
Study for *Neon Cloud* (2000). The installation on the roof of a hotel in Peccioli, Tuscany, is a neon light, fixed in the form of a permanent cloud, which changes colour according to the weather.

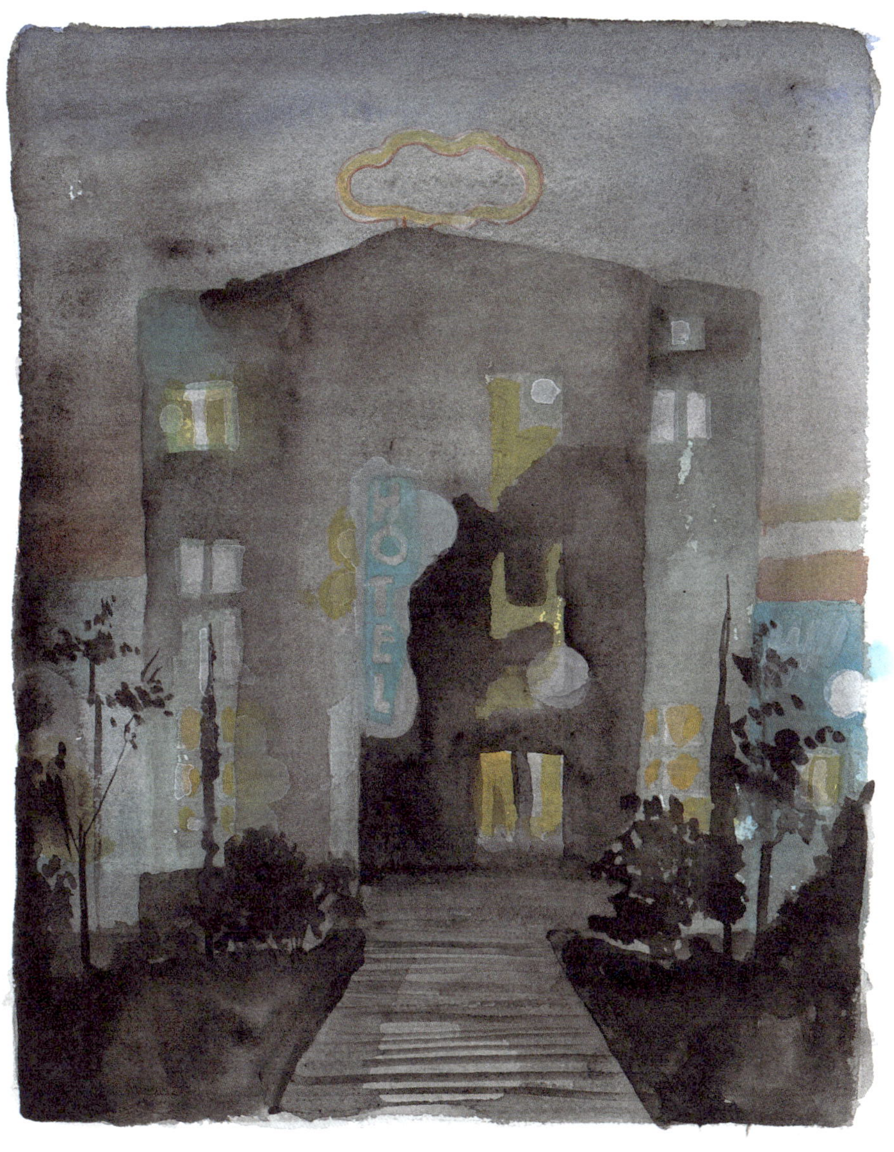
HOTEL

THE MYOPIC MIRROR

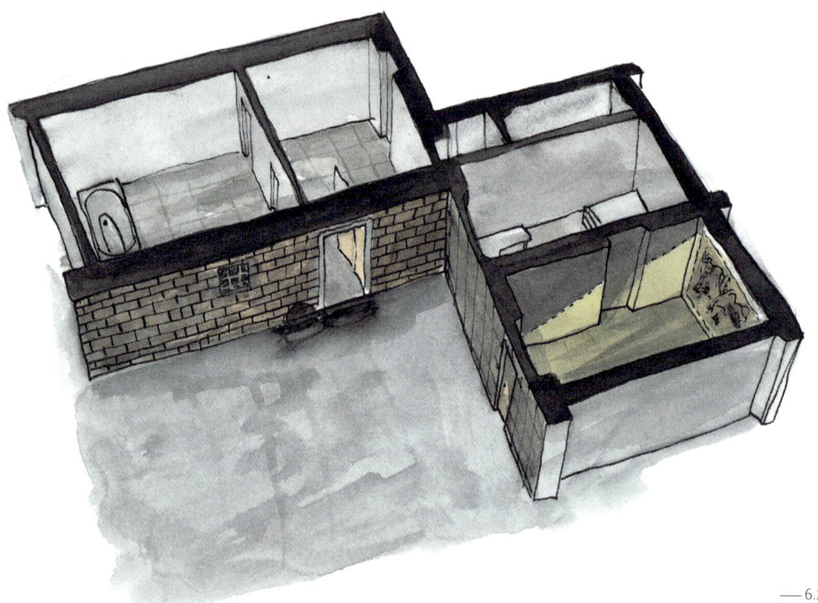

—6.20

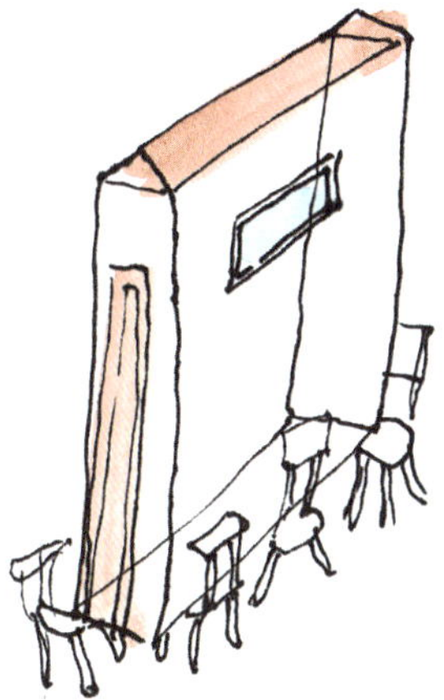

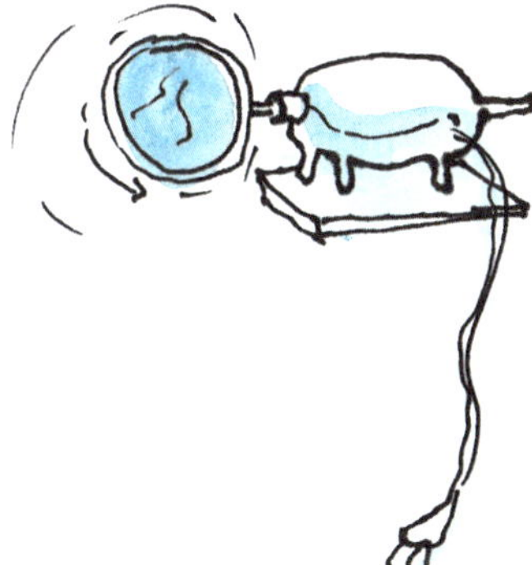

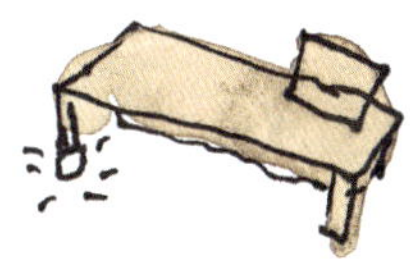

6.20 —

Study of Rome's Magazzino d'Arte Moderna gallery, seen by a seagull (2002). This is a model of the gallery containing the *Bathtub with The Ganges Traced in the Dirty Trickle* where *Novel* was later created instead. vedovamazzei design the space from the plan. They develop a series of hypotheses, with sketches and drawings, before obtaining the definitive space.

6.21 —

Picture of the *Myopic Mirror, Novel* and an illuminated desk, as a list of works to present in Rome's Magazzino d'Arte Moderna gallery (2002). The desk was not produced.

6.22 —

Technical drawing of the *Myopic Mirror* (2002) for the installation. The mirror, which is mounted on the wall like a normal bathroom mirror, vibrates imperceptibly, making the reflected image myopic.

6.23 —

The *Myopic Mirror* depicted on the workshop table where its mechanism was built.

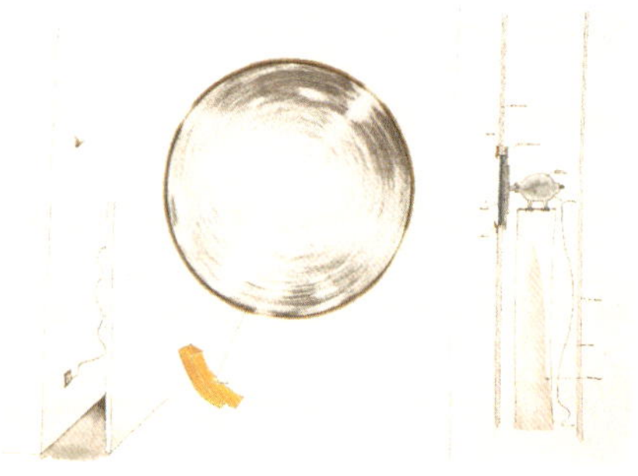

6.22 —

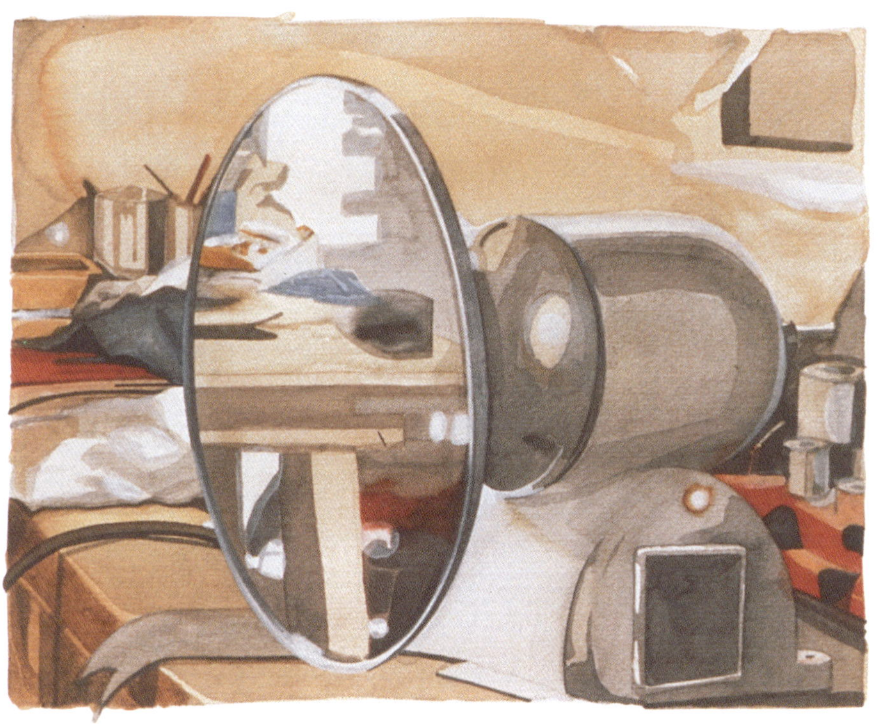

6.23 —

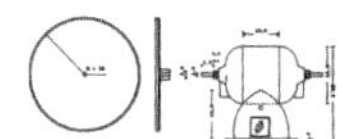

VII

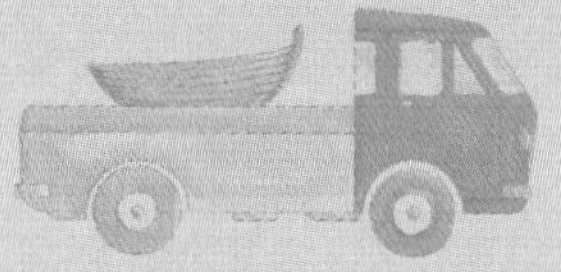

Processing of a System of Ideas in vedovamazzei's Mind

In the four following examples, we can see and compare how projects of a certain complexity are processed in vedovamazzei's mind by following them through the various stages of the relevant pieces' production. These projects differ from each other in both inspiration and outcome. The common factor in each of the four projects' development is the inspiration for them, which originates in a precise scientific fact. The elaboration of the different ideas leads to the unforeseen result of producing the final iconography in an image.

The city of Hann Münden, surrounded by three rivers, is subject to frequent flooding. In 1400 the flood reached a level of four metres, which corresponds to the height of the lorry in *Go Wherever You Want, Bring Me Whatever You Wish* (2000). This installation recreates an idealistic landscape from the past and the conditions for contemplating it. At the same time it presents two different, yet inter-related, temporal perspectives, namely the view from the past and that of the present, which change according to which space we are in. If we are in the little boat on top of the lorry, which are both visible from the bottom up of the present, we ourselves become part of a landscape of the past from which we can admire the view as it was six centuries ago. With the Leonardo-style mechanism created here, vedovamazzei declare themselves part of the fantastic and visionary tradition of Italian art, which is also evident both in *Marvellous Harmony* and in *Monte Marcello.*

HANN MÜNDEN

GO WHEREVER YOU WANT, BRING ME WHATEVER YOU WISH

Studies for the *Go Wherever You Want, Bring Me Whatever You Wish* installation in Hann Münden (2000). In the lorry, filled with 28 tonnes of water, a part of the nearby river has been created in its natural environment, with a little boat and its jetty. The lorry was parked in a field next to the river, for a collective exhibition of open-air installations.

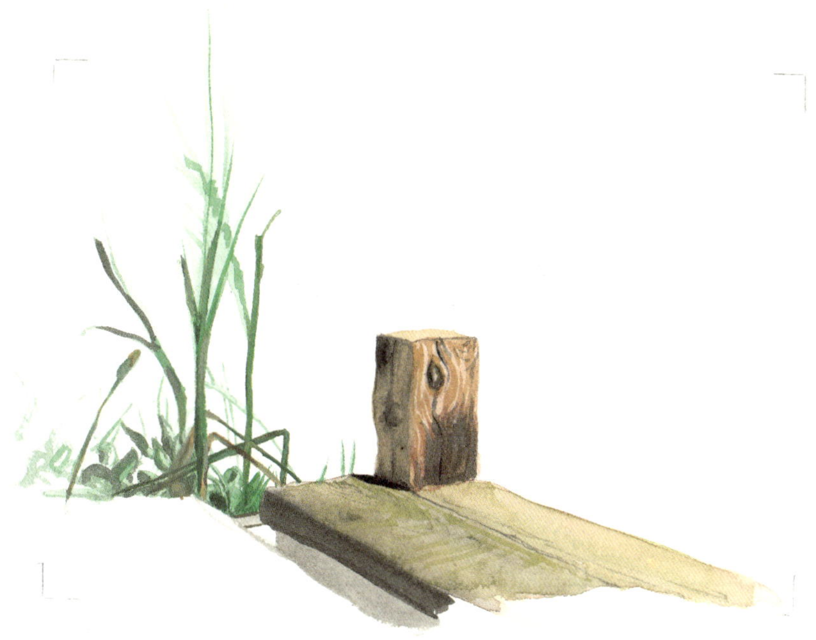

7.01 —
Detail of the wooden jetty inside the lorry in *Go Wherever You Want, Bring Me Whatever You Wish*.

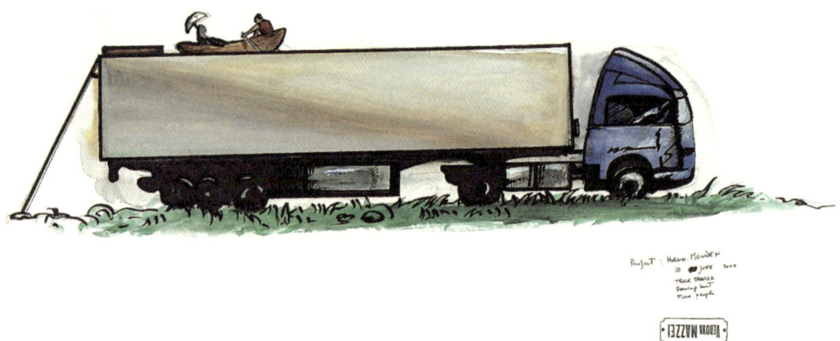

7.02 —

Study of the whole *Go Wherever You Want, Bring Me Whatever You Wish* installation in Hann Münden. The lorry is parked in the field.

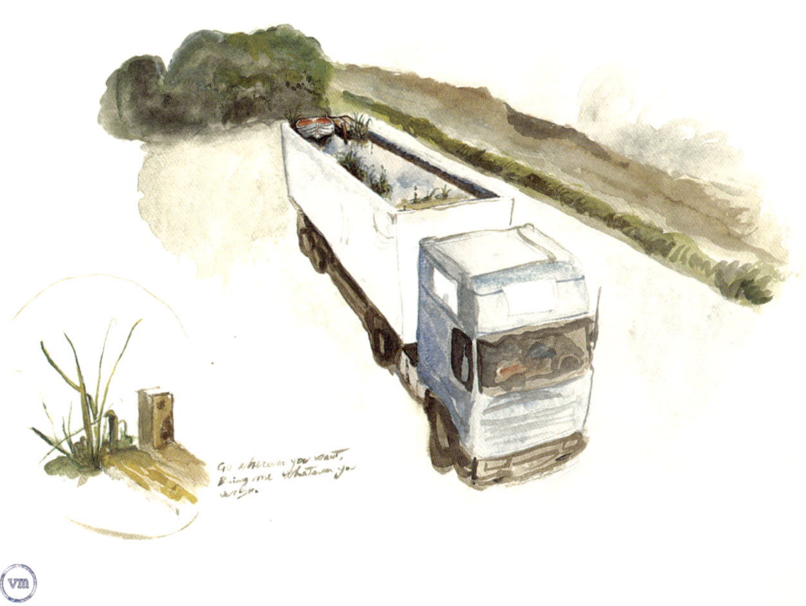

7.03 —

Study of the definitive *Go Wherever You Want, Bring Me Whatever You Wish* installation in Hann Münden. View from above of the installation in its setting.

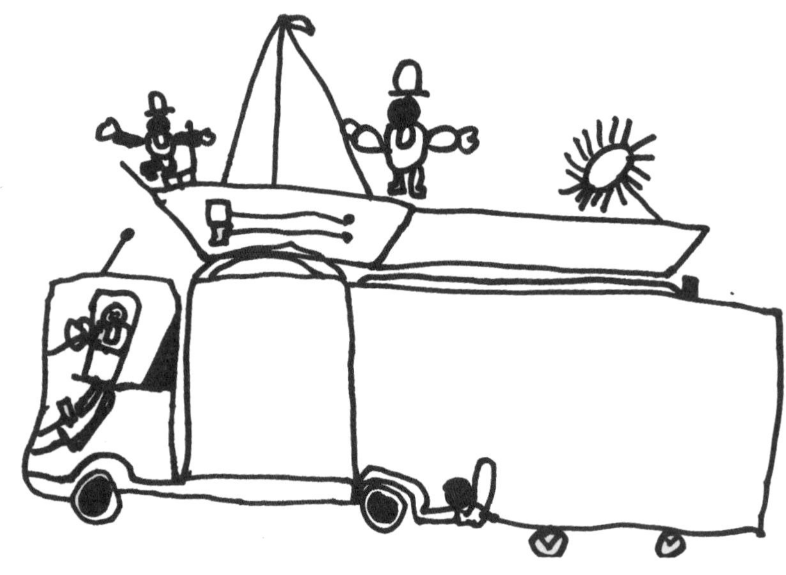

7.04 —

One example from a set of drawings of the lorry in
Go Wherever You Want, Bring Me Whatever You Wish
by children from Hann Münden.

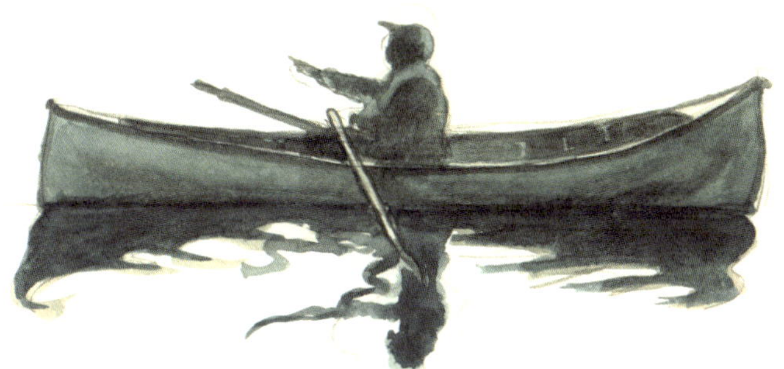

7.05 —

Study of a different type of boat for the installation
Go Wherever You Want, Bring Me Whatever You Wish
in Hann Münden.

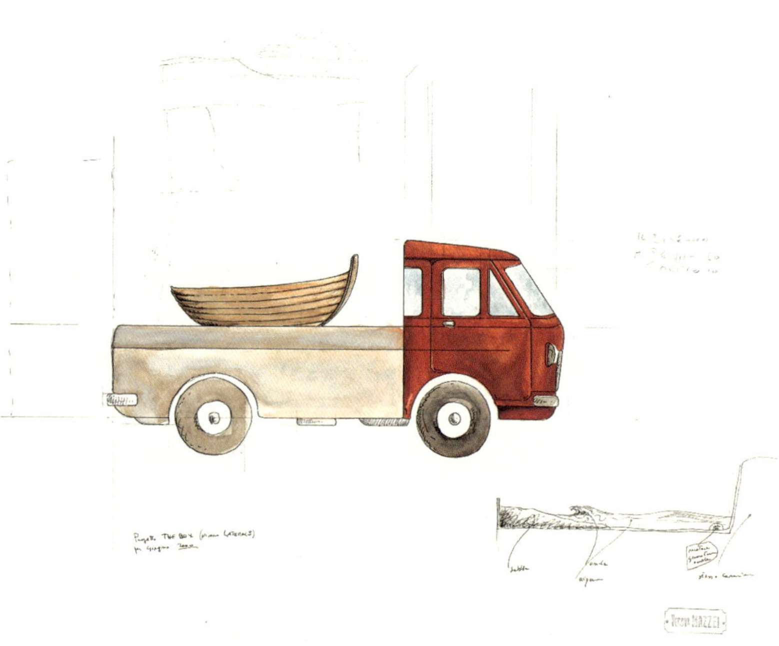

TURIN

7.06 —

Study of *Go Wherever You Want, Bring Me Whatever You Wish* (2000) for the installation of the lorry in Turin's The Box Gallery. The proportions have been inverted compared to Hann Münden to produce a small lorry and a big boat.

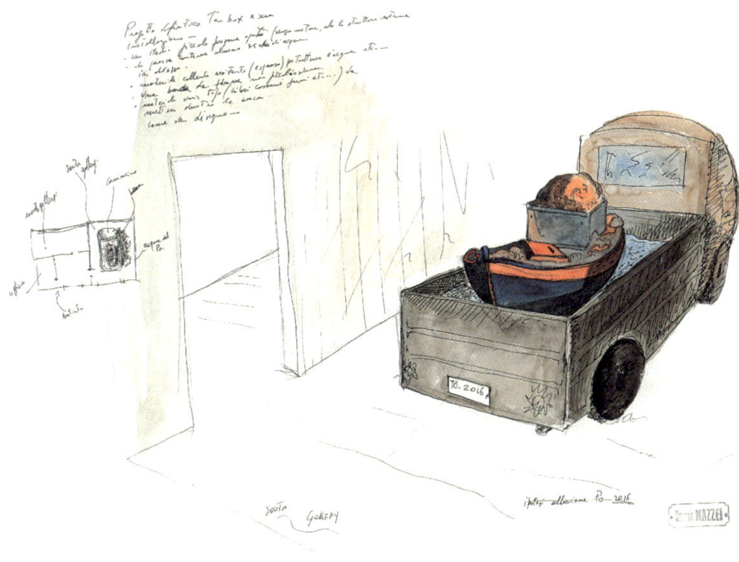

7.07 —

Study of the side of the lorry and a detail with the
variation of a wave instead of a boat in the lorry.

STRATEGY FOR AN ATTACK ON GENOA

Genoa as the scene of an imaginary naval battle with downpour and air raid. For a project in Genoa, vedovamazzei wanted to simulate a game of battleships between each other with drawings produced by each of them to compare together afterwards. Each had to choose their battle colours. The project was not completed.

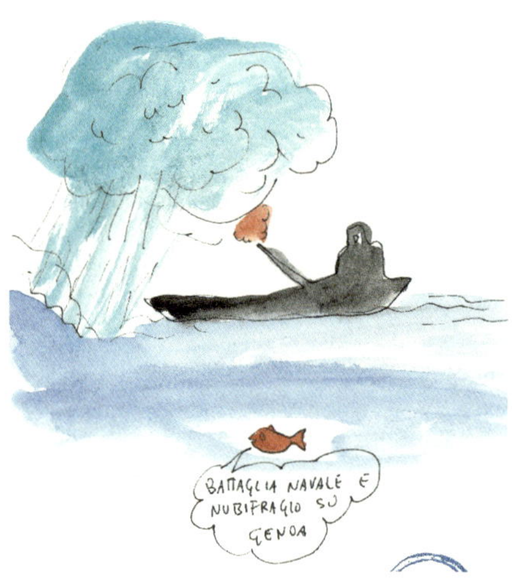

7.08 ——

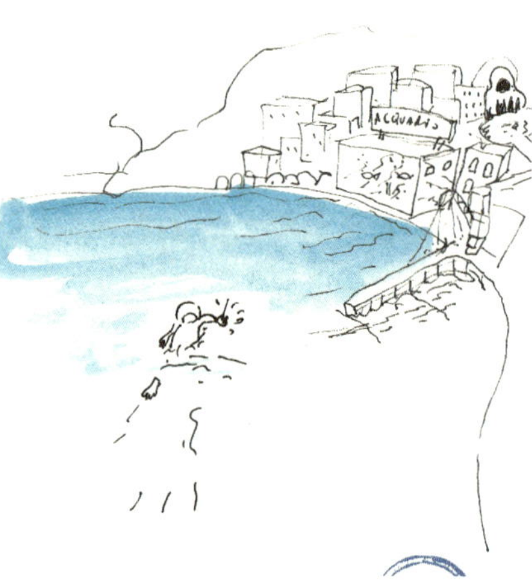

7.09 ——

NAVAL BATTLE
7.08 & 7.09 ——
Genoa as the scene of an imaginary naval battle between vedovamazzei in pictures. Attack near the port with view of aquarium.

AERIAL ATTACK
7.10 ——
Air raid on the Co-op in Genoa.

7.10 —

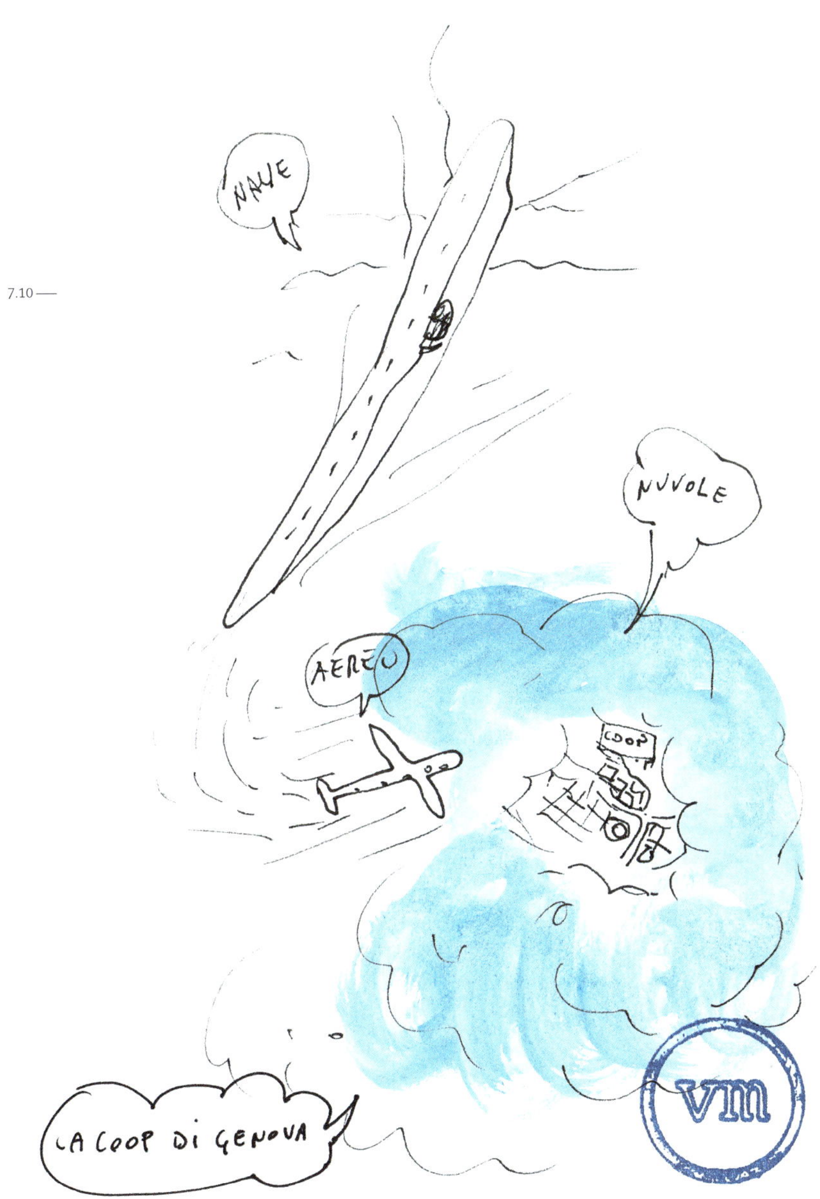

MARVELLOUS HARMONY

The idea for the *Marvellous Harmony* oil on canvas (1999) and installation (2000) comes from the Italian title of a book by biologist Robert O. Wilson on the ecosystem. For Wilson, nature is not ethical. What is marvellous is nature's independence and this is where its harmony lies. vedovamazzei recreate a real micro-climate as a microcosm in a puddle in which two genetically-modified lilies float. A detail of a Pollock painting is reproduced on the petal of one of the lilies.

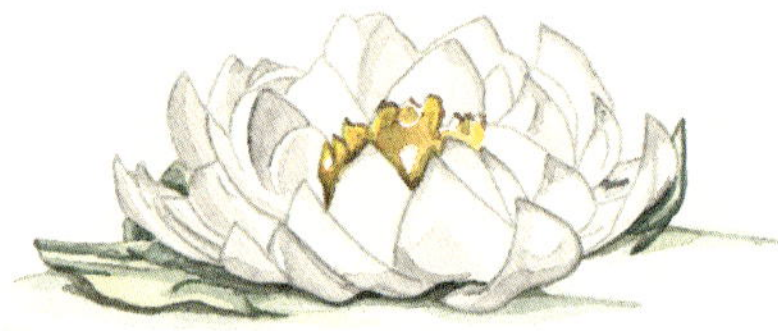

7.11 ——

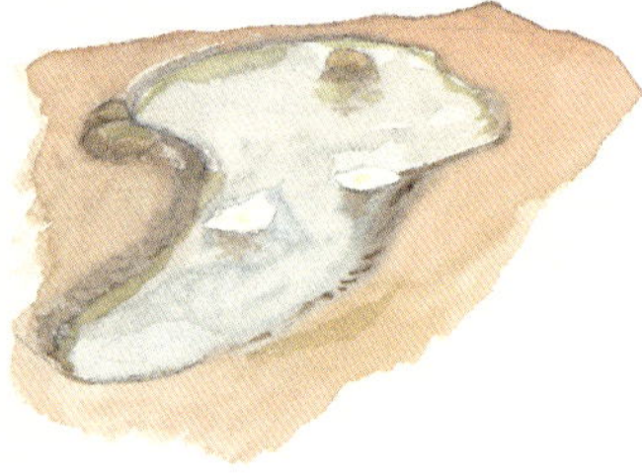

7.12 ——

7.11 ——
Study for the *Marvellous Harmony* installation (2000). Detail of the water lily.

7.12 ——
Study for the *Marvellous Harmony* installation. Detail of the puddle.

7.13 ——
Study for the *Marvellous Harmony* installation in Rome's Magazzino d'Arte Moderna gallery. The puddle in its natural habitat with water lilies, in the illuminated dark space.

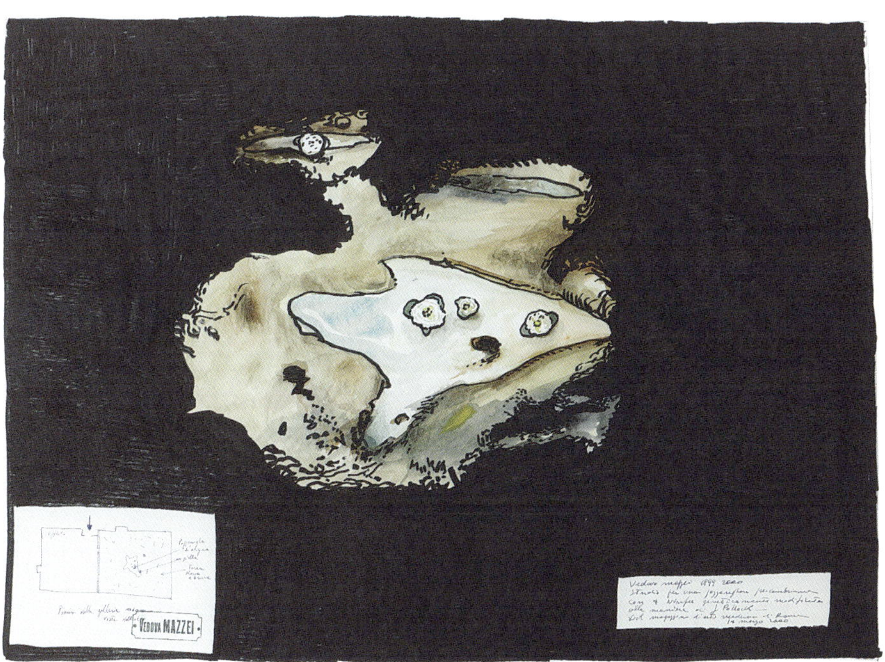

7.13—

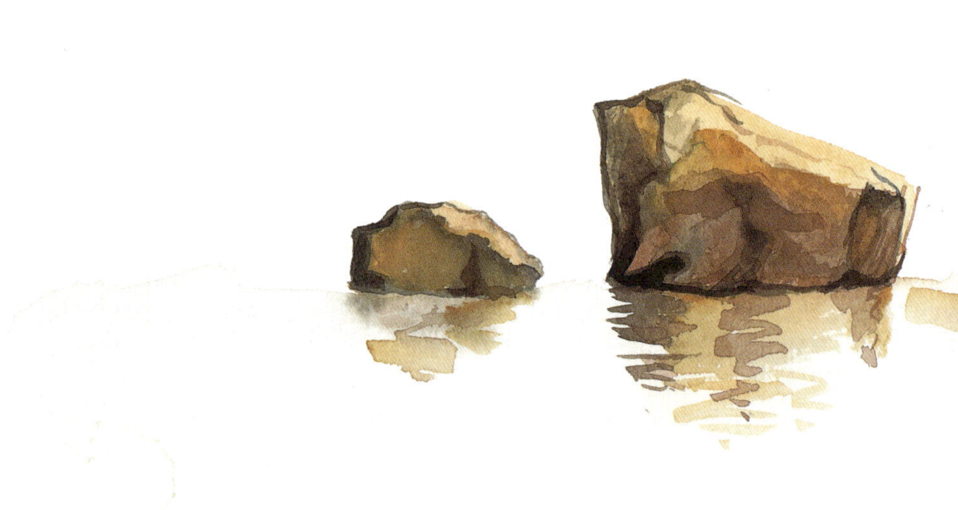

7.14 —

Study for the *Marvellous Harmony* installation. Detail
of the rocks.

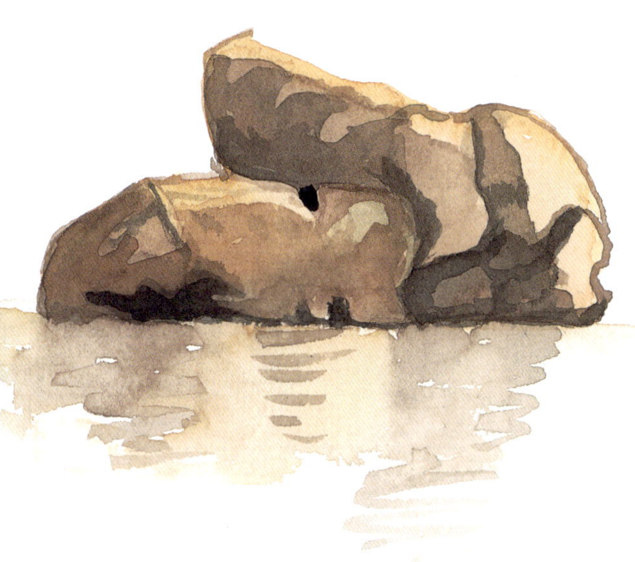

LE CAIRN

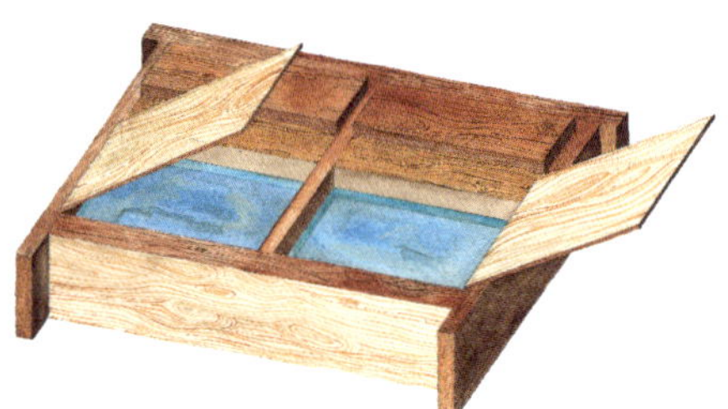

SYLVIE'S WARDROBE

7.15 & 7.16 —

Study for the *Sylvie's Wardrobe* installation, produced
in Le Cairn (2003). Variations of the open wardrobe
full of water in which a strawberry patch floats.

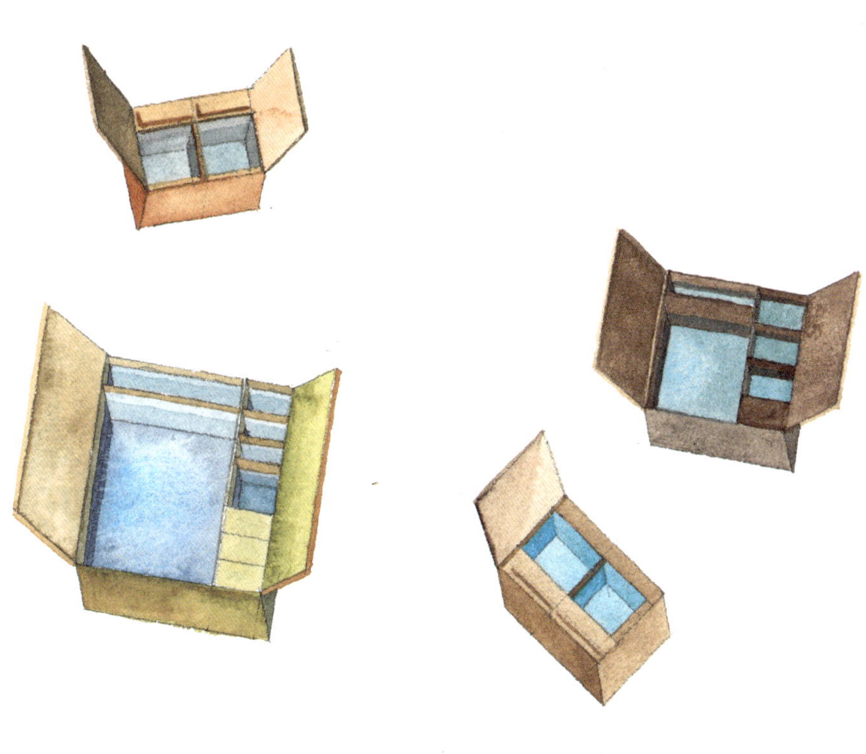

MONTE MARCELLO

STELLA MARIS G.M.O.

7.17 & 7.18 —

Section study of the hill for *Stella Maris G.M.O.* (2001).
A cubic metre of the Pacific Ocean, which has been
genetically modified, is recreated in an underground
space, dug out of the small hill at Monte Marcello,
Sarzana, La Spezia. This place corresponds to the
antipodes of the Chatham Islands (New Zealand) in
the Pacific Ocean.

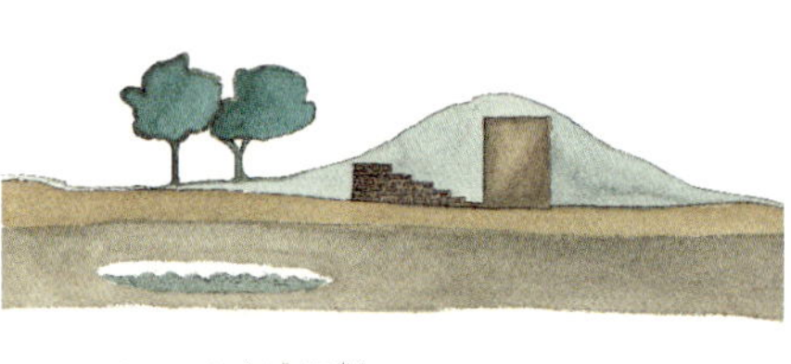

7.17 —

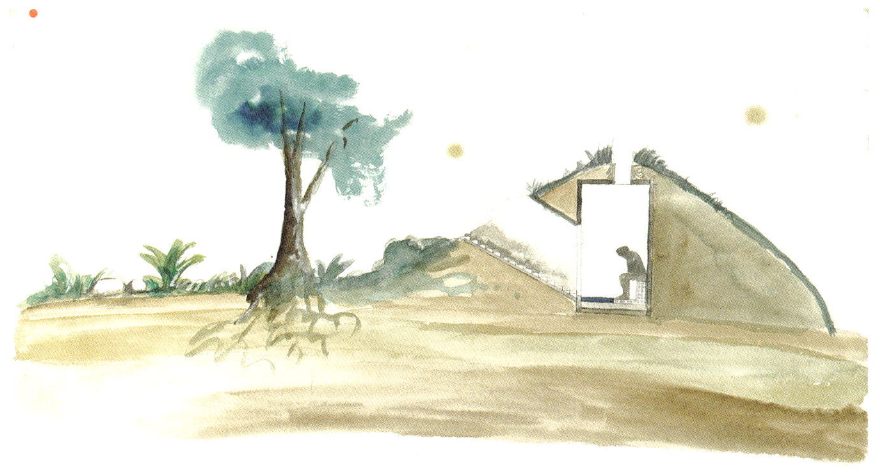

7.18 ——

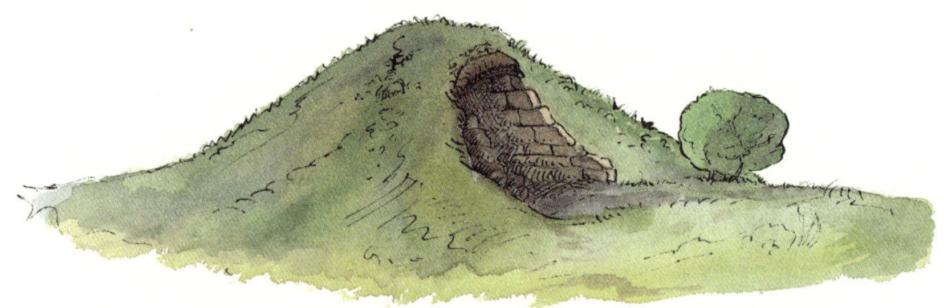

7.19 —

7.19 —

Detail of the hill in Monte Marcello, seen from the outside.

7.20 —

Watercolour study of *Stella Maris G.M.O.* Detail of the tank with motor always running which recreates the micro-climate with the biochemical composition of the ocean. Some prawns were born inside the tank. Descending into the hill, a photocell lights up the otherwise dark space.

— 7.20

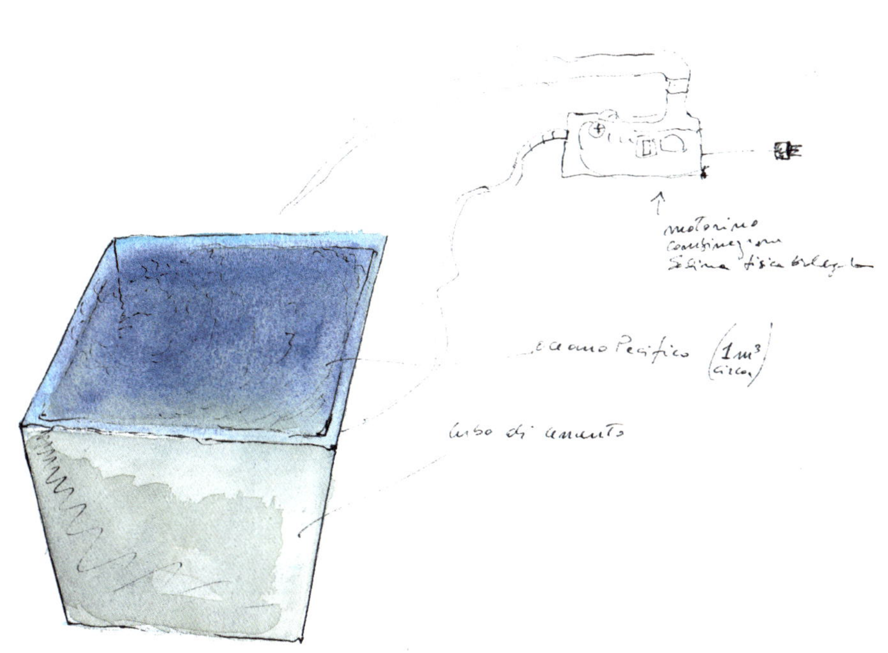

155 BC

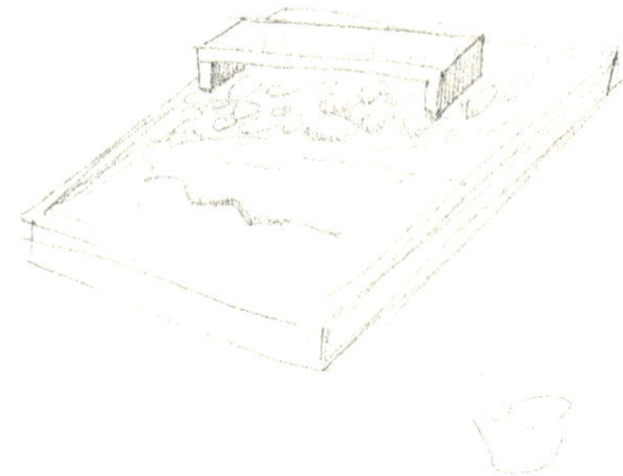

7.21 —

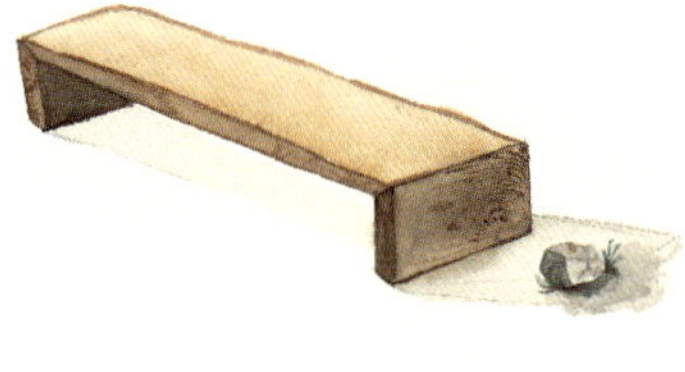

7.22 —

7.21 —
Study in pencil for *155 BC* (2001). Detail of the turf to put the speakers in.

7.22 —
Study for *155 BC*. Detail of the bench to place between two trees in a field in the Monte Marcello landscape. The visitor on the bench activates the speakers concealed under the grass and the installation plays the sound of a battle which echoes the battle that Consul Marcellus fought near here in 155 BC.

7.23 —
Study of the landscape in the *155 BC* installation with an early idea for a sound laser placed between two trees.

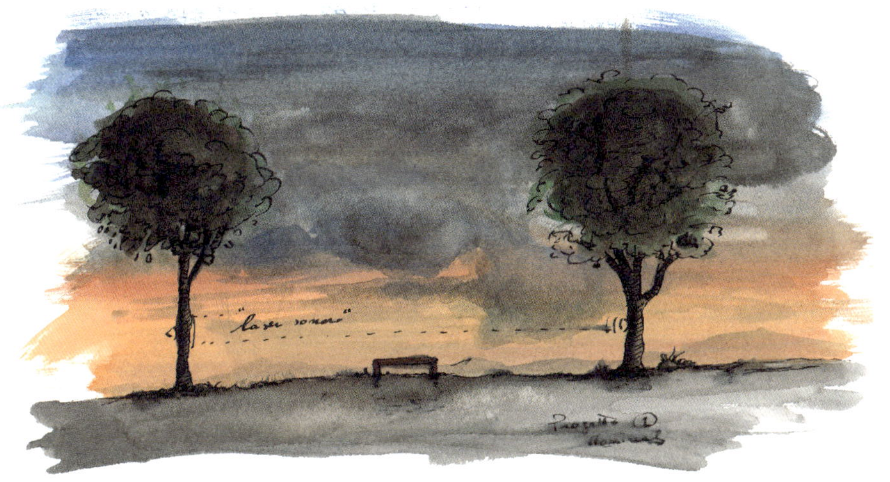

—7.23

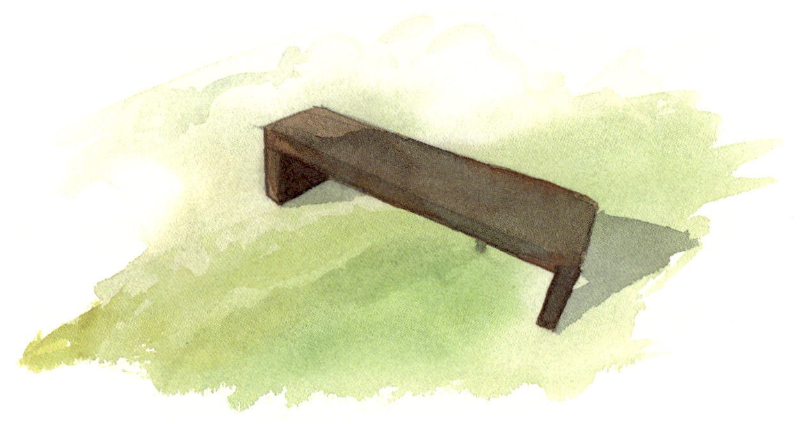

7.24 —
Detail of the bench in the field.

VIII

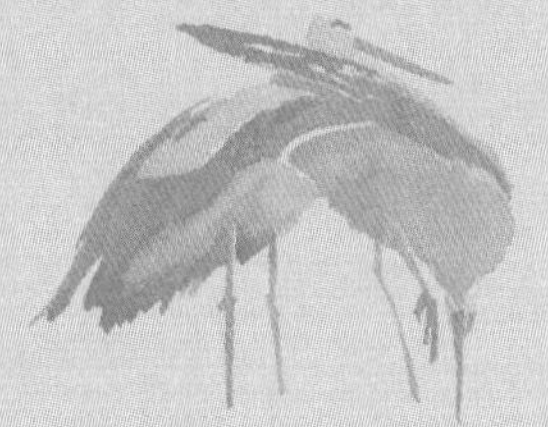

The Bird Class. Exceptional Ornithology

The Natural History of vedovamazzei closes with an entire chapter dedicated to the treatment of *Exceptional Ornithology* which brings together studies for two projects that were not realised. vedovamazzei are particularly interested in birds. The first project is an extraordinary affair inspired by C. Lombroso's treatise in which he recounts a true story witnessed by Vogt of homicidal mania displayed by a female stork that kills her mate to make space for a different male that had been courting her. It is a well-known fact that in the natural world, birds number among the few animals that remain faithful to their chosen mate. The second ornithological project is like a frenzied, dream-like vision drawn from an idea to put a flock of birds in flight into hibernation. This is still at the idea stage due to the considerable technical problems involved in producing it.

CRIME IN THE FEMALE ANIMAL

8.01 — 8.12 —

Storyboard for the video with the remarkable story
of a love triangle and homicidal mania as witnessed
in Bavaria by the ornithologist Karl Vogt, recounted
by Cesare Lombroso. Figure 8.03 contains notes by
vedovamazzei: '(Delinquent Woman) Lombroso…
crime in the female animal. Paragraph 5 / Sexual
Crimes: Vogt gives an account of a couple of storks
nesting near the village of Soletta. He noticed that
when the male was away hunting another, younger
male used to come to court the female. His advances
were at first rebuffed, then permitted, then accepted
and finally the two adulterers flew over the grassland
where the husband was hunting frogs and they pecked
him to death.'

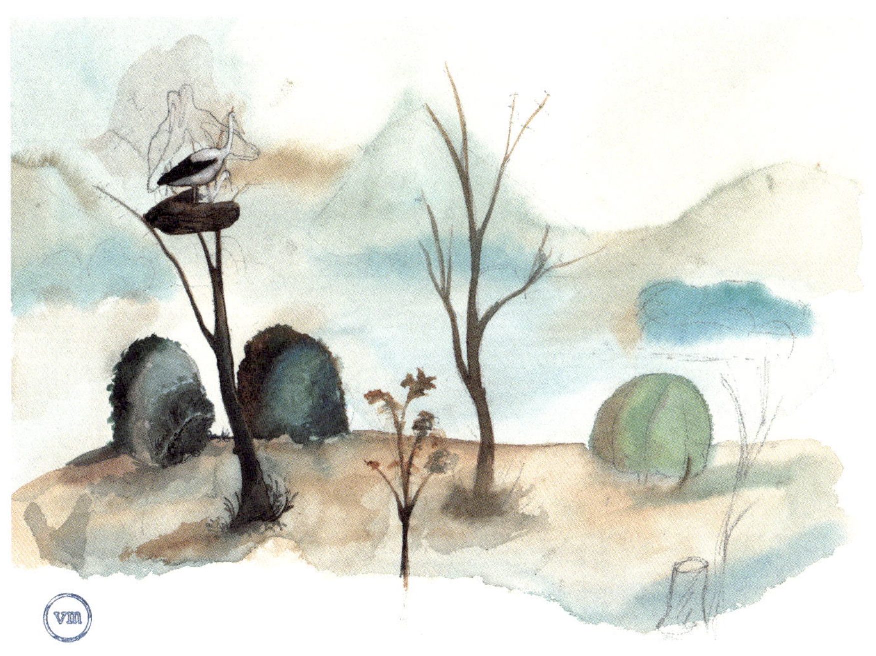

8.01 —

8.02 —

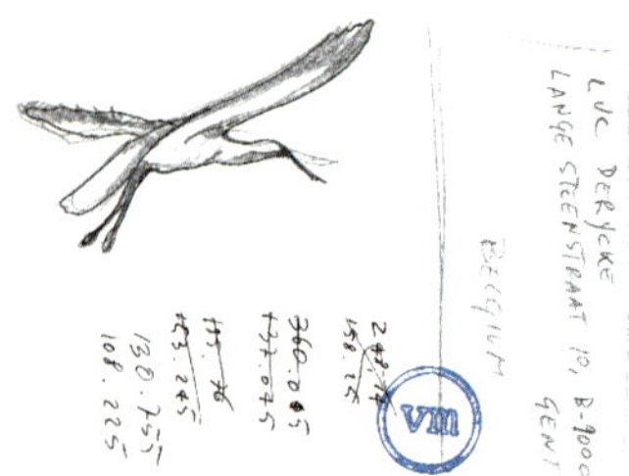

... il delitto nelle femmine animali / (Donna delinquente)
Lombroso

Paragrafo 5 / Delitti sessuali:

Carlo Vogt racconta che in una
coppia di Cicogne nidificanti
presso il villaggio di Solitta, si notò
che quando il maschio ere alla
caccia, un'altra più giovane
veniva a corteggiare la femmina.
In Principio fu respinto, Poi
Tollerato, poi accolto, e alle fine
i due adulteri volarono sulla
pasteria dove il marito cacciava
i ranocchi e lo uccissero a Beccate.

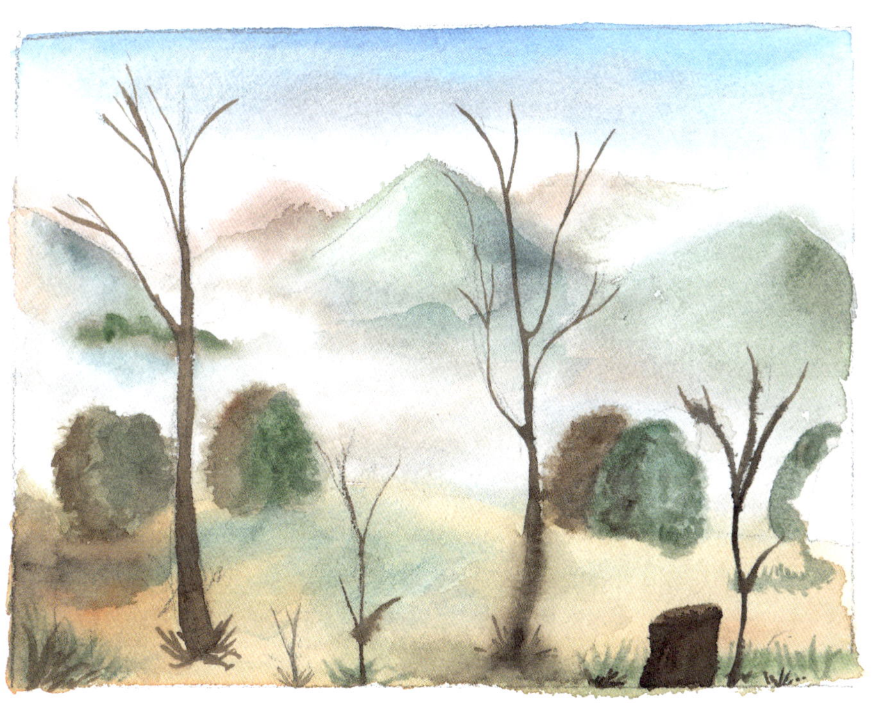

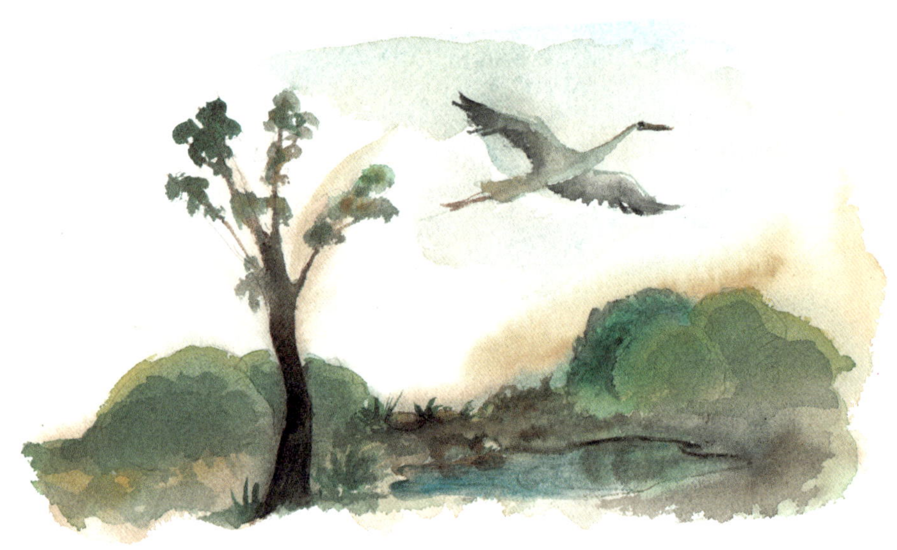

— 8.04

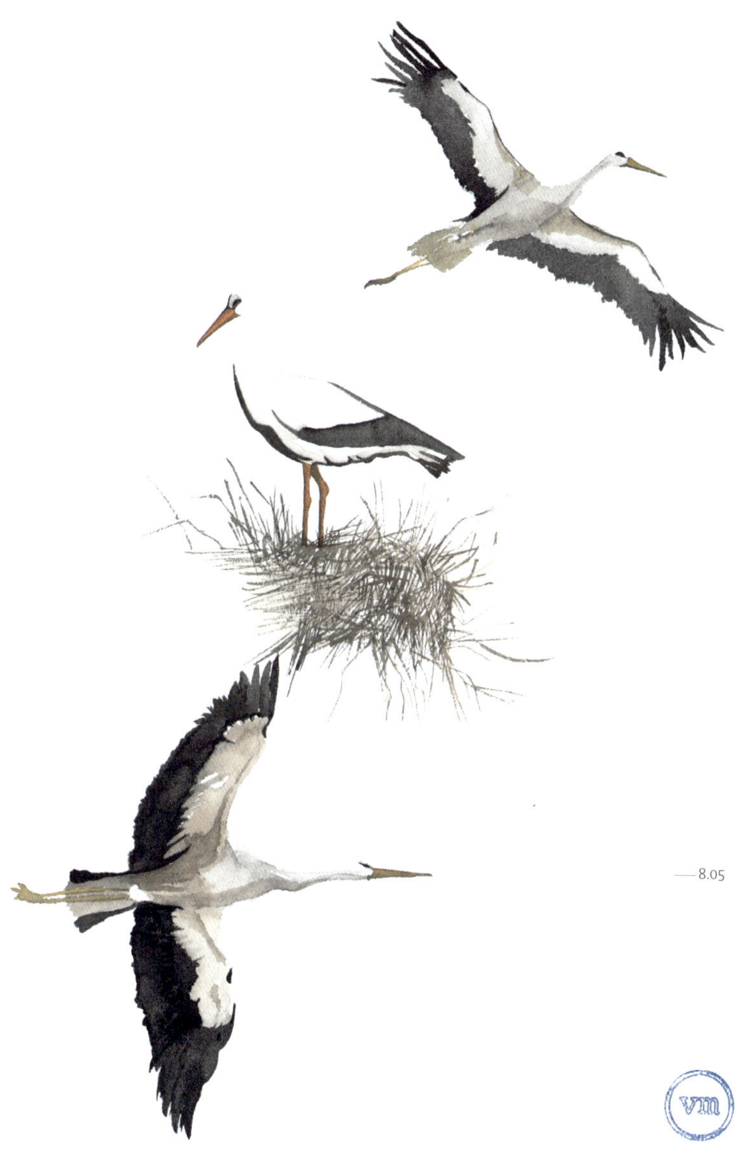

8.05

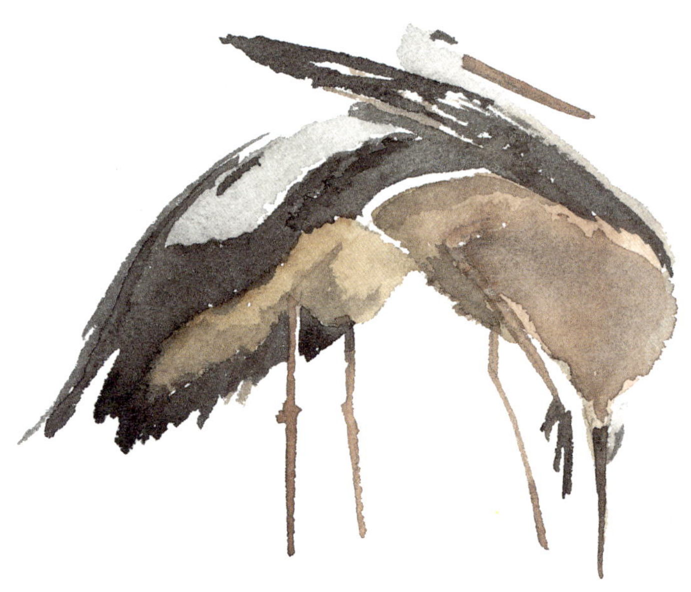

8.06 —

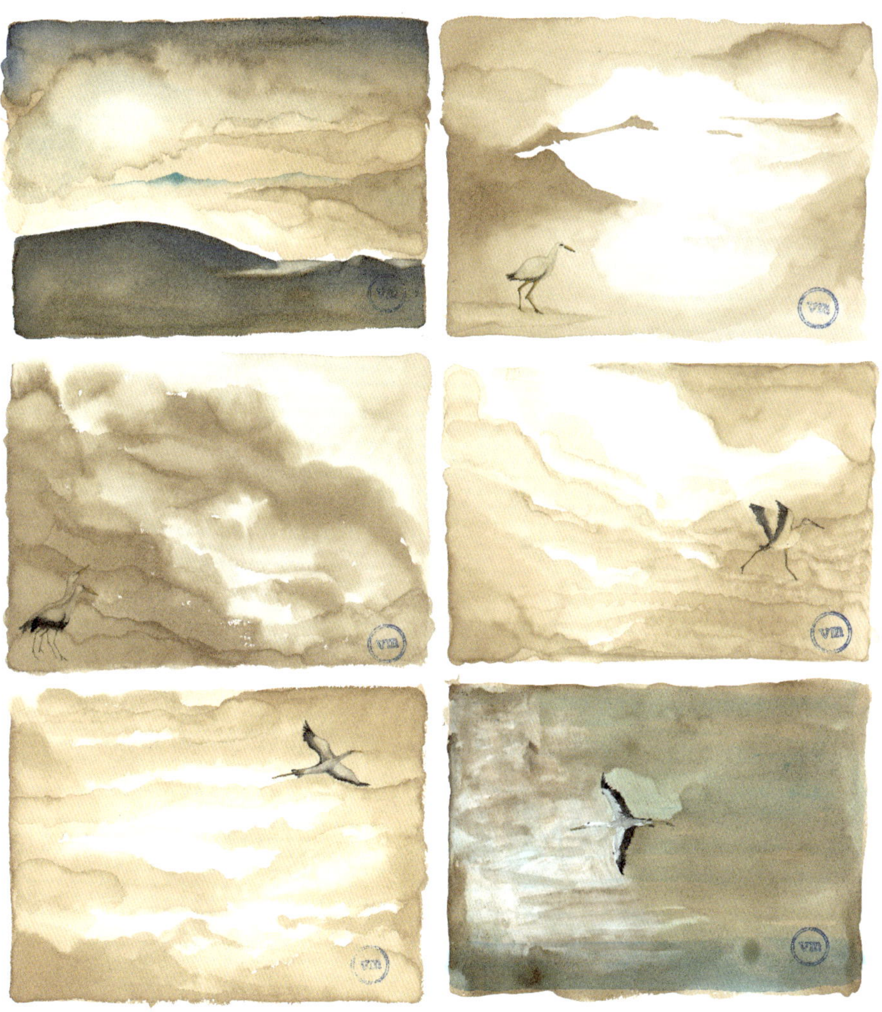

8.07 — 8.12 —

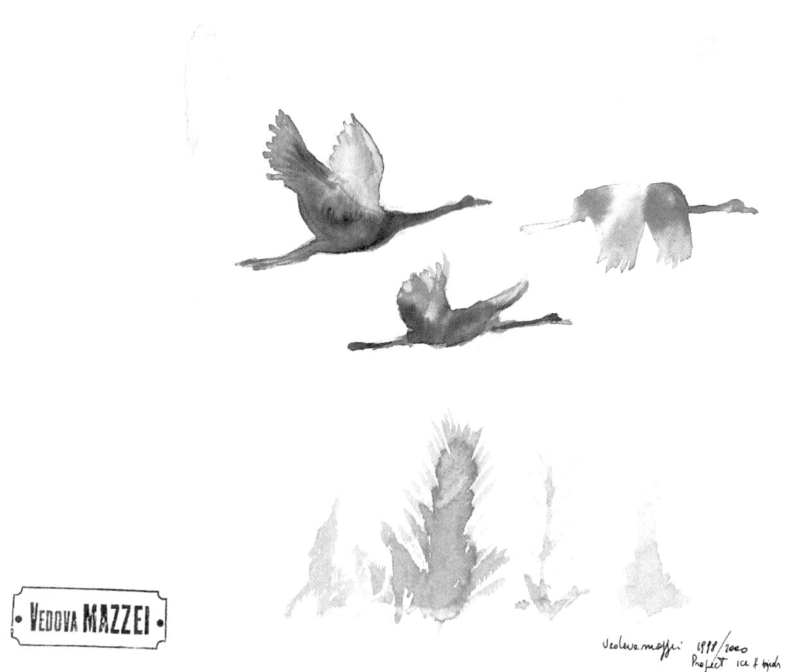

8.13 ——

THE HIBERNATION OF A FLOCK OF BIRDS IN FLIGHT

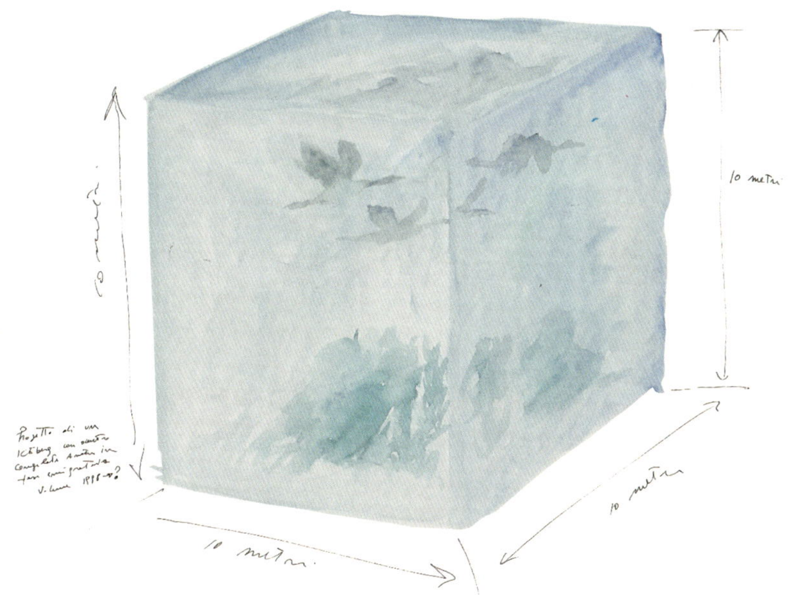

8.14 —

8.13 — 8.15 —

Studies of the hibernation of a flock of birds in flight.
Design and details for an installation with a ten cubic
metre block of ice with a flock of birds in flight inside
(1999–2000). Project not realised.

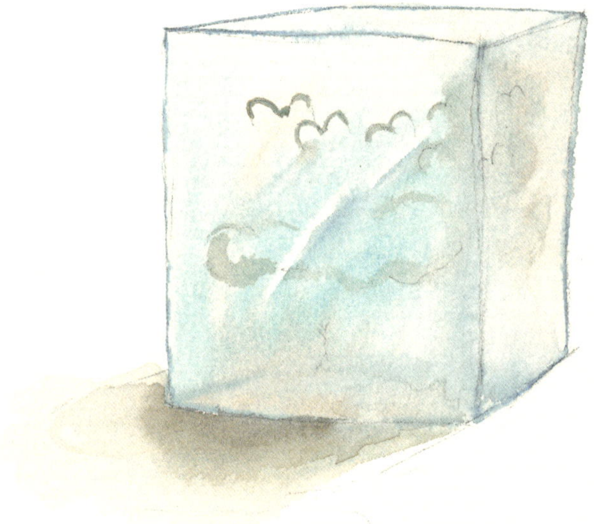
Ho visto uno stormo
d'icelli in volo
completamente ghiacciato

8.15 —

IX

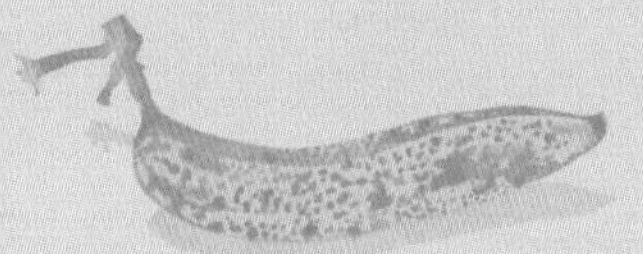

Miscellanea

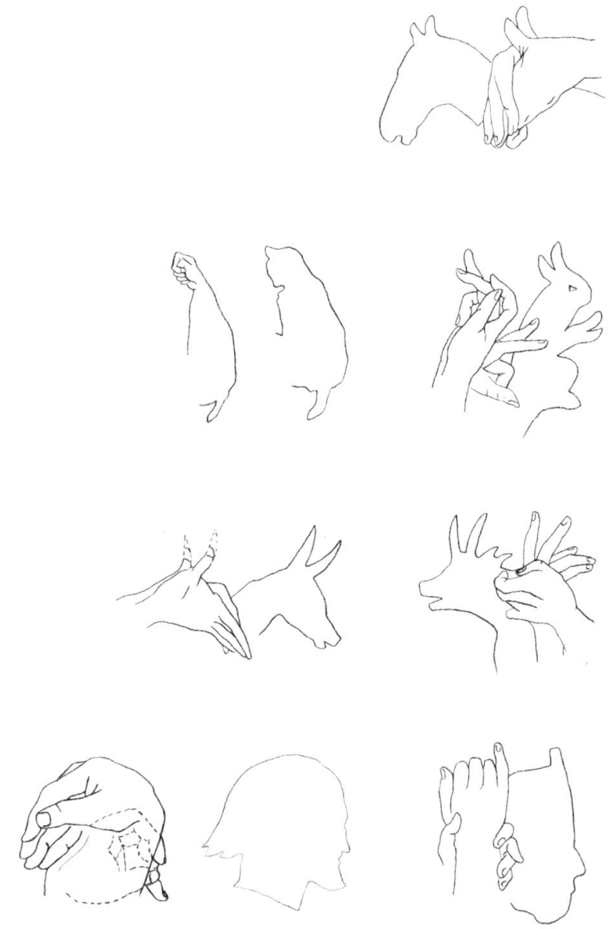

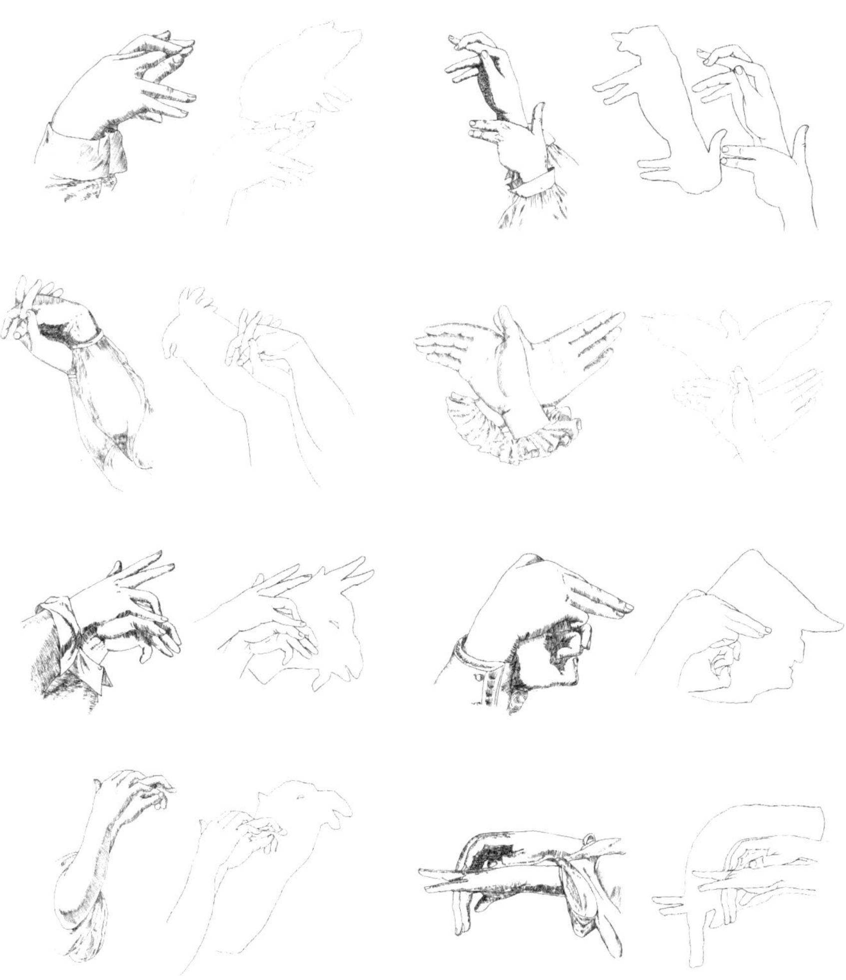

MORE CHINESE SHADOWS

9.01 — 9.15 —
The complete series of drawings for Chinese
Shadow sculptures.

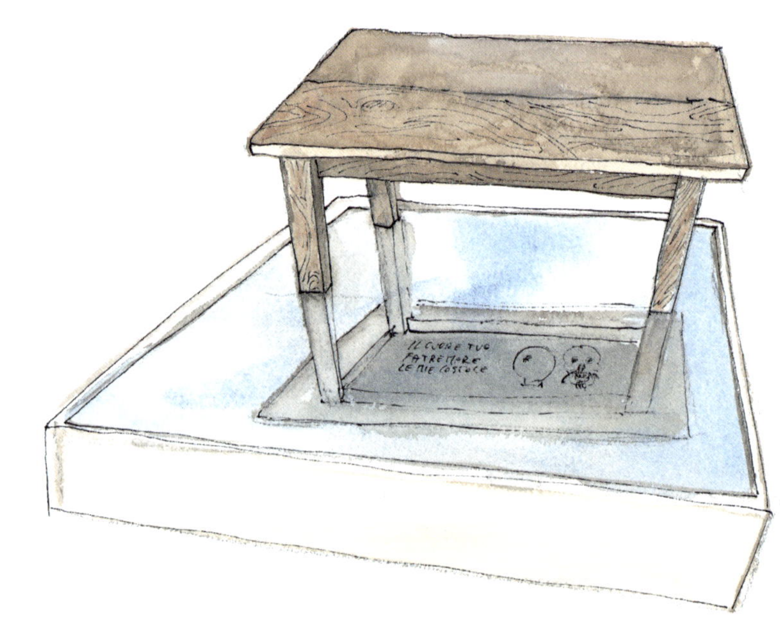

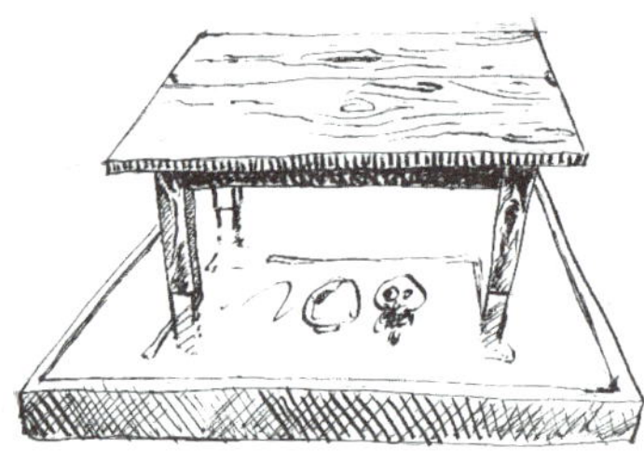

FRESCOS

9.16 — 9.18 —
Studies for frescos beneath a table to be looked at with a mirror.

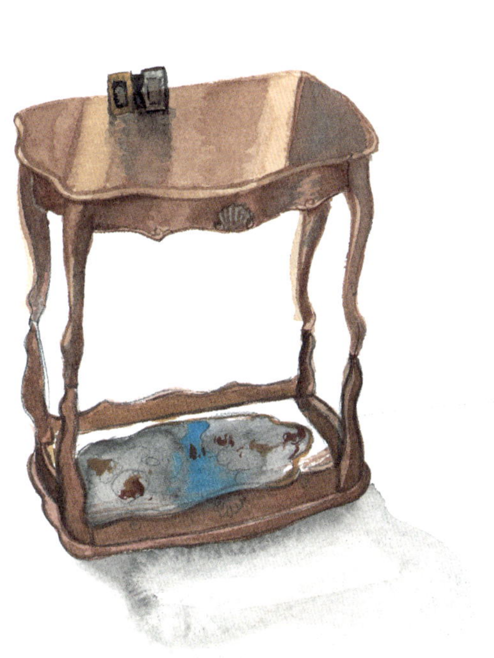

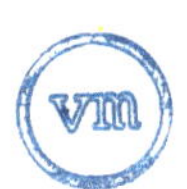

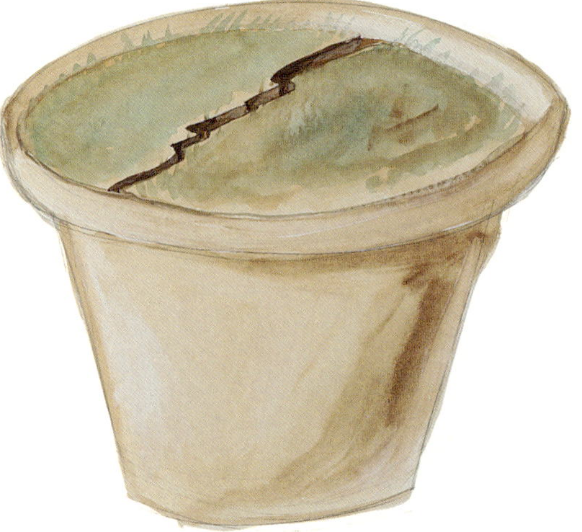

EARTHQUAKE

9.19 —

Home-made earthquake.

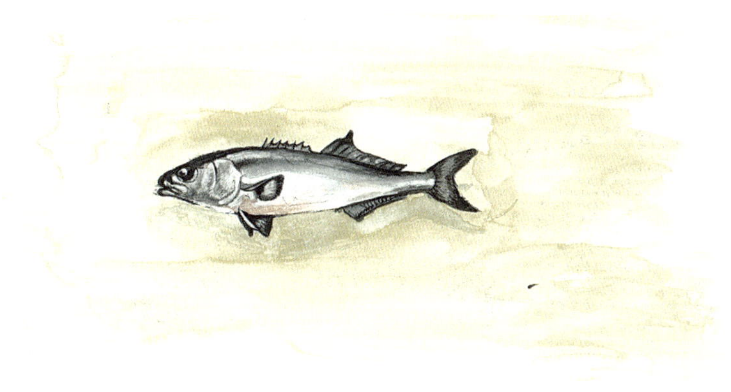

QUIVERING FISH

9.20 —

A fish quivering after its death.

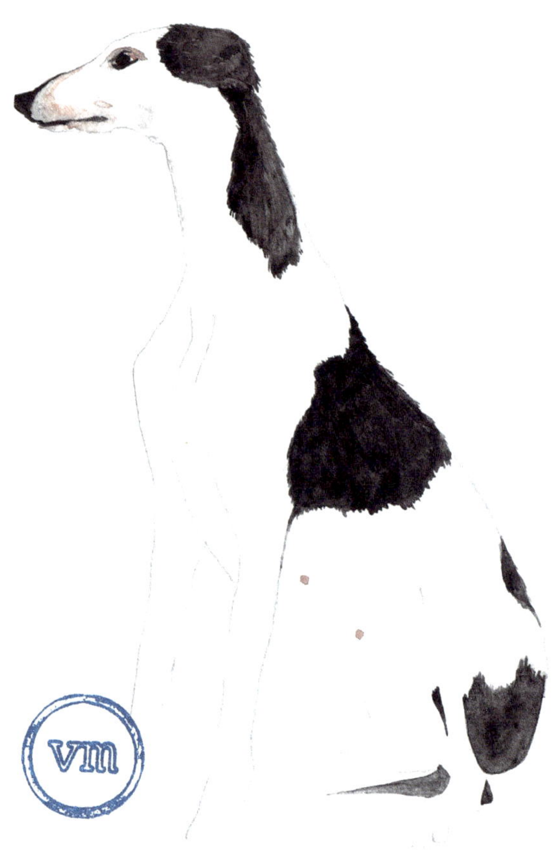

WATCHING DOG

9.21—

A dog watching Stella as she makes a phone-call.

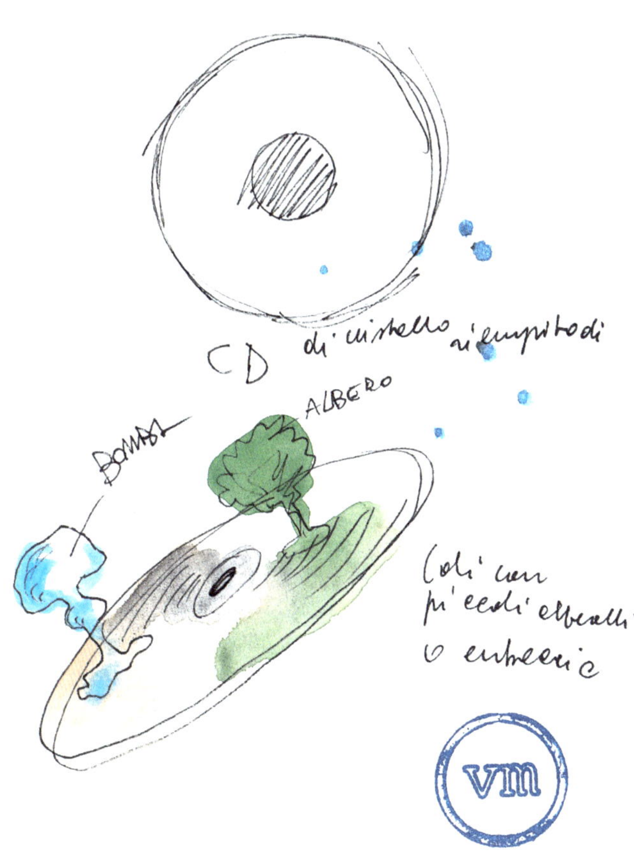

CD ROM BOMBING

9.22 —

Bombing of CDs and also of trees.

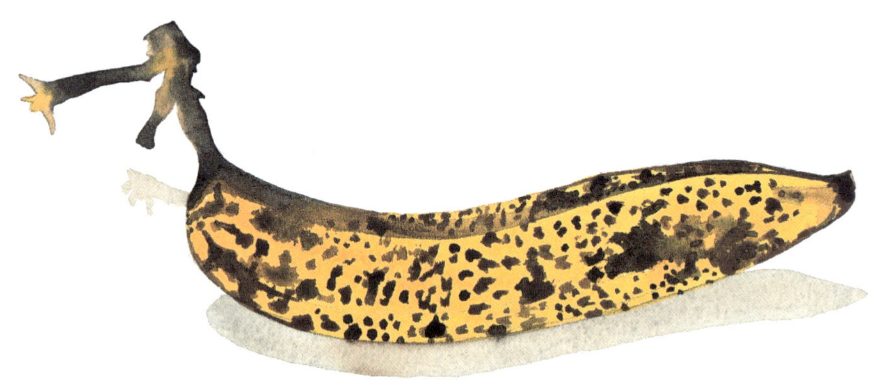

BANANA FROM APOLLO 11

9.23 —

The banana from Apollo 11 suspended in a gravitational
vacuum.

Published in Great Britain in 2003 by
Trolley Ltd.
Unit 5 Building 13, Long Street,
London E2 8HN, UK

Artwork © vedovamazzei
Text © Mirta d'Argenzio, 2003
Translation from Italian: Kate Davies

10 9 8 7 6 5 4 3 2 1

A catalogue record for this book is available from
the British Library

ISBN 1-904563-12-0

Design: Ben Weaver
Editing: redazioni, Venice
Reprographics: Fotolito Express
Printed in Italy by Soso

SPECIAL THANKS

Mauro Nicoletti, Alice Valli Bulgari, Alessia Bulgari,
Mario Alessandro and Andrea Codognato, Gigi
Giannuzzi, Maddalena Di Sopra, Maria Silvia Farci,
Steve and Claudio, Gennaro Bencivenga, Ruben
and Elisa, Nicholas Ward-Jackson, Athena Panni,
Maria Rosaria Rinaldi, Ruby Russell, Oliver Wood,
Carmen Foppiani and Max Renkel.